Luis Buñuel's *The Discreet Charm of the Bourgeoisie*

The first collection of critical essays on Luis Buñuel's 1972 Oscar-winning masterpiece, *The Discreet Charm of the Bourgeoisie,* this anthology brings fresh perspectives to the most sophisticated work by this filmmaker whose narrative experimentation was always ahead of its time. Combining some of the world's most distinguished scholars on Buñuel and Spanish cinema with new voices in cultural theory, this volume helps us to rethink not only *The Discreet Charm of the Bourgeoisie,* but also Buñuel's entire body of work. Among the topics examined are Buñuel's relationship to surrealism, the transnational (Spanish, French, Mexican, and American) nature of his work, and his dramatic and provocative rethinking of sex, narrative, and gender. Also included are vintage reviews of the film, as well as a selective Buñuel bibliography.

Marsha Kinder is Professor of Critical Studies in the School of Cinema-Television at the University of Southern California. She is the author of many books, including *Refiguring Spain: Cinema, Media, and Representation* and *Blood Cinema: The Reconstruction of National Identity in Spain.*

THE CAMBRIDGE UNIVERSITY PRESS
FILM HANDBOOKS SERIES

General Editor
Andrew Horton, University of Oklahoma

Each CAMBRIDGE FILM HANDBOOK is intended to focus on a single film from a variety of theoretical, critical, and contextual perspectives. This "prism" approach is designed to give students and general readers valuable background and insight into the cinematic, artistic, cultural, and sociopolitical importance of individual films by including essays by leading film scholars and critics. Furthermore, these handbooks by their very nature are meant to help the reader better grasp the nature of the critical and theoretical discourse on cinema as an art form, as a visual medium, and as a cultural product. Filmographies and selected bibliographies are added to help the reader go further on his or her own exploration of the film under consideration.

Luis Buñuel's *The Discreet Charm of the Bourgeoisie*

Edited by

MARSHA KINDER

CAMBRIDGE
UNIVERSITY PRESS

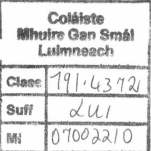
CAMBRIDGE UNIVERSITY PRESS
Cambridge, New York, Melbourne, Madrid, Cape Town, Singapore, São Paulo

Cambridge University Press
The Edinburgh Building, Cambridge CB2 2RU, UK

Published in the United States of America by Cambridge University Press, New York

www.cambridge.org
Information on this title: www.cambridge.org/9780521560641

First published 1999

A catalogue record for this publication is available from the British Library

Library of Congress Cataloguing in Publication data
Luis Buñuel's The discreet charm of the bourgeoisie / edited by Marsha Kinder.
p. cm. – (Cambridge film handbooks)
Includes bibliographical references and index.
ISBN 0–521–56064–0 (hb). – ISBN 0–521–56831–5 (pbk.)
1. Charme discret de la bourgeoisie.   I. Kinder, Marsha.
II. Series: Cambridge film handbooks series.
PN1997.C444L85   1999
791.43'72 – dc21   98–25859
                         CIP

ISBN-13 978-0-521-56064-1 hardback
ISBN-10 0-521-56064-0 hardback

ISBN-13 978-0-521-56831-9 paperback
ISBN-10 0-521-56831-5 paperback

Transferred to digital printing 2005

To the memory of Katherine Singer Kovács
Who shared my passion for Buñuel's discreet charm

Contents

Acknowledgments

I am especially grateful to all the contributors to this volume, including Julie Jones who translated the article by Agustín Sánchez Vidal and who, along with other distinguished international scholars, Peter William Evans, Emmanuel Larraz, and Gary W. McDonogh, contributed valuable ideas to the project.

I am also grateful to the series editor, Andy Horton, who recruited me to do this book; to my editor at Cambridge University Press, Anne Sanow, along with production editor Holly Johnson, who have seen the book through production; to Charles Tashiro, who assisted with the illustrations; to my assistant, Nithila Peter, who helped me obtain permissions and stills; to Monique Yamaguchi and Osa Hidalgo, who did the index; to Brian R. MacDonald, who did the copyediting; and to the students in my graduate seminar on "The Nomadic Subjectivity of Luis Buñuel" at the University of Southern California, who gave me insightful feedback on many of the ideas in my introduction.

FIGURE ONE
Luis Buñuel is a nomadic subject with a unique experience of
serialized exile. Courtesy of Agustín Sánchez Vidal and Caja de
Ahorros de la Inmaculada de Aragón.

MARSHA KINDER

The Nomadic Discourse of Luis Buñuel: A Rambling Overview

Luis Buñuel has a unique position in film history. This Spaniard, who experienced several periods of exile and who in his late forties changed his nationality to Mexican, is the only filmmaker in the world who has been described (however incorrectly) as the singular embodiment not only of a major film movement like French surrealism but also of two national cinemas, the Spanish and the Mexican. Since his death in 1983 those misperceptions have been corrected, partly through the global success of films by Spaniards such as Pedro Almodóvar, Carlos Saura, Fernando Trueba, Vicente Aranda, and Bigas Luna (all of whom were influenced by Buñuel) as well as by the commercial and critical triumphs of the New Mexican Cinema, especially in works like *Danzón* and *Like Water for Chocolate*.[1] Yet, since traces of these attitudes still remain, it seems timely to reassess Buñuel's relationship to his transnational contexts – Spanish, Mexican, French, and global – and to explore why he remains a pivotal figure in several other discursive contexts: the transition from modernism to postmodernism, the exploration of sound-image relations, the rehabilitation of melodrama as a viable political genre, and the redefinition of narrative as a cognitive mode.

1

Le charme discret de la bourgeoisie (The Discreet Charm of the Bourgeoisie, 1972) is the ideal film for exploring these conceptual issues, for it redefined Buñuel as the international auteur who was a consummate master of narrative experimentation. The playfulness of its tone and the glossiness of its visual surface partially disguised the pointedness of its satire – a dynamic that may have helped it win an Oscar for best foreign-language film. Ironically, while this film seemed to usher Buñuel back into the mainstream of the European art film, it actually pushed his earlier lines of thematic and formal exploration to their most illogical extremes. Moreover, it launched a final trilogy of films that enabled his career to end with a form of radical experimentation that matched, if not surpassed, that of his earliest surrealist productions.

This introductory essay is designed to perform two functions: to present my own take on what is most original and compelling in the works of Buñuel (particularly as exemplified in *The Discreet Charm*), and to provide an overview of the essays that follow.

A NOMADIC DISCOURSE: BUÑUEL AS EXILE

I am using the term *nomadic discourse* to refer to a form of mobil mentality one finds in the characters, plots, images, sounds, textual strategies, and life experiences of Luis Buñuel, a filmmaker who spent most of his years working in exile. Although he was born in 1900 in the small village of Calanda where (he reports in his autobiography) "few outsiders ever came,"[2] his later periods of exile always positioned him as paradigmatic outsider despite the differences in context: Paris as an international center of modernism in the late 1920s, when surrealism was a major artistic movement; Hollywood as the hegemonic center of filmmaking practice in 1930, when the conventions for the international sound film were being established; Paris in 1936 and then New York in 1938 as political sites for left-wing activism, where he worked on political documentaries or reedited those by others until being ousted by repressive right-wing forces (the German occupation of France and blacklisting in the United States); Mexico as a political refuge for thousands of leftist Spanish exiles fleeing from Franco's fascist Spain in the mid-1940s and 1950s, where he could make commercial movies in his own language within a thriving, small-scale industry; and France as the center of the politicized European art film in the 1960s and early 1970s, where he could make films with bigger budgets, better-trained actors, and more artistic freedom. These various periods of exile were motivated by virtually all of the reasons for which filmmakers have historically left home: to satisfy curiosity, fame, or hunger; to find a more stimulating artistic environment or better economic opportunities; to escape oblivion, censorship, harassment, political persecution, or death. His individual experience of exile represents the whole paradigm.

Buñuel's exile status has led some critics to exaggerate his powers, to see him not only as the singular embodiment of a movement or national cinema but, along with other famous Spanish exiles (such as artist Pablo Picasso and cellist Pablo Casals), as a one-man resistance who "fought the Franco regime from afar, as did other exiles in Paris, London, Mexico and New York, gradually creating in their minds the myth of a country in which no changes ever occurred, one that remained frozen in time in 1939, eternally Fascist."[3] The problem with this vision is that it also turns Buñuel into a frozen figure; it ignores the fact that although he was always a heretic who resisted what he called "the sectarian spirit," he was also a powerful shifter whose meaning changed according to which particular hegemonic system he was working to subvert. Anticipating several postcolonial critics, he inhabited what Hamid Naficy calls that "slipzone of indeterminacy" created by the hybridity of exile, one that "involves an ambivalence about both the original and the host cultures . . . a state of unbelonging, in effect a condition of freedom, nomadism, homelessness, or vagrancy – even opportunism."[4]

Partly because of this "indeterminacy," the Francoist government realized that Buñuel could be used as an effective international icon of Spanishness, an icon they tried both to exploit and repress, especially in the scandals that circulated around *Viridiana* (1961). Buñuel had been invited back to his homeland to make the film, partly to demonstrate to the rest of the world the growing liberalization of Francoist Spain. Although it remains one of the few feature films Buñuel made in Spain (with a script approved by Francoist censors, a story with Spanish characters and themes set in Spain, a cast and crew primarily Spanish, and even partial financing from Spain), and although it succeeded in winning both the prestigious Palme d'Or and the Society of Film Writers award at the 1961 Cannes Film Festival, as soon as *Viridiana* was denounced by the Vatican for sacrilege, it was immediately banned in Spain. The film's nationality suddenly was forced to change from Spanish to Mexican, as its director's had earlier in 1949.

Buñuel's career forces us to see that neither a national nor an auteurist context alone is sufficient for understanding the full resonance of his work.[5] His films demand a transnational perspective – one that considers the national-global interface. That is why the contributors to this anthology represent a diverse array of nationalities. His films also reward an engagement with theory, for despite Buñuel's avowed resistance to theoretical orthodoxy, his own early experimental work as a surrealist demonstrated how productive his use of the then relatively new psychoanalytic theory could be.

A PROLEPTIC DISCOURSE: BUÑUEL AS VISIONARY

The primary goal of this anthology is not to historicize Buñuel's work but to do the reverse: to highlight its *proleptic* power, its uncanny ability to prefigure future directions both in theory and filmic experimentation. That is one reason why Buñuel's work is so resistant to obsolescence – why its meanings are so mobile and nomadic, why it always challenges us to catch up with its experimentation. Like his restless characters strolling down an abstract highway in *The Discreet Charm* (a recurring image that prefigures the hypnotic framing image of Bill Pullman driving relentlessly forward on an abstract two-lane blacktop in David Lynch's experimental 1997 feature, *Lost Highway*), Buñuel's work always moves confidently into an uncertain future, shifting from one cultural and historical context to another while retaining its power to shock spectators out of their bourgeois complacency.

Even Buñuel's earliest experimental films, *Un chien andalou* (An Andalusian Dog, 1929) and *L'âge d'or* (The Golden Age, 1930) can be read productively not only against the surrealist movement of Paris in the 1920s and its reliance on Freud's dreamwork theory, but also, as Linda Williams persuasively demonstrated in *Figures of Desire* (1981), against Lacanian psychoanalytic theory of the 1960s and 1970s and its theorization of desire, which was influenced by the surrealists as well as by Freud.[6] A collaborative effort with his fellow Spaniard, surrealist painter Salvador Dali, *Un chien andalou* still remains one of the best dramatizations of that tension between the desire to immerse oneself totally in the raw perceptions of subjective dreams and the drive to narrativize them, that is, to provide a rational interpretation that tames their corrosive power. As Buñuel and Dali put it in the leaflet they distributed at the film's Paris debut, "NOTHING, in the film, SYMBOLIZES ANYTHING. The only method of investigation of the symbols would be, perhaps, psychoanalysis." Like other orthodoxies (such as Catholicism, communism, and even surrealism) to which Buñuel refused to submit himself totally but which profoundly marked him nevertheless, psychoanalysis frequently came under his attack, even though he was significantly influenced by Freud's method of interpreting dreams: its attentiveness to concrete sensory perceptions, repetitions, juxtapositions, and discontinuities and its suspiciousness of the drive toward linear narrative and rational explanation.

In *L'âge d'or*, one of the first sound films made in France, Buñuel experimented with sound-image relations (just as Alfred

Hitchcock was then doing in England, Fritz Lang in Germany, and Sergei Eisenstein in the Soviet Union), but in his case he called attention to the ways in which these sensory channels were being gendered, as feminist film theorists like Mary Ann Doane, Kaja Silverman, and Amy Lawrence would later do in the 1980s and early 1990s.[7] Like Eisenstein, Buñuel experimented with disjunctive relations between sound and image – to enhance the power not of montage (as in the case of Soviet expressionism) but of subversive desire, what the surrealists called *l'amour fou* (mad love). Rejecting the reassuring redundancy and realism of a unifying synchronization sought by Hollywood, Buñuel explored an acoustical expression of subjectivity that could represent the kind of split subject that had been theorized by Freud – one constituted through two different language systems: the primary process language of the unconscious that worked toward immediate gratification versus the more linear, rational language of secondary revision used by the ego. Thus, in *L'âge d'or* when the "off camera" interior monologues of his outrageous lovers ("the first time spoken thoughts were used in film") help block the physical consummation of their passion, it was as if film's new capacity for sound were being used to postpone the gratification demanded by the driving materiality of the visual image. According to Buñuel, "The characters are seated in a garden, but the dialogue indicates they are in a bedroom. . . . 'Move your head closer, the pillow is cooler over here. Are you sleepy?' "[8] This conversation transports them to some imaginary future that takes the edge off their desire. Yet this acoustic subjectivity could also function subversively in service of primary process thinking, for earlier in the film it features disjunctive animal cries that help express the two-way flow of intersubjective desire across traditional barriers of gender (the desiring male pursuing the desired female) and sensory channels (the erotic image heightened by an accompanying and thereby subordinate musical track).

In one sequence (which occurs shortly after the lovers had been found wallowing in the mud noisily making love a few yards away from an official ceremony in progress, heavily attended by the bourgeoisie), the lustful male (Gaston Modot) is being led by his bourgeois captors through the streets of the imperial city. As if anticipating the perceptions of contemporary cultural theorists who have linked the mobile gaze of window shopping in modernist arcades with the visual dynamics of early cinematic spectatorship,[9] when this reluctant *flâneur* sees erotic visual images of women – first in an advertising poster on a sandwich board and then in an artistic photograph in a shop window – the image dissolves to his beloved (Lya Lys), who is now in her bourgeois mansion with her mother. Consistent with traditional classical cinema, this visual dissolve positions her as the erotic object of *his* desire, which seems to evoke her. Yet when the mother notices that one of her daughter's fingers is heavily bandaged, we begin to suspect masturbatory activity which is a sign of the female's own desire.

Then, in the longest speech thus far in this transitional sound film (whose earlier sequences function more like silent cinema), Lys begins to describe technical strategies for handling sound at a forthcoming party (positioning musicians close to the microphone to compensate for their small numbers), a juxtaposition that surprisingly links her erotic desire to the new fetishized apparatus that controls the sound track. This association is strengthened when she retreats to her bedroom and finds a huge cow (wearing a bell around its neck) seated on her bed (one of Buñuel's most amusing surrealistic jolts). What is equally surprising is that Lys seems accustomed to finding the animal there. Yet in her current state of aroused desire the tinkling bell acquires a new function, helping to evoke an image in her boudoir mirror of a sky full of moving clouds, out of which emerges the stirring sound of wind. Her acoustical experience (of cowbell and wind) suddenly brings forth the image of her lover (just as her image was earlier evoked by his erotic gaze), thereby completing the circle of intersubjective desire. Over this image of her strolling lover we continue to hear the tinkling cowbell and stirring wind, now joined by a barking dog, a constructed "natural" cacophony that expresses (or arouses) an erotic ecstasy, which reaches an acoustical climax, presumably experienced simultaneously by both lovers, despite their physical separation in space. Hence, like Doane, Buñuel demonstrates the power of the sound track to smooth over spatial gaps – not for the purpose of creating an illusory narrative continuity as in Hollywood cinema but to heighten the intensity of subjective desire and the subversive power of *l'amour fou*. He demonstrates that the desiring machine (like its analogue, cinema) is accessible to both genders and capable of using any sensory channel.

Consistent with the arguments of Gilles Deleuze and Felix Guatarri in *Anti-Oedipus*, the subversive power of this desiring machine is not restricted to the domestic realm of the patriarchal family; rather, it is a mode of imagination that permits total freedom and is capable of threatening the whole bourgeois order.[10] As Buñuel put it in defending the film's final subversive figure, a conflation of Jesus Christ and the Marquis de Sade (who was a hero of the surrealists): "The imagination is free, but man is not."[11] The fact that *L'âge d'or* was banned for nearly half a century demonstrates the lasting power of its subversiveness.

Buñuel's first Spanish film, *Las hurdes* (also known as *Tierra sin pan* and *Land without Bread*, 1932), had the distinction of being banned both by the Republican government (which was in power when the film was made) and by Franco's right-wing Nationalist government (which displaced it after winning the Spanish Civil War). Both political sides agreed that this documentary about an impoverished region depicted Spain in a very bad light.[12] It is the film's ironic voice-over (cowritten with Pierre Unik) that makes this documentary surreal, for, while sympathizing with the poor inhabitants and implicitly criticizing isolated absurdities, its tone is patronizing and emotionally detached (an inadequacy underscored by the use of Brahms's Fourth Symphony as background music). Not only is the commentary contradictory and pseudoscientific, but it is also politically impotent for it fails to address the economic inequities that cause the Hurdanos to live and die in such misery. Yet, despite its absurdity, on screen we are still confronted with devastating visuals, including haunting images of starving children. The juxtaposition frequently makes some spectators laugh, perhaps, as Buñuel suggests, to relieve their own distress and feelings of impotence. They laugh not at the misery of the Hurdanos but at the incongruity between image and commentary – a dynamic that enables Buñuel to call *Las hurdes* "the least gratuitous film I have made."[13] We know this commentary was vital to the film's conceptualization for, before the sound track was added in 1936, Buñuel used to read it aloud at screenings.

This incongruity between image and sound track (both the commentary and music) also enabled the film to parody ethnographic filmmaking even before it was widely perceived as a genre. According to F. T. Rony, in early ethnographic films such as R. C. Nicholson's *The Transformed Isle* (1920); Robert Flaherty's *Nanook of the North* (1922) and *Moana* (1926); Léon Poirier's *La croisière noire* (The Black Cruise, 1926); Meriam C. Cooper and Ernest B. Schoedsack's *Grass* (1925) and *Chang* (1927); and H. P. Carver's *The Silent Enemy* (1930), this genre was infused with a "redemptive potential" that excused colonizers (including anthropologists and ethnographic filmmakers) for the various forms of misery and exploitation that were inflicted on subject people.[14] Although Buñuel's film operated on the register of class rather than that of race or ethnicity, it was precisely this "redemptive potential" that his parody destroyed. Thus, his "proleptic parody" enabled him to prefigure the new postmodernist anthropology and reflexive documentaries of the 1970s and 1980s that would question the ideological position of the traditional complacent ethnographer.[15]

Las hurdes was not Buñuel's only film to utilize proleptic parody. Also focusing primarily on class issues, his 1962 Mexican feature *El ángel exterminador* (The Exterminating Angel) parodied the disaster film before it was widely perceived as a genre.[16] Here the privileged members of Mexico City's haute bourgeoisie are trapped in a drawing room following an elegant dinner party, while their servants are just as inexplicably seized with a desire to flee. Their mysterious inability to leave the room is experienced as a failure of will – perhaps no more mysterious than the one that prevents citizens from changing the totally corrupt economic, social, and political system on which their privileges (as well as the miseries of the servants and the Hurdanos) are based. The thin veneer of civilization quickly breaks down and these bourgeois guests descend into a brutal savagery, breaking down walls to get at water pipes, committing suicide and demanding the sacrificial death of the host, and turning to magic, dreams, and narrative for consolation and release – a scenario that has many similarities with that of *The Discreet Charm of the Bourgeoisie*, released a decade later.

What makes *The Exterminating Angel*, like *Las hurdes*, so visionary is Buñuel's ability to explore the ideological implications of these emerging genres, particularly with respect to the power relations between insiders and outsiders. That is why they engage many issues that were to be addressed by later theorists. In the case of *The Exterminating Angel*, they include issues that would be pursued by French narratologists (like Roland Barthes and Gerard Genette) in the 1970s and 1980s, for this is the first of several Buñuel films in which humor depends on a serious engagement with narrative theory.[17] Buñuel plays with the subversive potential of repetition and its paradoxical ability to avoid narrative closure while appearing to fulfill it. As in *Un chien andalou*, we are confronted with a series of incongruous perceptions that raise unanswerable questions: for example, why are certain scenes repeated without the characters noticing them, why are there visual discontinuities in backgrounds, why are sheep and a bear wandering through an elegant mansion, why is there no motivation for the guests' inability to leave the room? Like the guests, we have a strong desire to find a rational explanation that will free us from the anxiety aroused by such disturbing questions.

This cognitive struggle is even dramatized in the plot: at one point, the character known as "the Virgin" commands everyone to stand still, for she claims they are all standing in precisely the same spot as when this strange condition first emerged. Through a communal "faith" in this absurd narrative premise (how could they all be in the same place when some have already died?), the guests are miraculously released from the drawing room, only to have the same kind of entrapment reimposed within the cathedral where they soon go to give thanks. As in *Las hurdes*, though the insiders at first seem to be the only ones who are trapped, the film eventually reveals that the trap extends outward to encompass outsiders (including us spectators) who are all caught in the same network of structures but on a much larger scale.

In these few examples, I have chosen issues and textual strategies that receive greater elaboration in *The Discreet Charm of the Bourgeoisie* – the pull between an experiential immersion in the phenomenology of raw perceptions versus a rational drive toward narrative coherence, the experimental play with the disjunctive relations between sound and image, the strategic deployment of laughter to address corruption and class struggle, the entrapment of a group of characters in social rituals and arbitrary narratives, and the destabilizing power of repetition and dreams in revealing both the manipulative rhetoric and subversive potential of cinema as a desiring machine.

A NOMADIC TEXT: THE DISCREET CHARM OF THE BOURGEOISIE

In *The Discreet Charm of the Bourgeoisie* plot is minimal. A group of six affluent characters living in Paris – two married couples, the Sénéchals and Thévenots; Madame Thévenot's younger sister Florence; and their friend and associate, the ambassador of Miranda – repeatedly get together for a social meal, which is always interrupted. During the course of these events, we learn that Madame Thévenot is having an affair with the ambassador and that he is involved in a drug-smuggling scheme with her husband and Mr. Sénéchal. The final interruption leads to the murder of all six characters, at which point the ambassador awakens from a nightmare and has a late night snack, perhaps implying the whole film is a series of dreams inspired by his voracious hunger. Partly because of the minimalism of the plot, our attention is drawn to the way the story is told, the narrative discourse, which is rich and complex.

The film opens on the road in the dark – with four of its bourgeois characters en route to their first abortive dinner engagement at the Sénéchal home. This opening introduces three tropes that structure the narrative design of the film: on the level of thematics, the organizing social ritual of the recurring lunch or dinner party, which is inevitably interrupted by unpredictable events related to sex, death, or dreams; on the level of mise-en-scène, the dark lighting that will subsequently signal a shift in ontological or generic status away from the glossy surface of light bourgeois comedy to a more somber oedipal melodrama embedded within a morbid back story about death or an uncanny inset dream; and on the level of narrative, a vehicle (in this scene, the chauffeur-driven luxury car) that literally drives the plot from one episode to another. Like the frustrated guests who must learn to read the signs of their recurring frustration (the unlit fire, unset table, and inappropriately dressed hostess that signal Mrs. Sénéchal does not expect them; or the locked door, lack of patrons, change of management, and sounds of weeping that signal the death of the restaurant owner), we too must learn to read the signs of how this film is to be consumed. One valuable hint occurs in that peculiar moment when Florence (the youngest and most unconventional of the guests) seems to examine the frame line of the camera lens or screen, perhaps signaling we must be more attentive to percepts than to plot if we are to understand this reflexive text.

The film repeatedly demonstrates that specific cultural expectations are crucial for contextualizing the reading of signs. In a later scene, when a restaurant's menu offers coffee and tea, its female patrons expect those options to be available, and the violation of these expectations proves to be far more disturbing to these bourgeois consumers than the adultery and patricide that

occur in the inset story of a young lieutenant's unhappy childhood, which he, for some mysterious reason, insists on telling
them without having been asked. Thus, these three bourgeois
ladies receive both more and less than what they ordered, and
both deviations violate their expectations. As with Buñuel's experience of exile, the film presents us with an entire paradigm of
violations – ranging from a minor breach of etiquette (gulping a
martini) to drug trafficking, murder, and revolution – all strung
together as if to simulate a plot.

The disjunctive relations between sound and image in this
film are directly related to the suppression of political discourse.
Virtually every time there is a political discussion (such as the
revelation of which ambassador was recently caught using his
diplomatic pouch to smuggle drugs, or the young terrorist's
speech quoting Mao that proves he does not understand Freud,
or the minister's explanation of why the police must release the
charming bourgeois dope dealers), it is drowned out by some
familiar urban noise (traffic, a typewriter, or a plane passing
overhead) that is foregrounded in the kind of aural close-up Buñuel first used in *L'âge d'or*. To make sure that spectators realize
the suppression of this information is intentional, the pattern of
censorship is repeated. Although Buñuel was deaf by the time he
made this film, he still takes credit for sound effects, which anticipates the function of "sound design," an important characteristic of most of his films from *L'âge d'or* onward. Thus, in contrast to most conventional film narratives where substantive and
stylistic choices are made to seem natural or inevitable, here the
spectator is constantly made aware of the implications not only
of what is included but also of what is excluded both from the
audio and visual tracks (e.g., the sex scene between the Sénéchals
that is discreetly hidden behind a bush, the scars of the adulterous wife that are concealed behind her expensive organdy
blouse, the soldier's train dream that we do not have time to
hear, and the reasons why the poor woman hates Jesus, which
she promises to tell the murderous bishop). As a result, despite

the film's emphasis on repetition and the literalization of the narrative vehicle, it is always impossible for us spectators to predict what will happen next.

One of the most intriguing series of images is that of the six bourgeois characters walking down a highway, a wordless scene that recurs three times and that provides the closing image of the film. The image is very concrete – with obvious variations in camera angle, editing rhythms, blocking, props, and ambient sounds. The variations in angles and movement might suggest the dialectic choreography of a choral ode in Greek tragedy with its three contrapuntal movements (strophe, antistrophe, and epode). The first version moves top-down, opening with an upward angle shot of a cloud-filled sky that tilts down to the characters on the road and then cutting to two more shots (one from the side and the other from behind) that move increasingly closer to the figures. Conversely, the second version is bottom-up, starting with an overhead shot of the pavement that tilts upward as the characters walk into the frame, then cuts to four shots from in front and behind the figures, ending with a tilt back down to the pavement as they walk out of the frame. The third mediating version starts with a close frontal shot, then cuts to five shots presenting alternating views from the side and behind and ending with an extreme long shot of the figures over which the credits roll as they move out of the frame and the image goes out of focus while the ambient sounds – of footsteps, wind, and birds – remain crystal clear. The costuming of the women (which is the same in all three versions) prevents us from seeing the action as flowing out of any scene that immediately precedes or follows: for, while Mrs. Thévenot is dressed in the discreet organdy blouse and black jumper that she will wear in the later adulterous scene, her sister Florence is wearing the same outfit she had on in the opening sequence, and Mrs. Sénéchal's costume is worn only in these scenes on the road.

It is possible to read this walk as another form of social ritual, like an after-dinner stroll or a suburban form of flânerie. Yet these scenes lack narrative coherence, for we never discover where these flaneurs are going, why they are going there, whether they ever reach their destination, or how this movement relates to any of the preceding or following actions (except for the two other scenes just like them). Thus, unless we offer the kind of allegorical reading that Buñuel strongly discourages ("I regret to say there is no message there"),[18] these scenes seem to have no connection to the social-political satire or to the narrative.

Yet, from another perspective, they have everything to do with narrative discourse, for like the hydrangeas that the bishop-gardener proposes to plant as a decorative border on both sides of the pathway that leads from the street entrance to the Séné-chal mansion (where the main social rituals occur), these three scenes divide the rest of the narrative symmetrically into three discrete acts of approximately equal length, each of which contains at least one embedded oedipal mininarrative (see Table 1). Paradoxically, they both punctuate and violate the boundaries between the parts, just as they both evoke and depart from the picaresque tradition. Their very lack of narrative coherence is what qualifies them to function as narrative markers in place of the climaxes within the traditional three-act structure of Holly-wood classical cinema. Like the car on the road in the opening sequence, they function as narrative vehicle.

In contrast to these abstract scenes on the road, the series of five embedded oedipal mininarratives all center on generational conflicts in scenes that are darkly lit like the opening and that contain strange ambient sounds (including weeping and church bells). They too have variations, but in this case they are functional differences signaling a thematic shift of emphasis from a psychoanalytic to a political discourse: moving from the death of the good patriarch (in the restaurant funeral), to patricide (in the lieutenant's childhood memory of poisoning his stepfather to avenge his mother), to incestuous desire (in the soldier's dream of reuniting with his dead mother), to class conflict (in the bishop's deathbed shooting of the murderer of his parents, a poor gardener whom they treated "like a beast" and whom the

Table 1. *Charting parallel scenes in the narrative*

Act 1	Act 2	Act 3
Number of scenes (linked pairs) after opening		
Dinner party/wrong date	Restaurant/no tea, etc.	Bishop's borders
Restaurant funeral	Lieutenant's sad story	Gardener's murder
Visit to embassy	Adulterous rendez-	Dinner/arrest po-
Shooting at terrorist	vous	lice station/
	Encounter with ter-	Story of June 14
	rorist	
Lunch/hosts have	Dinner/war games	Dinner/murder
sex	Sergeant's dream	Acosta awakens
Hiring the gardener		(shift in light-
		ing)
	Colonel's party/dream	
	1 (shift in lighting)	
	Colonel's party/dream	
	2 (shift in lighting)	
Punctuated by recurring image of 6 characters on the road		
On the road –	On the road –	On the road –
top down	bottom up	head on
Information (sound) drowned out		
Name of ambassa-	Why Mao hates Freud	Why prisoners
dor		must be freed
Information (narrative or visual) omitted		
How restauranteur	Mlle. Thévenot's scars	Why woman
died	Train dream	hates Jesus
Darkness		
Opening in traffic	Lieutenant's story	Gardener's murder
Restaurant funeral	Sergeant's dream	Dream of ghost
	Dream of party/stage	Acosta's murder
	Awakening from sec-	Awakening from
	ond dream of party	dream of mur-
	with murder	der
Oedipal mininarratives		
Death of restaurant	Lieutenant's story of	Bishop's revenge
owner	patricide	Story/dream of
	Sergeant's incestuous	policeman's
	dream	ghost

bishop paradoxically comes to emulate in vocation, garb, and revenge), to overt political action associated with May 1968 (in the cries of the student activist who was tortured by the repressive police sergeant whose ghost returns every 14 June).

Again, Buñuel displays the whole paradigm or, as narrative theorists like Roman Jakobson and Roland Barthes put it, projects a paradigm onto the syntagmatic plane, a form of semiotic transgression around which a great number of creative innovations are organized.[19] Instead of merely selecting one alternative from each paradigm and then combining these choices to create a conventional linear narrative, Buñuel tends to string all of the alternatives from a single paradigm together as if to simulate a plot. This principle of serial organization also applies to his depiction of eating and dreaming, two daily activities that help structure our lives.

The eating trope is not merely a displacement of erotic desire, but the quotidian bodily function arbitrarily selected for social sanction, a carnal pleasure (in contrast to sex or excretion) that can be communally satisfied in polite company. Its compulsive repetition in *The Discreet Charm* makes us look both backward and forward within Buñuel's body of work to realize the full resonance of the trope and its subversive connotations.

In his surrealist classics Buñuel was still outraging audiences primarily with a display of aggressive sexuality, which begins to be contextualized within the bourgeois dinner party in *L'âge d'or*, for the sublimation and self-control demanded by this heavily conventionalized setting further intensify the desire to commit outrage – whether it's a small fire in the closet, a slapped hostess in the parlor, sex in the garden, or murder on the grounds. In *Las hurdes* the eating trope is fraught with the social perversions of mortal lack and entrapment – an absence of bread, and cruel choices between polluted water or fatal thirst, dysentery or starvation. In *Los olvidados* (The Young and the Damned, 1950) these deprivations are most vividly dramatized in an erotic dream. The displacement from sex to eating is revealed in the young boy's oedipal nightmare of mother's meat going to his murderous rival. By using this kind of Freudian dreamwork in a realistic text on social poverty, Buñuel exposes the limits of the neorealist aesthetic, which, in focusing only on the surface, fails to address the subversive power of the desiring machine. As he put it, "Neorealist reality is partial, official, above all reasonable; but poetry, mystery, are absolutely lacking in it."[20] This mysterious power of the desiring machine is exposed in *The Exterminating Angel*, where a failed dinner party turns catastrophic, leading to a complete breakdown of civilization, and also in *Viridiana*, where a sacrilegious parody of the Last Supper makes all Christianity succumb to erotic desire.

All of these dynamics are operative and intensified in *The Discreet Charm* and in the final trilogy of films it introduces. *The Phantom of Liberty* exposes the arbitrariness of choosing eating (as opposed to excretion, the other end of the biological process) for social ritual; in a parodic lecture on comparative ethnography that references anthropologist Margaret Mead (a lecture delivered to a classroom of rebellious police), the professor demonstrates the social constructedness of all conventions. This sequence also reveals the ethnographic project that lies at the heart not only of a documentary like *Las hurdes* but of Buñuel's entire canon, a project that demands a sharp break from the kinds of emotional identification on which the pleasures of Hollywood's aesthetic regime are propped. In his final film, *Cet obscur objet du désir* (That Obscure Object of Desire, 1977), Buñuel returns to the direct sexual referent with all of its political reverberations. Despite the "obscurity" in the title, Conchita (the male protagonist's elusive object of desire) is first encountered while serving him his supper and later found and regained in a restaurant from which she is fired for violating the establishment's taboo against workers fraternizing with customers. The repeated frustration of the bourgeois narrator's erotic desire proves analogous to the serial deprivation of the lower classes. Both become explosively violent as they reach the level of metanarrative in this story built on serial displacement and suspension, which is literally blown apart at the end. Thus, in the case of eating and sex the primary anxiety-arousing question is whether you will be able to rid yourself of the pain brought by hunger or be interrupted before you reach satisfaction. In other words, it is a narrative question involving timing, sequence, suspension, repetition, and pleasure.

In the case of dreams, on the other hand, the key question is a matter of agency – who is the dreamer, source, or enunciator? – which inevitably (or, at least, according to Freudian dreamwork theory) changes our interpretation of its meaning. Nowhere is this dynamic better illustrated than in the series of interlocking dreams in *The Discreet Charm* that begins with Sénéchal's dream of the colonel's dinner party, which has him stranded on a stage performing a play whose lines he doesn't know, a dream that is embedded within Thévenot's dream version of the colonel's party where Don Rafael deAcosta, the ambassador of Miranda, insults the French army and fatally shoots his host. Similarly, in the final act of Buñuel's film, the story of the 14 June ghost begins as a flashback told by one policeman and concludes as the police captain's dream; the final dinner party (which is interrupted by the murder of the guests by a rival drug gang) concludes with the shooting of Acosta – an action from which both he and we spectators are provided two routes of escape. We can move outward either intertextually to the dream sequence in *Los olvidados*, which contains virtually the same image of bloody meat that leads both dreamers to their death at the hands of rivals, or intratextually out of this nightmare into the waking reality of the ambassador who satisfies his hunger with a midnight snack of meat before he, along with his resilient bourgeois friends, is thrust back on that recurring dreamscape of the road leading nowhere. Since the ambassador of this fictional Latin American nation (despite his elegant demeanor) functions as the slightly less civilized Other and Miranda as an imaginary Hispanic dystopia where all charges of political corruption can be conveniently displaced, we might conclude that this murderous dream is actually a French fantasy being displaced onto a Third World foreigner, yet the ambassador is played by Spaniard Fernando Rey who was a close friend of Buñuel and his alter ego in several films, which might lead us to suspect Don Luis of this act of displacement. In any event, this pattern of structural embedding moves outward (as in *Las hurdes* and *The Exterminating Angel*) to include the whole film; that is, leading us to read all the episodes as a series of closely interrelated fantasies embedded within a cross-cultural dream of multinational corruption spun by an exiled Spaniard (cum Mexican) and his French cowriter Jean Claude Carrière, as well as by the dominant ideology in Western culture that is the object of their satire. Again, Buñuel provides us with the whole paradigm of possible answers, whose variations are strung together as a plot.

As in *Un chien andalou*, this emphasis on dream makes us aware of the tension between our immersion in raw perceptions and our drive toward narrativization. Narrative enables us to select certain perceptions and arrange them in elegant structures of meaning, but in this drive toward coherence and closure we ignore many details – subordinating them as minor, casting them as extras, or simply not perceiving them at all. As a medium that mediates between biological programming (through our rhythmic cycles of REM sleep) and cultural imprinting (reprocessing images we have absorbed in waking life), dreams daily bombard us with a flood of fragmentary percepts, which are narrativized (inevitably with distortion and censorship) only later in the wake of the dream. Thus dreams force us to confront this tug of war – between the quotidian repetition that keeps enabling us to awaken into a fresh version of the familiar fiction, and the finality of death that forces us to accept this particular version as the end.

A PREVIEW OF THINGS TO COME

This volume is divided into four sections. The first, "Overtures and Overtones," contains brief contributions from two well-known Hispanic artists who are also masterful teachers of writing – Spanish filmmaker José Luis Borau and Chicano novelist John Rechy. These dual overtures put us in the right spirit for savoring *The Discreet Charm* and relishing its unique tone.

In "Laughs with Buñuel" Borau describes the way Spaniards characteristically respond to Buñuel's films, particularly in contrast to the French. As his primary example he uses the Paris premiere of *The Discreet Charm of the Bourgeoisie*, the film that beat his own *Mi querida señorita* (which he produced and coscripted) for the best foreign-language Oscar in 1973.

In "How Marilyn Monroe Profoundly Influenced *The Discreet Charm of the Bourgeoisie*," John Rechy creates an apocryphal account of an alleged meeting between the glamorous Hollywood movie star and Buñuel, which, according to Mexican filmmaker Arturo Ripstein (who was then a young assistant to the maestro) occurred in Mexico City on the set of *The Exterminating Angel*. In this boldly imagined recreation (which builds on his earlier novelistic representation of the star in *Marilyn's Daughter*), Rechy ingeniously reveals how this meeting illuminates the most baffling mysteries in *The Discreet Charm*.

Section 2, "Recontextualizing *The Discreet Charm*," contains essays by three Hispanic scholars who teach in different parts of the world – Mexico City; Zaragoza, Spain; and Santa Barbara, California. Each contextualizes his reading of *The Discreet Charm* not only against other films by Buñuel but also against various art forms, cultures, and historical movements.

The section opens with "Buñuel, the Realist: Variations of a Dream," a comprehensive essay by Mexican filmmaker and scholar Juan Roberto Mora Catlett, which serves as an effective transition from the artistic overtures in Section 1. Attending very closely to the filmmaker's own statements as well as to his experimental practice, Catlett claims that he developed a special form of film dramaturgy, one that purposely kept a growing distance from its literary origins as it helped to define and expand the unique language of cinema. According to Catlett, this line of experimentation led Buñuel to explore the proximity of filmic language to music and dreams. More specifically, Catlett develops an illuminating analogy between the musical form known as the *rondo* and Buñuel's narrative development of recurring motifs, an analogy that enables him to examine the subversive implications of these stylistic choices in considerable detail. Catlett claims Buñuel believed the rhythm of a film is based not merely on the pace of the images themselves but also on the harmony created by their lights and shadows. This musical rhythm produces a flux of irrational images that comes close to poetry and dreams and thereby acquires considerable power in challenging the bourgeois order.

In "A Cultural Background to *The Discreet Charm of the Bourgeoisie*" (an essay translated into English by Julie Jones), Agustín Sánchez Vidal (Spain's most distinguished and prolific Buñuel scholar) reads *The Discreet Charm* as the central work in a triptych of French films that also includes *La voie lactée* (The Milky Way, 1969) and *The Phantom of Liberty* (1974). He argues that this triptych marked a new stage of artistic freedom in Buñuel's troubled career and that all three films feature an experimental episodic structure based on the Spanish picaresque novel. The essay explores the cultural and artistic sources for these works and also considers how they relate to the rest of Buñuel's canon.

In "The Discreet Charm of the Postmodern: Negotiating the Great Divide with the Ultimate Modernist, Luis Buñuel," Spanish film and literary scholar Victor Fuentes argues that Buñuel can be seen not only as "the ultimate modernist" whose classic surrealist films from the 1920s and early 1930s were definitive but also as a precursor of postmodernism, particularly in his later films made in Paris – from *Belle de jour* (1966) through *That Obscure Object of Desire* (1977). Comparing the two contexts of Paris in the 1920s and the 1970s, Fuentes analyzes how Buñuel updated surrealist concepts, such as "the unity of opposites" and "art in the service of revolution," and the political implications of these changes. More specifically, he explores Buñuel's playful negotiation of the boundaries between modernism and postmodernism in *The Discreet Charm*. In positioning Buñuel within these broader cultural and theoretical debates, this essay provides a transition to Section 3.

Titled "Retheorizing Buñuel," Section 3 contains three essays by North American scholars (two of whom are young cultural theorists completing their doctoral degrees) that demonstrate how certain recent theoretical discourses can lead us to rethink Buñuel and his entire body of work, which prefigures many of the assumptions on which those discourses are based. Far from being static or fixed, the meanings of his texts prove amazingly mobile and hence still very useful in addressing key issues of the 1990s.

In "Buñuel in the Cathedral of Culture: Reterritorializing the Film Auteur," distinguished Hispanist Marvin D'Lugo analyzes "Buñuel! The Look of the Century," a retrospective exhibit of the life and films of the filmmaker at the Spanish Centro de Arte Reina Sofía, which was part of the nation's commemoration of the birth of cinema. D'Lugo sees this exhibit as an attempt to reposition the exiled Buñuel firmly within Spanish national culture – a move that transforms him into a cultural commodity and demonstrates the mobile constructedness both of authorship and nationality. Building on his earlier sophisticated studies of other Spanish filmmakers (such as Carlos Saura and Bigas Luna), D'Lugo explores the parallel theoretical interrogations that have deconstructed the closely related discourses of auteurism and national cinema.

In "Unraveling Entanglements of Sex, Narrative, Sound, and Gender: The Discreet Charm of *Belle de jour*," Harmony Wu roots her feminist analysis of Buñuel in readings of two books published in 1990 – the memoirs of his widow, Jeanne Rucar (a rival account of their life, which portrays her husband as a domestic tyrant), and Susan Suleiman's *Subversive Intent* (a feminist critique of the misogyny of avant-garde movements, including surrealism). Wu addresses the puzzling question of how a possible misogynist like Buñuel could create two such pleasurable models for subverting narrative and its patriarchal structures from within. By reading *Belle de jour* (a film about female masochism) through *The Discreet Charm* (a film about narrative), she succeeds in provocatively rethinking not only the representations of gender in these two films by Buñuel but also more generally the complex relations between narrative and sexuality.

Finally, in "Buñuel's Net Work: The Detour Trilogy," interface designer James Tobias explores how the notion of network functions within and across Buñuel's own films as well as with several fictional and theoretical works by others. In contrast to the trilogy of the road described by Sánchez Vidal, Tobias reads Buñuel's last three films as a triad of intimately linked detours that focus on movement in the form of the network, which is most powerfully represented in the recurring scene from *The Discreet Charm* of the main characters tramping down a country road. Tobias sees this trilogy moving from a meandering toward the network in *The Discreet Charm*, through a clear exposition of the concept in *Phantom of Liberty*, toward a compression of wandering and exposition in *That Obscure Object of Desire*. Rather than using the figure of the network solely in the service of interpretation, Tobias demonstrates how it functions within a variety of influential twentieth-century discourses. Comparing Buñuel's narrative network of effects with the power-oriented networks of Michel Foucault and the cognitive communication networks of Marvin Minsky, he concludes that these figures are three of the most important agents of construction in our era.

A final section contains appendixes that extend the international network of readings generated by Buñuel's work. It contains three vintage reviews by well-known writers: Hungarian-born scholar-filmmaker Steven Kovács, author of one of the best historical studies of surrealist films; prolific popular critic Jonathon Rosenbaum, best known for his insightful studies of cult films and of narrative experimentation in the European art film; and Yugoslavian-born reviewer John Simon, notorious for his ascerbic wit. These reviews were published around the time of the film's original release in influential journals: *Film Quarterly*, the oldest surviving American film journal; *Sight and Sound*, the monthly published by the British Film Institute; and the *New York Times*, whose reviews are widely quoted by other newspapers across the nation. This section also contains a selective bibliography by Taiwanese-Chinese scholar Yungshun Tang. Both appendixes support the claim made by Tobias, Wu, and Borau that one of Buñuel's most notable achievements is his ability to make *our* work as readers such a pleasure, especially given that his films are so demanding. Apparently many critics have tracked his nomadic trail *avec plasir* – a phrase that recurs like a refrain in his last three films. It is the hope of the contributors to this volume that reading our critical works will heighten the pleasure of *your* engagement with Buñuel's *Discreet Charm*.

NOTES

1 These misperceptions have also been critiqued in several recent books on these two national cinemas as well as in several new studies of Buñuel. For Spanish cinema, see Peter Besas, *Behind the Spanish Lens: Spanish Cinema under Fascism and Democracy* (Denver: Arden Press, 1985); Marvin D'Lugo, *Carlos Saura: The Practice of Seeing* (Princeton: Princeton University Press, 1991); Marvin D'Lugo, *Guide to the Cinema of Spain* (Westport, Conn.: Greenwood Press, 1997); John Hopewell *Out of the Past: Spanish Cinema after Franco* (London: British Film Institute, 1986); Marsha Kinder, *Blood Cinema: The Reconstruction of National Identity in Spain* (Berkeley: University of California Press, 1993); Marsha Kinder, ed., *Refiguring Spain: Cinema, Media, Representation* (Durham, N.C.: Duke University Press, 1997). For Mexican cinema, see Charles Ramirez Berg, *Cinema of Solitude: A Critical Study of Mexican Film, 1967–1983* (Austin: University of Texas Press, 1992); Carl Mora, *The Mexican Cinema: Reflections of a Society, 1896–1980* (Berkeley: University of California Press, 1982). For recent studies of Buñuel, see Peter Evans, *The Films of Luis Buñuel: Subjectivity and Desire* (Oxford: Clarendon Press, 1995); Victor Fuentes, *Buñuel in Mexico* (Teruel: Instituto de Estudios Turolenses, 1993); and Agustín Sánchez Vidal, *Luis Buñuel: Obra cinematografica* (Madrid: Ediciones J. C., 1984) and *Buñuel, Lorca, Dali: El enigma sin fin* (Barcelona: Editorial Planeta, 1988).
2 Luis Buñuel, *My Last Sigh*, trans. Abigail Israel (New York: Vintage, 1983), 9.
3 Besas, *Behind the Spanish Lens*, 51.
4 Hamid Naficy, "Cross-Cultural Syncretism and Hybridity in Exile," paper delivered at the Society for Cinema Studies, 1990.
5 For a fuller discussion of this issue, see chapter 6, "Exile and Ideolog-

ical Reinscription: The Unique Case of Luis Buñuel," from my book *Blood Cinema*, passages of which have been recontextualized within this essay.

6 Linda Williams, *Figures of Desire: A Theory and Analysis of Surrealist Film* (Urbana: University of Illinois Press, 1981).

7 Mary Ann Doane, "The Voice in the Cinema: The Articulation of Body and Space," *Cinema/Sound, Yale French Studies* 60 (1980): 33–50; Kaja Silverman, *The Acoustic Mirror: The Female Voice in Psychoanalysis and Cinema* (Bloomington: Indiana University Press, 1988); and Amy Lawrence, *Echo and Narcissus: Women's Voices in Classical Hollywood Cinema* (Berkeley: University of California Press, 1991).

8 Buñuel, as quoted in José de la Colina and Tomás Pérez Turrent, *Objects of Desire: Conversations with Luis Buñuel*, ed. and trans. Paul Lenti (New York: Marsilio Publishers, 1992), 23.

9 See Anne Friedberg, *Window Shopping: Cinema and the Postmodern* (Berkeley: University of California Press, 1993); and Giuliana Bruno, *Streetwalking on a Ruined Map: Cultural Theory and the City Films of Elvira Notari* (Princeton: Princeton University Press, 1993), both of which draw on Walter Benjamin's theorization of the *flâneur* in his essay, "Paris, Capital of the Nineteenth Century," trans. Edmund Jephcott, in *Reflections* (New York: Harcourt Brace and Jovanovich, 1979). The *flâneur* is a modernist urban figure who leisurely strolls through the streets or arcades, looking through shop windows and at other passers-by. According to Friedberg: "As a social and textual construct for a mobilized visuality, flânerie can be historically situated as an urban phenomenon linked to, in gradual but direct ways, the new aesthetic of reception found in 'moviegoing.' . . . The imaginary flânerie of cinema spectatorship offers a spatially mobilized visuality but also, importantly, a temporal mobility. This use of the historical model of the *flâneur* will also draw attention to the gendering of power and visuality in the configurations of modernity. It is here that we can find the origins of the *flâneuse*, the female counterpart to the male subject in modernity" (3).

10 Gilles Deleuze and Felix Guatarri, *Anti-Oedipus: Capitalism and Schizophrenia* (Minneapolis: University of Minnesota Press, 1983).

11 Colina and Turrent, *Object of Desire*, 28.

12 According to Buñuel, "The film was banned during the so-called Black Biennium [the two years of the Republic when the right wing won the election] . . . with Lerroux and Gil Robles. Later, in 1936, the war broke out, and then the Republican government gave me money to add a sound track. The ban was only during the Republic's reactionary phase. . . . Lerroux's government issued a communiqué

to the Spanish embassies in every country instructing them to lodge an official protest before the government of any country where *Las hurdes* was shown. Later, during the war, Franco's rebels had a file on me which stated that I had made a film that was defamatory to Spain and that if I were arrested, I was to be taken to the Generalisimo's headquarters at Salamanca. The file was found at a Civil Guard barracks that the Republican troops took." Colina and Turrent, *Objects of Desire*, 33–35.

13 Ibid., 36

14 F. T. Rony, "Time and Redemption in the 'Racial Film' of the 1920s and 1930s," in *The Third Eye: Race, Cinema and Ethnographic Spectacle* (Durham, N.C.: Duke University Press, 1996), 131.

15 For a perceptive essay describing the development of the new anthropology, see James Clifford's essay, "On Ethnographic Authority," in *The Predicament of Culture: Twentieth-Century Ethnography, Literature and Art* (Cambridge, Mass.: Harvard University Press, 1983), 21–54. The films I have in mind are works like Dennis O'Rourke's *Cannibal Tours* (1987) and Trinh T. Minh-Ha's *Naked Spaces – Living Is Round* (1985) and *Surname Viet Given Name Nam* (1989).

16 Although there were several precursors to the disaster genre before *Exterminating Angel* – such as *San Francisco* (1936) and *Green Dolphin Street* (1947), which both featured spectacular earthquakes; *The Rains Came* (1939) and its 1955 remake, *The Rains of Ranchipur*, and *Hurricane* (1937), the source for the 1979 remake, which all featured floods or typhoons; and Hitchcock's *Lifeboat* (1944), an adaptation of a John Steinbeck story that anticipates the genre by presenting its ensemble of survivors as a microcosm for society – these films were usually seen as melodramas with disastrous attractions rather than as constituting their own disaster genre, which coalesced in the 1970s.

17 See Roland Barthes, *S/Z*, trans. Richard Miller (New York: Hill and Wang, 1974); and Gerard Genette, *Narrative Discourse: An Essay in Method*, trans. Jane E. Lewin (Ithaca, N.Y.: Cornell University Press, 1980). Also see Susan Suleiman, "Freedom and Necessity: Narrative Structure in 'The Phantom of Liberty,' " *Quarterly Review of Film Studies* 3 (Summer 1978): 277–295.

18 Colina and Turrent, *Objects of Desire*, 210.

19 See Suleiman, who was the first to note how this principle applied to Buñuel's narrative innovations.

20 Luis Buñuel, as quoted by José Francisco Aranda in *Luis Buñuel: A Critical Biography*, trans. and ed. David Robinson (New York: Da Capo Press, 1976), 165.

Overtures and Overtones

JOSÉ LUIS BORAU

Laughs with Buñuel

I have always been struck by the different welcome Buñuel's films receive from foreign audiences as opposed to Spanish ones. The former usually receive the Aragonese's tales with a respect bordering on the religious, especially if they are French, while the latter, on the other hand, have no compunction about celebrating what goes on, if it is deserved, with a loud guffaw.

Obviously on occasion such gaiety has a suspicious origin and owes itself not so much to the attractiveness of what the Spanish see and hear but rather more to the eagerness to demonstrate to the rest of the audience that the maestro has been "hunted down," that his divine teasing, unreachable perhaps to the rest of the audience, is shared by them. I remember with particular distaste the stentorian, malicious hoots of laughter with which some of the pupils of the now defunct Official School of Cinema in Madrid dotted the screenings of the director who at that time was still the "bad boy," almost unknown to us.

However, I now wish to make reference to the healthy, direct laughter that Don Luis's events normally produce in his countrymen; laughter that implies a natural and, on the other hand, very logical approach to the author, for whom, according to the known testimony of those who were involved with him from his infancy, it was a prime objective to amuse by means of jokes and bumps, sometimes bloody ones.

I remember specifically the commercial first night of *The Discreet Charm of the Bourgeoisie* in Paris in the spring of 1973. It was the first evening screening in one of those cinemas where the film was being put on. Nobody had seen it yet and there was a logical expectation when you bear in mind the prestige that Buñuel enjoyed among his Parisian devotees. The film progressed in general silence, but from time to time you could hear isolated, intermittent laughter right around the room. This was not the pedantic laughter of the Old School, but spontaneous, open, and genuine. At times the rest of the audience turned around to look with a certain surprise at those who with so much joy – and, of course, with such cheek – allowed themselves to underscore what was happening on the screen. My partner Luis Megino and I, who had gone to Paris precisely to contract one of the foremost figures in the film, the actress Stéphane Audran, for our film *B. Must Die*, tried in the darkness to identify those responsible for this disrespectful merriment, in some cases succeeding. Then, once the screening was over, and as the public streamed out of the cinema, we managed to get near them. All, without exception, were Spaniards who were still commenting among themselves with delight on the episodes of their illustrious fellow countryman.

I think that such differences between the welcome displayed by one audience as distinct from another, extended to Buñuel in general and to this film of his, *The Discreet Charm of the Bourgeoisie*, in particular, deserve a certain analysis because this could hold an important key to the purpose of revealing what Buñuel's work is implying jokingly, in fun, and, on occasion, with iconoclastic hooliganism, for those who can get to know him better through affinity.

Shortly after writing this statement, I chanced upon another concrete example of the kind of cultural affinity I was describing. I found it in the most important book on the history of Mexican film, *Historia documental del cine mexicano*, by the distinguished Mexican scholar Emilio García Riera, who happened to be born in Spain just before the Civil War. Riera recounts an incident that happened to him in a movie theater in Chapultepec in Mexico City where "a female spectator condemned [him] for laughing during the screening of *El discreto encanto de la burguesía*: 'More respect for the master Buñuel,' she demanded."[1]

NOTE

1 Emilio García Riera, *Historia documental del cine mexicano* (Guadala-jára: Universidad de Guadalajára, 1993), 287.

JOHN RECHY

How Marilyn Monroe Profoundly Influenced *The Discreet Charm of the Bourgeoisie*

In 1961, Marilyn Monroe visited Luis Buñuel on the set of *The Exterminating Angel* in Mexico. The following is one account of what *may* have occurred – but probably did not – between the legendary movie star and the master of surreal realism.

On the set, Marilyn extended her hand to Buñuel and, in her inimitable manner, said, "Hel-low, Mr. Bu-nu-ell," hugging each syllable. "What an honor to meet you." And it was. Herself an unwanted child, she had wept throughout *Los olvidados*.

Buñuel, an elegant socialist and always a gentleman, kissed the star's hand graciously. "Señorita Monroe." (He never lost his Spanish formality.) "The honor is mine" (*El honor es el mio*).

Marilyn, who was humble as she was gorgeous, blushed under her light makeup (she had attempted to be "modest" so Buñuel would not think her brash), and said, "Thank you – and please – *please!* – don't let me interrupt." Gathering all her courage, she added: "May I watch?"

"Naturally, yes" (*Naturalmente que si*). Buñuel bowed – and went back to direct the mysterious bear that roams a shadowy mansion while a gathering of absurd bourgeoise remain baffled

FIGURE TWO

"An account of what *may* have occurred – but probably did not – between the legendary movie star and the master of surreal realism." Original drawing by Nicolás Bautista, inspired by various photographs of the illustrious pair.

as to how they could be entrapped in a room without constraint whatever. Buñuel, who had a way with animals, was patiently teaching the bear (the director had less patience with actors who wanted their "motivation" explained) to growl while perched on a chandelier. The bear growled expertly, and the scene was finished in one take. The director returned eagerly to the movie star.

"What a superb scene!" Marilyn said. She meant it; she was always honest. Then she added: "When you whispered to the bear . . ." Buñuel had indeed whispered to the bear. "Did you tell him his motivation?" (Marilyn had been a pupil at the Actor's Studio under the tutelage of the tyrannical Lee Strasberg, who had not been able to squelch her wit.) The director lifted his hand lightly to cover his mouth. Interpreting that as disapproval of her remark, that he had considered it disrespectful, Marilyn Monroe retrenched: "But what does it mean?" she asked the director. *That* was the kind of question she was expected to ask.

Buñuel quickly understood what had happened; that the movie star was much more intelligent than she was allowed to be, even by herself. So he asked her, seriously, "What does it mean to *you*?"

Oh, he *hadn't* misunderstood! "It means that the growls a bear makes while hanging on a chandelier make more sense than all the noise of the tiresome, uncaring people trapped in" – she delivered the next words as a sensual breath: "the room."

Buñuel applauded. His beloved mother – a beautiful woman whose Catholicism he had respected even while he himself derided the Church, but never within her hearing – had taught him not to contradict a lady. But it was not his background that had produced the applause; it had been produced by the astuteness of the movie star. "Exactly what I intended," he told her.

She kissed him on the cheek. Because he was hard of hearing by then, he only felt the kiss, didn't hear the delicious sound it made, by which she had wanted to call attention to it, for everyone on the set to know that she *and* Buñuel – she never hesitated to adjust reality – had kissed *each other*.

Buñuel took both of her hands in his and led her cordially to a corner of the set. If only all actors and actresses were this intelligent, he rued. All eyes were of course on them, the Mexican crewmen posturing for the movie star, unsuccessfully, since she was captivated only by the great director. "Now tell *me*," Buñuel said earnestly to Marilyn Monroe, "how do *you* see life?"

She had always hoped someone would ask her that question! Instead, they asked what perfume she wore to bed. Oh, she had longed to be asked about the meaning of life – longed for years, ages! Not only had that now happened, but it had been asked by this great man! "I see life as," Marilyn cherished each syllable. "I see life as a long meaningless . . . *talking*, everybody just talking

. . . obliviously." (The first time she had used that word, "obliviously," she had been with Arthur Miller – they were not yet married – and he had raised his eyebrows. Intimidated, she had quickly withdrawn the word and said "obviously," giving him what he wanted – the opportunity to correct her.)

As it so happened, when Marilyn Monroe had pronounced the word "talking" on the set of *The Exterminating Angel*, an airplane had flown noisily overhead. That, and the difficulty Buñuel had with his hearing – though he had strained to listen by subtly cocking his ear as if he were rubbing a place behind it – distorted the word "talk" into "walk." Of course! he thought. It was just as the magical movie star had said, life reduced itself to "tiresome, uncaring people" – clearly the bourgeoisie – just walking, obliviously.

So it followed that in *The Discreet Charm of the Bourgeoisie* Buñuel pays homage to the movie star's sagacious observation. To depict the bourgeoisie's deadly "discreet charm," he interrupts the action and cuts to a squadron of "bourgeois" walking, just walking along a barren landscape, just walking with brisk, indomitable intrepidness; and that is their "discreet charm" – their dull, terrifying, *oblivious* endurability.

When he told an assistant the origin of that structuring device – "the gorgeous *and* brilliant Marilyn Monroe" (la hermosa y brillante Marilyn Monroe) – the assistant informed him that the movie star had said "talking," not "walking." (The assistant had "overheard" them, that day on the earlier set.) Remembering the noisy airplane that had smudged her word (Buñuel had an astonishingly retentive memory and could describe the exact location and the somber box where his mother had kept her favorite rosary, to be brought out only once a year, during Good Friday), the director immediately incorporated the new information into his film – a further homage to the grand star: at key points, narrative information is drowned out by the roar of an airplane, throwing ambiguous events into greater ambiguity.

When Marilyn Monroe saw the film, in a New York theater with Arthur Miller, by then her husband, she turned to him and said: "The bourgeoisie! Always walking, just *walking* . . ." She had paused before she added the last word, which she pronounced precisely: "*obliviously.*"

Miller arched his eyebrows at the word and waited for her to convert it into a wrong one so he could explain it all over to her.

She did not.

The greatest movie star of all time was exulting in the knowledge that her view of life had influenced the great director. It didn't matter that no one else might know that. The thrilling interlude would be kept between her and Mr. Buñuel, like a secret love affair.

Recontextualizing
The Discreet Charm

JUAN ROBERTO MORA CATLETT

Buñuel, the Realist:
Variations of a Dream

At the movies, unfortunately, it is customary
to narrate things that one already knows before one enters. I like to be told things that I
don't know. If not, why bother to go to the
cinema at all?

Luis Buñuel[1]

When we speak of Luis Buñuel's work, his contributions to film art come to mind because he opened a new road,
setting signposts that showed the way to a form of cinematic
storytelling that increasingly differentiated itself from the dramaturgy of theater and created one more akin to the essence of
film.

Historically, fiction film has taken many of its expressive tools
from older art forms, mainly literature. If we compare cinema
with its sister art form, photography, we see that at its beginnings photographers borrowed from painting and graphic arts,
until, step by step, they were able to find and develop photography's own aesthetic essence, which characterized it as an autonomous art form. A similar process occurs in film language, where
the gap between cinema and theater or novel widens constantly,

41

thanks to the work of filmmakers like Buñuel, Fellini, and Tarkovski, to mention just a few.

It is in this light that we attempt an analysis of Buñuel's 1972 film *Le charme discret de la bourgeoisie*,[2] as one example of his search for a film dramaturgy.

The word *drama* derives from the Greek word δρᾶμα which means action.[3] The distinctive characteristic of film, what makes it unique among other art forms, is its capacity to record action and movement in their duration (i.e., the passing of time) in such a way that, when the recording is reproduced, it creates an illusion of movement in the mind of the spectator. That illusion is so believable that it can be taken for a re-creation of reality, that evokes it with such strength that an audience might react to it as if it were facing real stimuli in a real space-time continuum.

We can then consider that the plastic material of cinema is an illusory space-time continuum, created in the spectator's mind by means of audiovisual stimuli. Unlike reality, that continuum can be manipulated through the means of registration (camera, microphones, etc.), the arrangement of the reality that is being recorded (the process of staging for the camera and/or microphone), and the rearrangement of the recorded material in the editing process. In this way an individual's perception of the world is expressed.

The concept *drama* has been understood in theater as a literary composition that "presents in dialogue or pantomime a story involving conflict or contrast of character,"[4] made with the purpose of being acted on a stage. The word *dramaturgy* refers to the craft of dramatic composition and when we use it in the context of cinema, it refers to the composition of dramas to be recorded in this medium. Hence, if for a play the dramaturgy must be based upon the essential characteristic of theater (i.e., the relationship between a live actor and a live spectator), in film it should be based upon its capacity for recording and reproducing movement (i.e., the passing of time).

Buñuel has done exactly that, with true artistic integrity,

while creating a body of work that reflects his search for a film dramaturgy and that keeps a growing distance from its literary origins.

If we look into the genesis of *Le charme discret de la bourgeoisie*, we find that Buñuel once said: "I have always felt attracted, both in life and in my films, by things that repeat themselves. In *El ángel exterminador* there are, at least, a dozen repetitions."[5] And referring to the idea for *Le charme* he wrote:

> We were searching for a pretext for a repetitious action, when Silberman (the producer of the film) told us what had just happened to him. He had invited some friends to dine at his home, let's say on a Tuesday, but he forgot to mention it to his wife and he also forgot that on that same Tuesday he had to dine out. The guests arrived around nine, loaded with flowers. Silberman was not in. They found his wife in a robe, completely unaware, having already dined and getting ready to go to bed. This scene became the first one of *Le charme discret de la bourgeoisie*. All we had to do was to work on it, to imagine different situations where, without pressing verisimilitude too much, a group of friends try to dine together without being able to do so. Our work was very long. We wrote five different script versions. We had to find the precise equilibrium between the reality of the situation, . . . and the accumulation of unexpected obstacles, which, nevertheless, should never seem fantastic or extravagant. Dreams came to our aid, and, even, a dream inside a dream.[6]

In constructing a film with variations of the same theme, Buñuel's aim, we find a new structural narrative proposal. The original dramatic situation is based on a traditional conception of drama: a group of characters (the bourgeois friends) pursue an objective (to dine together), motivated by their needs and desires (to enjoy gourmet food in a sophisticated social environment), and to achieve their objective they have to confront a variety of obstacles. But the development of the plot does not follow conventional rules, it only "mimics" them, misleading the spectator into believing that he is watching a commonplace feature, until he arrives to that point when narration departs radically from convention, introducing poetic or dreamlike associations among the scenes.

The Spanish critic, Agustín Sánchez Vidal, states that: "The questioning of the bourgeoisie through the misfortunes of these 'Six guests in search of a host' implies, therefore, the questioning of its narrative codes, its dramaturgy, and its social 'staging.' That is why *Le charme discret de la bourgeoisie* not only shows us as its *theme* a series of frustrations, but through its *form* frustrates our consumption of the film."[7]

When Luis Buñuel Portolès, who was born of a wealthy, bourgeois landowning family, was preparing to shoot *Le charme discret de la bourgeoisie*, he wrote film critic and Jesuit Manuel Alcalá with certain irony: "I am going to start my *panegyric* of the bourgeoisie."[8] Meaning by this that he was about to launch a vicious attack on the prototypes of bourgeois hierarchy. To understand Buñuel's position, we have to remember his convictions as a surrealist that date back to his first films. He once remarked: "Surrealism has made me see something very important: that man is not free."[9] Buñuel saw, in the forms of social intercourse, a trap that kept man prisoner. Sánchez Vidal points out that, for Buñuel, "good breeding is a form of behavior that guarantees the survival of the oppressive system. A change of those forms is a revolutionary change."[10] This observation coincides with Jean-Luc Godard's appreciation of Buñuel's second film, *L'âge d'or*, where Buñuel presented social forms as the main obstacle for the consummation of love.[11] The French filmmaker wrote:

> I believe that the most difficult thing to change is not the essence, but the form. . . . to change a man, to change the form, it would take millennia. *L'âge d'or* might be classified as a political film because it certainly addresses changes in detail, to change those forms that we know as the most powerful, which are merely social relations or good behavior. . . . And real changes only happen when those forms change.[12]

Le charme discret de la bourgeoisie tells a story of a group of well-to-do friends who are immensely preoccupied with social form, because it is form that makes them "better" than the common-ers. For example, in one scene when they are carefully preparing a dry martini (Buñuel's own recipe), they mock their chauffeur's lack of upbringing because he just empties the glass in one gulp. "It must be sipped and flavored," says one of the characters, and Rafael de Acosta, ambassador of Miranda, adds: "No system can help the masses to acquire refinement." In another scene, a cou-ple about to make love in their bedroom prefers to escape through a window and make love in the garden behind some bushes, for their luncheon guests in the living room might be disturbed by the wife's cries of pleasure.

Buñuel's attack on social forms was done through cinema. The constant scandals, censorship attacks, and turmoil that his films aroused are proof of this. Buñuel said, about his 1964 film, *Journal d'une femme de chambre*: "Bourgeois morality is immoral for me, it is what we have to fight against. It is a morality founded upon our extremely unjust social institutions, such as religion, the fatherland, family, culture, in short, what is called 'the foundations of society.' "[13] But more than in the themes per se, the aggressiveness of his work was in the formal solutions of his filmmaking. Nevertheless, his fight was not only aesthetic but, above all, ethical.

At the beginning of *Le charme discret de la bourgeoisie*, the only thing that we know about the main characters is what we learn from their appearance; and that is that they are rich, refined, and very decent. By the end we have learned that they are nothing but a gang of drug dealers with connections in high places: Ra-fael, the ambassador of Miranda, is also a ruthless politician and an impulsive and violent man, full of lust for women and food; Mrs. Thévenot is cheating on her husband by having an affair with Rafael; Mr. Thévenot is obsessed by a caviar that he zeal-ously keeps at home; the bishop is a murderer; Mr. and Mrs. Sénéchal are a lustful couple that can't control their urges; and Florence, maybe the most humanized character of the lot, is a drunkard who hates cellos and loves astrology. In their last con-versation at the table, before being wiped out by what seems to be a rival drug gang, they discuss the apprehension of a Nazi war criminal who was the head of a concentration camp. They say that to call the Nazi a butcher is an exaggeration, Rafael once met him and found him a perfect gentleman; Mrs. Sénéchal adds: "It's not incompatible, one can be poor and a thief." And Mr. Thévenot concludes: "And rich and honest, my dear."

During his film apprenticeship in France as an assistant director to Jean Epstein, Buñuel refused to embark on a career as a commercial filmmaker. Instead, he made films that questioned the establishment and joined the surrealist movement.

Their leader, André Breton, in his 1924 "manifesto," had defined the new movement as "dictated by thought, on the fringe of all rational control and of all aesthetic and moral preoccupation."[14] Contrarily, the Spanish critic Agustín Sánchez Vidal is of the opinion that Buñuel's adhesion to the group, at the end of the twenties, "implied above all an ethical option whose duties aimed toward the subversion of bourgeois values, in order to substitute them by new ones that were more respectful toward the uncontaminated motor of desire."[15]

Desire drives most of Buñuel's films. In *Le charme*, for example, the death of the ambassador of Miranda at the hands of a gang of heavily armed thugs occurs while he is hiding under the dining room table, because of his inability to control his urge to eat a slice of meat from his plate. In fact, the main theme of the film, the continuously frustrated dinner party, is a continuously frustrated desire.

We find ourselves face to face with a seemingly complex film, which disorients many spectators. *Le charme* is defined as a fiction film, in the sense that it narrates fictional events enacted by characters portrayed by actors, and in that aspect it fulfills the audience's idea of what an entertainment film should be. But it does not follow the conventional solutions of commercial film that are based on theatrical drama. Instead it proposes a form of narration that, even when dealing with themes wrung from reality, breaks away from the traditional dramatic framework and approaches a configuration that I find very near musical form.

The structure of the film gravitates around the idea of *repeti-*

tion or, more precisely, *variation*. Its construction is not unlike one of the fundamental musical forms: *variations of a theme*. According to composer Aaron Copland:

> The theme that is adopted to be subjected to variations, can be a composer's original or it can be taken from any other source. As a general rule, it's simple and of a frank character. It is better if it is so, then the audience can hear it, in its most simple version, before the beginning of the procedures that are going to vary it.[16]

Buñuel's film contains ten variations on "the frustrated dinner party" theme, intertwined in a rondolike[17] fashion with other stories and themes: "the drug smugglers' dealings with the authorities and the rival gang" story, "the bishop's revenge" story, "the stroll on the country road" leitmotif, "the policeman's and soldiers' death and ghosts" stories, and "Miranda's terrorists" story. The themes and stories are loosely linked together, as if we were following a lifelike logic where chance plays an important role. But even so, the different plots comment on each other. As spectators, we feel compelled to make sense of this composition, of this mingling of the real and the fantastic.

It is enlightening to review some of Buñuel's comments on film language, especially those that suggest its proximity to music. In an article in *Del plano fotogénico*, he stated that:

> Film, being movement above all, will have to become rhythm in order to be photogenic. If we limit ourselves merely to imprint a running man, we will have achieved the objective of film. But if during the projection, in the middle of the race everything disappears and we watch a couple of fast feet, the landscape parading vertiginously, the runner's anguished face and in successive shots . . . the main elements of the race . . . , we'll have the objective of that which is photogenic. Not only a movement or a sensation is being described, . . . but in the harmony of their lights and shadows a series of images, which given their dissimilar duration in time and different values in space, will bear the same pure enjoyment as those of a sym-

phony, or the abstract forms and volumes of a modern still nature.[18]

In a 1928 article in Madrid's *La gaceta literaria*, Buñuel criticized a superficial transposition of musical forms to film, claiming:

> A great deal has been said about the role of the shot in the architecture of film. . . . There are even those who see all cinematic virtues as based upon what is usually called the *rhythm* of a film. . . . It is not difficult to see the trick when the structure, norms, or, at least, the resemblance of film to the classic arts, mainly music and poetry, is frequently imposed onto cinema.[19]

Buñuel saw film as a "marvelous instrument to express poetry and dreams – the subconscious."[20] While watching the last part of *Le charme discret*, the audience feels that he has fulfilled this potential. Buñuel has said about cinema:

> It's the best instrument to express the world of dreams, emotions, instinct. The film-image producing mechanism . . . is the one among all means of human expression most similar to the human mind . . . the one that best mimics the workings of the mind in a dream state. B. Brunius has made us observe that the gradual night that invades the theater is the equivalent of closing the eyes: then both on the screen and in man the incursion through the night of the unconscious begins; the images, as in a dream, appear and disappear through dissolves and fade-outs; time and space become flexible, they contract or extend freely; and chronological order, as well as the relative values of duration, do not correspond to reality.[21]

His script collaborator, Jean-Claude Carrière, has testified to "Buñuel's mastery of film technique, but also – and above all – of those techniques that allow one to unblock the flux of irrational images, from the subconscious toward consciousness, training imagination as an athlete does his muscles."[22] For Buñuel, not only are the images produced important but also the way in which they relate to each other – the process that psycho-analysis calls "free association."

The constant return to "the frustrated dinner party" theme creates a spinal chord that gives the audience the impression of tagging along the trail of a plot, but the persistent interruptions by the other themes and stories, which don't follow conventional film logic (i.e., a chain of cause-effect) and which don't create any other kind of direct link with the main theme, disorient the spectator, especially the one who fell into the trap of believing that the film was being narrated in a conventional fashion.

Sánchez Vidal has noted the connections between music and dreams in Buñuel's work:

> Marcel Oms has underlined the way his scripts work like a musical score: with reiterated scenes, situations that are resumed, repeated, or modulated. All of this makes rhythms impose themselves with a peculiar logic in the editing, temporarily interrupting rational control, for the conjugation of visual rhymes. Thanks to this particular fluency, no one but him has been able to reconstruct the inner cadences of dreams, establishing shortcuts by way of the unconscious. . . . Fellini declared, not without admiration, that while watching films like *Le charme discret de la bourgeoisie*, one had the impression that cinema was made to come to grips, in an almost natural way, with the universe of dreams which is really very difficult to grasp with a camera.[23]

According to Sigmund Freud, dreams are mainly the expression of repressed desires and needs that emerge from the unconscious in a disguised form. The individual recognizes the urgency of those profound desires while simultaneously feeling the anguish that stems from their antisocial character. Because they strive against the established order and its system of ethics, they are unsettling.

In *Le charme discret de la bourgeoisie*, from the seventh variation on, the transitions between the sequences are presented as dreams within dreams, a common human experience. It is as if, instead of watching a film, we were dreaming it. Buñuel has said, although in another context, that "film audiences are lazy and they are always half asleep during the movie,"[24] and "due to that category or kind of hypnotic inhibition, [they] lose a high percentage of [their] cognitive faculties."[25] He was interested in a technique of filmmaking that would make unusual or incredible situations seem natural and believable. He resorted to what appear to be traditional solutions, while at the same time doing weird things with time, space, his actors, and the plot. As he anticipated those in the audience to be half asleep, he expected them not to notice consciously these things as they happened but foresaw a delayed effect that would come about when the accumulation of strange happenings would create in the audience members' subconscious an unrest that would jolt and provoke them, while being perceived as a dreamlike atmosphere.

Buñuel's film teacher, Jean Epstein, thought that "film dramaturgy means a dramaturgy of space, of a changing space, that differentiates itself from theatrical dramaturgy, which presupposes fixed distances and a continuous time dimension."[26] In Epstein's case, this reasoning made him modify chiefly the time factor by the use of slow- or fast-motion cinematography. Buñuel preferred to play with the spatial factor. Space in film is rendered mainly through lighting and photography: with light we can create, or eliminate, contrasts between figure and background and we can model an object by means of very hard shadows or a delicate chiaroscuro. Different lenses let us see not only a certain quantity of space but, together with filters or selective focus, they also emphasize or flatten perspective. Buñuel wrote: "The lens – 'that eye with no tradition, morality, prejudices, capable, nevertheless, of interpreting by itself' – sees the world. The filmmaker, orders it afterward. Machine and man. The purest expression of our age, our art, our daily authentic art."[27] We also have access to many of the resources of line and color developed by painting to represent space, as we are also dealing with a flat surface (the screen) that is going to be interpreted in a three-dimensional way. In *Le charme discret de la bourgeoisie*,

Buñuel uses space distortion in a subtle way to induce the feeling of dream.

     In the scene when the group of friends arrives to dine at the colonel's place, the walls of the dining room are painted backdrops and, although we see them as such, due to the flatness of the screen and the actions of the players, we acknowledge that they are part of a scenery only when the characters themselves realize that they are on a stage, being watched by an audience. It would seem that, by a sheer act of magic, a real room suddenly became a stage. What really happens is that, in perfect accord with Buñuel's dramaturgy, we stop perceiving flat surfaces as three-dimensional and start seeing them as they are. In the sergeant's dream, after introducing it with the words, "I was taking a stroll at dusk, along a very busy street," we see a contradictory image: the sergeant strolls along an empty street while we hear on the soundtrack, at a very low volume, the clamor of a crowd inside a large hall and the faraway sound of a church bell tolling; although the sergeant walks near the camera, we don't hear his footsteps. Buñuel creates an eerie feeling by the use of color (everything is tinted in a bluish scale) and, although we have an evident vanishing point in the frame composition (the street walls diminishing in the distance), he flattens the perspective by eliminating the shadows and by excluding reddish colors in the foreground. The contradicting audiovisual and spatial information, supported, of course, by the actors' performance, creates the dreamlike quality of the scene; afterward, when the sergeant is talking with his dead mother, Buñuel cuts to a close shot of the mother's hands, folded upon a cross, while she is being buried. This method, of creating a synthetic continuity between different spaces or times so the spectator will perceive it as a continuum, serves Buñuel not only to make ghosts appear and disappear but also to reproduce a flow of thoughts composed of logical ideas, free associations, feelings, and emotions.

Several times in this film, a loud noise prevents the audience from hearing a piece of dialogue: a passing car covers Rafael's statement that the American ambassador was arrested for smuggling cocaine, a passing plane and office noise cover up the home minister's and the superintendent's explanations as to why they are releasing the ambassador and his friends from jail, and so on. Actor Roberto Cobo, who played "Jaibo" in Buñuel's 1950 film *Los olvidados,* narrated the following story during a television interview:

> One day, when Buñuel was shooting a scene, the sound engineer asked to cut the camera because the noise of a passing plane was drowning out the dialogue, Buñuel, who was upset by this interruption, told him that being in a city, it was natural for planes to fly by and he gave the sound engineer permission to cut a take only if a ship sailed by.

Frankly, Buñuel's themes are quite familiar to us from the press, literature, and everyday life. We often find comments on the depravity and corruption of the upper classes, the collaboration between governments and drug dealers, guardians of morality who place themselves above it, and the like. It is interesting to notice that the only scene cut out from the film by the Spanish censors was the one where the bishop shoots the murderer of his parents after giving him Christian absolution. But what is important in his work is how he presents these themes as a mixture of the rational and the irrational, because then we see them in their profound meaning and not as socially conscious clichés. In that context Buñuel wrote:

> Surrealism is not something nonexistent that is added to reality. . . . The Academy accustomed us to think rationally, but man is not rational. . . . Surrealism is what was missing to complete our vision of reality, taking into account that reality holds a terrible and extraordinary sense to be discovered. I am not a surrealist, because surrealism, as a school, has already . . . laid its egg. . . . Surrealism's . . . foundation was laid on humor as a liberating force, . . . the last poetic and subversive element in present society. . . . But we must not confuse humor with irony. Irony is a partial, individual, and isolated element. . . . I am against irony. Humor is tremendous, violent, and liberat-

ing. It's an escape to produce subversive and disagreeable sensations through laughter. . . . Sentimentality is the opposite of humor. Sentimentality is conformism, it pleases people's emotional habits. . . . On the other hand, surrealism is a mixture of tenderness and cruelty, and precisely in this mixture resides its quality.[28]

In this film, we find the class struggle as a constant, underlying all the themes: the have-nots against the have-alls. Buñuel underlines it with discrete strokes: Miranda's ambassador shooting at the female terrorist, the shabbiness of her clothes set against the elegant decoration of the ambassador's apartment, the bread and lettuce that she carries in her handbag as opposed to the gourmet food of the ambassador and his friends, the murder of the bishop's parents at the hands of their gardener (who claims they treated him like a beast), the story of the French soldiers being forced to drink three liters of wine a day to prevent them from deserting, the home secretary liberating the rich drug dealers while the police torture a young student, the First World citizens slandering or being completely ignorant about the Third World, and so forth. André Breton has said: "The most admirable thing of the fantastic, is that the fantastic does not exist, everything is real."[29]

"At the end of his film career," points out Sánchez Vidal, "Buñuel confessed: 'The thought that still guides me today, at the age of seventy-five, is the same that guided me at twenty-seven. It's an idea from Engels: the artist describes authentic social relationships with the objective of destroying the conventional ideas on these relationships, to place the optimism of the bourgeois world in a crisis and to force the audience to doubt the perenniality of established order."[30] Also, at a conference at Mexico's National Autonomous University, Buñuel concluded the idea with more of Engels's words: "even if he [the artist] does not show us a conclusion directly, or even if he does not take sides ostensibly."[31]

For Buñuel film is an "instrument of poetry, with all the liberating sense that this word holds as a subversion of reality, a disagreement with the narrow society that surrounds us."[32] The concept of reality that Buñuel has expressed in his films has much to do with the poetics that Salvador Dalí coined under the motto of the "Holy Objectivity." When he visited Barcelona, to collaborate with Buñuel, he wrote about *Un chien andalou*:

> It deals with . . . the establishment of facts. What makes it abysmally different from other films resides only in that such facts, instead of being conventional, fabricated, . . . are real facts or similar to them and because of that, enigmatic, incoherent, irrational, absurd, with no explanation. . . . Only the imbecility and cretinism shared by the majority of the writers and by people from especially utilitarian ages have made it possible to believe in real facts as having a clear meaning. . . . The appearance of the facts of life as coherent is the result of an accommodation process, very similar to the one that also makes thought appear as something coherent, being incoherence by itself.[33]

Buñuel's characters don't act logically all the time but follow sudden impulses. For example, in the beginning of the film, when the friends arrive for dinner at the Sénéchals' home, they give Mrs. Sénéchal a bouquet. As soon as she tells them that there is no dinner and hands their gift to the maid, Florence snatches it back for no apparent reason and holds on to it until they arrive at the restaurant. Just as in life, his characters sometimes behave in unpredictable ways.

On this subject, Buñuel tells us that when he was having a conversation with the Italian neorealist film director and script writer Cesar Zavattini, he stated his disagreement with neorealism:

> We were having a meal together and the first example that came to my mind was the glass of wine from which I was drinking. To a neorealist, I told him, a glass is a glass and nothing else; we watch how it is brought out of a cupboard, how it's filled with a drink, how it's taken to the kitchen to be washed, and how it's broken by the maid, who can be dis-

missed from the household or not, etc. But that same glass can be a thousand different things when it's contemplated by different men because each of them charges with affection what he beholds, and not one of them sees it as it is, but as his desires and his emotional condition want him to see it. I support a kind of cinema that will make me see that kind of glass because that cinema will give me an integral vision of reality.[34]

Delving into these concepts, we find that in an article titled *Del plano fotogénico*, there is a paragraph that complements this idea:

> Let's remember an episode from *The Merry Widow*: three men gathered in a theater box, desiring the same woman who is dancing on the stage. . . . Suddenly, she stops. According to how she is seen by each of the men, she is shown to us fragmented in three shots: feet, abdomen, and eyes. Immediately, three psychologies are explained by cinema: a refined sadist, a sexual primitive, and a pure lover. Three psychologies and three motives. The rest of the film is a comment on these three attitudes.[35]

Reality processed by the subconscious is the spring of Buñuel's themes. And as all human beings grow and are educated in a social milieu, the reality he deals with is essentially a social reality. The struggle between the id (as the place where all that is instinctive resides) and the superego (as the place where all the social prohibitions reside) dictates his dramaturgy. It is interesting to notice that in Constantin Stanislavski's acting method, the origin of dramatic action is placed precisely on this struggle; a physical motivation rises from the id as an impulse and becomes a psychological motivation in the ego, urging the person to satisfy a need or a desire, but the superego, finding the desire or the plan to satisfy it unacceptable, creates an obstacle that the ego must overcome through proper action.

In this film, Buñuel's characters feel hunger (physical motivation) so they want to have dinner (psychological motivation), but their upbringing tells them that they can only do so if certain conditions are met (the social obstacle). They have to eat food suited to their rank, and they have to follow precise rules of behavior and good manners. Since those conditions are never fulfilled, the characters are not able to satisfy their hunger; they are condemned by the same social forms that give them rank. At the end of the film, only Rafael is able to get something to eat when, defying the rules of good upbringing, he gets a midnight snack from the refrigerator.

If we list the obstacles that block the main line of action of the film (i.e., the attempts of the friends to celebrate their dinner party), we find they are: (1) the host forgets to tell his wife that he is having guests for dinner; (2) a wake over the dead is taking place in the restaurant where they want to dine; (3) the guests flee a feared police raid; (4) the tea shop is out of tea and coffee; (5) a battalion of soldiers arrives to stay at the Sénéchals during military maneuvers; (6) a sergeant arrives with an urgent message for the colonel, ordering him to initiate the maneuvers; (7) when they are about to start dining, a curtain rises and they realize that they are on a stage; (8) Miranda's ambassador assassinates the host of the dinner party; (9) the police apprehend the friends, on drug-dealing charges, when they have just sat at the table; (10) a group of armed hoods (probably the rival Marseilles gang) machine-guns the friends while they are eating a leg of lamb.

Most of the obstacles have to do with violence or death, which are also the underlying themes of the film. Could the main dramatic conflict of the picture be hunger against death and violence, or the libido opposing destruction?[36] According to Nicola Abbagnano, "In *Civilization and Its Discontents* . . . , Freud considered all of human History as a struggle between two instincts, *eros* or the life instinct and (*thanatos*), the death instinct. 'This struggle,' he wrote, 'is, in short, the essential content of life. That is the reason why it is necessary to define evolution by this brief formula: humankind's fight for life.' "[37] And, if cinematographer Gabriel Figueroa (who worked with Buñuel in Mexico) is correct when he states that "Buñuel made only one film and then kept repeating it all through his life,"[38] could it then be the main dramatic conflict of all of his films? The only answer that I can give is that each of us sees in a film a unique and very personal meaning. In that way a film is like a house of mirrors, where we see ourselves in new and different ways.

The film is punctuated by a leitmotif that is repeated three times: the group of friends aimlessly strolling on a country road. They don't get anywhere and there isn't even a continuity that would let us affirm that they are advancing. The second time it appears, we see Mr. Sénéchal tying his shoelace and then running to catch up with his friends. In the following two shots that seem to occur in temporal and spatial continuity with the previous ones, we see two of the friends carrying branches that suddenly appear in their hands; in the following shots, they don't have the branches any longer. It is as if we were watching different variations of the same action, occurring in the same place. They don't get anywhere, they are not going anywhere. It is a visual parable and, with this same parable, the film ends. Buñuel does not include the "The End" title because the friends' stroll does not have an end: they are condemned to it for eternity.

As a corollary, I would like to point out that Buñuel wrote, among his likes and dislikes, that "I like to observe animals, mainly insects. But I'm not interested in their physiological performance, their concrete anatomy. What I like to observe are their habits."[39]

NOTES

1 *Griffith* Magazine, no. 1, Madrid, June 1965, as quoted in J. Francisco Aranda's *Luis Buñuel, Biografía Crítica* (Barcelona: Editorial Lumen, 1970), 356–57.
2 For this essay, we consulted a Beta NTSC format copy of *Le charme discret de la bourgeoisie*, Cinematheque collection, CC 8000, Media Home Entertainment, Inc., Los Angeles, 1985.
3 Santiago Rodríguez Castro, *Diccionario etimológico griego-latín del Español* (Mexico: Editorial Esfinge, 1996), 39.
4 *The Random House Dictionary of the English Language, College Edition* (New York: Random House, 1968), 401.
5 Luis Buñuel, *Mi último suspiro*, trans. Ana María de la Fuente (Barcelona: Plaza & Janes, S. A., 1982), 231–232.

6 Ibid., 240.
7 Agustín Sánchez Vidal, *Luis Buñuel* (Madrid: Editorial Cátedra, 1991), 99.
8 Manuel Alcalá, *Buñuel, cine e ideología* (Madrid: Cuadernos para el diálogo S. A., EDICUSA, 1973), 99.
9 Aranda, *Luis Buñuel*, 199.
10 Sánchez Vidal, *Luis Buñuel*, 25.
11 It is interesting to note that in *Le charme discret de la bourgeoisie* there is a reference to *L'âge d'or's amour fou*, in the scene when Mr. and Mrs. Sénéchal try to make love in their bedroom, while they fight with their clothes that don't seem to be made to allow lovemaking (just as in *L'âge d'or*), and then escape through a window into the garden, to make love behind some bushes.
12 Jean-Luc Godard, *Introduction à une véritable histoire du cinéma*, as quoted in Sánchez Vidal, *Luis Buñuel*, 26–27.
13 Sánchez Vidal, *Luis Buñuel*, 79.
14 J. Pierre, *El surrealismo* (Madrid: Aguilar, 1969), 98, quoted in Manuel Alcalá, *Buñuel*, 59.
15 Sanchez Vidal, *Luis Buñuel*, 14.
16 Aaron Copland, *Cómo escuchar la música* (Havana: Instituto del Libro, Havana, 1970), 162.
17 "The *rondo* is a type of musical composition in which a section is repeated at certain intervals. . . . A simple *rondo* is constructed with an *a-b-a-c-a-d* . . . (etc.) outline, in which *a* is the section that is repeated and *b,c,d* . . . are the contrasting sections." Ibid., 446, 447.
18 Luis Buñuel, quoted in Aranda, *Luis Buñuel*, 319.
19 Luis Buñuel, "Decoupage o segmentación cinegráfica," in *La gaceta literaria*, Madrid, December 1928, quoted in Aranda, *Luis Buñuel*, 324.
20 Sánchez Vidal, *Luis Buñuel*, 10.
21 "El cine, instrument de poesía," *Revista Universidad de México 13*, no. 4 (December 1958), quoted in Aranda, *Luis Buñuel*, 334–335.
22 Sánchez Vidal, *Luis Buñuel*, 22.
23 Ibid., 21–22.
24 Interview by Fausto Carrillo in *México en la Cultura*, 478 (May 11, 1958), quoted by Aranda, *Luis Buñuel*, 341–42.
25 Aranda, *Luis Buñuel*, 333.
26 Yvette Biró, *Teorie filmové dramaturgie* (Prague: Cs. filmovy ústav, 1975), 113.
27 Aranda, *Luis Buñuel*, 324–25.
28 Sánchez Vidal, *Luis Buñuel*, 68.
29 Ibid., 17–18.

30 Ibid., 31.

31 "El cine, instrumento de poesía," *Revista Universidad de México*, 13, no. 4 (December 1958), as quoted in Aranda, *Luis Buñuel*, 336. This quotation by Buñuel is from the famous letter that Engels wrote Minna Kaustky from London, on September 26, 1885. Sánchez Vidal tells us: "The author had sent him her novel, *Die Alten und die Neuen*, a work with social pretensions, and Engels praised it with a final reproach: the 'message,' the writer's taking of sides, was too explicit. He proposed, instead, less conditioned reality grasping procedures: 'The novel addresses mainly readers from the bourgeois milieu, that is, those who don't directly belong to ours, and among them the novel will fulfill its mission very well, according to my judgment, if through a faithful picture of life's true conditions, it breaks the conventional illusions that exist about them, crushes the optimism of the bourgeois world and makes inevitable the doubt about the eternal validity of everything that exists, even if the work by itself does not offer an immediate solution, and in certain circumstances, there isn't even need to take sides ostensibly.' " Quoted by Sánchez Vidal, *Luis Buñuel*, 30.

32 "El cine, instrumento de poesía," quoted in Aranda, *Luis Buñuel*, 332.

33 Sánchez Vidal, *Luis Buñuel*, 17–18.

34 "El cine, instrumento de poesía," quoted in Aranda, *Luis Buñuel*, 336.

35 Aranda, *Luis Buñuel*, 321.

36 "The libido is not the specific sexual drive, but merely the tendency to produce or reproduce voluptuous sensations related to the so-called 'erogenous zones'; which is a tendency that manifests itself from the first instants of human life." Nicola Abbagnano, *Diccionario de filosofía* (Havana: Instituto del libro, 1960), 56.

37 Ibid., 966.

38 Alain Derbez, "Figueroa mira a Buñuel," *Suplemento cultural de La jornada*, no. 4443 (19 January 1997), 10.

39 Luis Buñuel, quoted in Aranda, *Luis Buñuel*, 222.

AGUSTÍN SÁNCHEZ VIDAL   *Julie Jones, translator*

A Cultural Background to *The Discreet Charm of the Bourgeoisie*

At the end of the 1970s Luis Buñuel's film career settled into its last French phase. This new equilibrium came from the experience of filming *Le journal d'une femme de chambre* (The Diary of a Chambermaid, 1965). It was here that he began to work with Jean-Claude Carrière on screenplays and with Serge Silberman as producer. Before *Le journal* his efforts to break into the Francophone market had been less successful. Films like *Cela s'appelle l'aurore* (1955), *La mort en ce jardin* (Death in the Garden 1956), and *La fièvre monte à El Pao* (1959), as well as *The Young One* (1960), his second attempt at entering the English-speaking market, had not fared well. After *The Young One*, Buñuel returned to Spain in order to film *Viridiana*. This renewed contact with his native land led to a period of heightened creativity that produced *Viridiana* (1961), *El ángel exterminador* (The Exterminating Angel, 1962), and *Le journal*. But he had to leave his next film, *Simón del desierto* (Simon of the Desert, 1965), unfinished because of problems with funding. This setback, following hard on the heels of the *Le journal* experience, convinced him that he should

Portions of this essay appeared in my *El mundo de Luis Buñuel* (Zaragoza: Caja de Ahorrus de la Inmaculada, 1993).

go back to making French films. The commercial success of *Belle de jour* (1966) provided him with a freedom that he had hardly enjoyed since his first films – *Un chien andalou* (An Andalusian Dog, 1929) and *L'âge d'or* (The Age of Gold, 1930). The result was that peculiar triptych made up of *La voie lactée* (The Milky Way, 1969), *La charme discret de la bourgeoisie* (The Discreet Charm of the Bourgeoisie, 1972), and *La fantôme de la liberté* (The Phantom of Liberty, 1974).[1]

A number of different stimuli contributed to this trilogy. The peripatetic structure was inspired by the picaresque novel and its progeny, especially *Gil Blas de Santillana* by Alain René Lesage (1715–1735) and *The Manuscript Found in Saragossa* (1797) by Waclaw Potocki. Both Potocki's original narration (published in Roger Caillois's collection of 1958) and the magnificent 1964 film version by the Polish director Wojciech J. Has interested him. Buñuel must have recognized his own techniques in Has's inventive use of flashbacks to create the effect of a mise en abîme, like the Russian dolls that nest one inside the other. The digressive structure that characterizes the picaresque was dear to Buñuel. The episodes in *L'âge d'or* are linked by means of fortuitous details, and *Ilegible, hijo de flauta* (Illegible, Son of the Flute, 1947) is also governed by a logic of chance.[2] The journey is the raison d'être of *The Milky Way*, where the external pilgrimage along the Camino de Santiago is matched by the internal pilgrimage through the different heresies, and *The Phantom of Liberty*, which depends on a series of chance encounters. In *The Discreet Charm* the journey reappears in the leitmotif of the road.

Dreams provide another important structural element in *The Discreet Charm*. They take the form here of flashbacks within flashbacks. Buñuel had used oneiric sequences very effectively throughout his career, most notably in films such as *Los olvidados* (The Young and the Damned, 1950) and *Subida al cielo* (Mexican Bus Ride, 1952). But it was not until *Belle de jour* (1967) that he used them to structure the work so that they erase the boundary between "dream" and "reality," thereby challenging the bourgeois conceptions of world and narrative. This approach allowed him to treat the bourgeois social conventions as a form of fiction (*The Discreet Charm* inherits this extensive use of oneiric scenes and flashbacks; the whole film can be seen as a series of dreams narrated in flashback.[3])

The work of contemporary directors, like Godard, provided an additional stimulus for the trilogy. When Buñuel attended the 1967 Venice Film Festival to present *Belle de jour*, he saw *La chinoise*. "If this is what people are doing now," he remarked to Carrière, "I think we can make the movie about the heresies." It was a project that had been on his mind since he had read Marcelino Menéndez Pelayo's *La historia de los heterodoxos españoles* (The History of the Spanish Heretics), and the result was *The Milky Way*. After that, in 1970, he filmed another old project – Benito Pérez Galdos's novel *Tristana* – and then resumed the trilogy, making *The Discreet Charm* in 1972 and *The Phantom of Liberty* in 1974.[4]

In the triptych Buñuel recapitulates a good part of his cinematic career, returning to a surrealism that is now very different from the militant frenzy of his early work. The tone, too, is gentler, more ironic, not so harsh as his Mexican phase, as though it stemmed from a Cartesian revision of earlier works. *The Milky Way* bears much the same resemblance to *Simon of the Desert* as does *The Discreet Charm* to *The Exterminating Angel*. The last two share a common hidden structure, a very Buñuelesque form or antiform, a string of bourgeois rituals that link mass to meat, altar to table, with all the connotations, both fascinating and sinister, that these ceremonies have for the filmmaker.

BLACK MASSES, SATANIC SUPPERS

As an explicit theme, the black mass appears only in a screenplay that Buñuel never filmed: *Là-Bas*, written in 1976 and based on Huysmans's novel of the same name. However, in covert form, it crops up in a number of his films, forming a kind of subterranean link among sequences. The one in *Belle de jour* is obvious; here the necrophiliac duke invites Séverine to his mansion, where he draws her into a strange ceremony that was originally presided over by the amazing Christ of Grünewald. The hints of a black mass are equally hard to miss in *La fièvre monte à El Pao* (1960) when Alejandro Gual surrounds the bed with candles and lays out priestly robes on a chair just before Ines surrenders to him. The relation between the religious and the erotic is also clear in the washing of the feet sequence with which *El: This Strange Passion* (1952) begins. But there are other similar, if more secret, ceremonies in Buñuel's filmography that hint at a possible explanation for these dances of desire, which, I believe, intensify eroticism by interjecting religion. It is as though Buñuel had to orchestrate a whole ritual in order to exorcise his fear of that inseparable couple: sex and death.

Buñuel first formulates this notion of the interference of religion with the erotic in *Un chien andalou*; here the protagonist has to drag priests and donkey carcasses behind him in order to reach the woman. In *L'âge d'or*, all of society gets in the way of the lovers. The rotten bishops on whose remains Rome is built are a deadweight, and the lovers are finally separated in the name of the church. At the end of *Abismos de pasión* (also called *Cumbres borrascosas* and *Wuthering Heights*, 1953), sex is treated as a secret ceremony that must be performed, as André Breton pointed out, in a tomb. In *Tristana*, Don Lope Garrido seduces the protagonist after she visits the tomb of Cardinal Tavera in Toledo.

These are the ceremonies related to the Altar. The ceremonies related to the Table are also critical in Buñuel's world. These primal scenes that take place at the dinner table have a subversive function. Buñuel uses them to question the social rituals on which they are based. As Godard, who himself defied the conventions, argues,

> The critics failed to realize that *L'âge d'or* is a political film. In fact, it is probably the only film that caused a scandal in its time and – I have to admit it – is still powerful. *L'âge d'or* interests me because it is a film that deals with the conventions. I think the hardest thing to change isn't the content, it's the form. . . . The form is the hardest thing to change that there is: to change a man, to change the form, that takes millennia. . . .

Diplomas, or the way a person dresses, these things are incredibly important. If you dress badly, they won't receive you in certain places. The conventions tell us how a head of state should be received at the airport, or a newborn baby baptized or how people should get married.[5]

The marriage ceremony, to use one of Godard's examples, really does matter to Buñuel's characters. In *Ensayo de un crimen* (The Criminal Life of Archibaldo de la Cruz, 1955) a police inspector, a priest, and a colonel (forming a trinity of civil, religious, and military authority) step outside the church during a marriage service in order to vent their feelings:

INSPECTOR: I had to leave the chapel because I was on the point of tears. Weddings, baptisms, even confirmations always make me cry.

PRIEST: It's because there is nothing else like the pomp and circumstance of the Catholic Church. Why not say it? – the mantle of poetry it bestows on all its ceremonies is unique. How would you feel if this were a civil ceremony?

CHIEF: It would be common and ordinary. . . .

COLONEL: You're absolutely right, father, but, apart from that, I think our friend, the honorable inspector of police, is a sentimentalist.

CHIEF: It's true, it's true, thank God. Can you believe it – if I see a regiment go by with the flag unfurled, I feel a knot in my throat, and my eyes fill up with tears?

COLONEL: Of course, that's natural in well-bred people. It's patriotic emotion.

The reception in *L'âge d'or* is the earliest version of this primal scene based on the bourgeois rituals, but it also surfaces in the parties in *El, The Criminal Life of Archibaldo de la Cruz*, and *Cela s'appelle l'aurore* (all of which are broken up by shootouts, murders, or other forms of violence). In relation to the Table, the situation reaches parodic heights in *The Phantom of Liberty*. Here the guests are invited to a collective defecation while they have to eat shut up in narrow booths that isolate them from each other as if they were involved in an embarrassing, private act.

The rituals of the Altar and of the Table converge for the first time in *Viridiana*, a film with two halves: the first, starring Fernando Rey, culminates in Don Jaime's Black Mass and the frustrated rape of the novice Viridiana; the second, starring Francisco Rabal, ends in a kind of Satanic Supper with the beggars' orgy and another effort to rape Viridiana. In this case, the transformation from Altar to Table is explicit, thanks to the gloss of Leonardo da Vinci's *Last Supper*. The Last Supper is, of course, the first Mass, and this facilitates the passage from dark dinner to Black Mass. *Viridiana* depends on this dialectic between the picaresque and the mystic modes that are critical to Spanish literature and thought.

It's not surprising that Buñuel should fall back on the same formulation in his next film, *The Exterminating Angel*. Here a select group of upper middle-class Mexicans who have gotten together for dinner discover that they cannot leave the dining room until, a few days later, they repeat the situation that led to their paralysis. The film ends when they gather in church to offer a Te Deum of thanks for their release only to find the situation repeating itself. Again, as in *Viridiana*, the rituals of the Table and the Altar converge. *The Exterminating Angel* turns on a notion that will be essential to understanding *The Discreet Charm*: Buñuel regards the upper middle class as a caste that has no choice but to repeat its rituals; it cannot survive without them, but it is imprisoned within them.[6]

The Discreet Charm is a kind of popularized version in lay form for Cartesians of *The Exterminating Angel*. In it the explicit religious elements are no longer foregrounded, but they remain essential to this film and to *The Phantom of Liberty* as well. An awareness of Buñuel's "hidden agenda" – his reliance on ingredients that are part and parcel of Hispanic tradition – is fundamental to any understanding of the two films.

A GUEST MADE OF STONE

The central idea of *The Discreet Charm* – the interrupted dinner – comes from Buñuel's favorite play: *Don Juan Tenorio*, written by the Spanish Romantic José Zorrilla in 1844. This drama became so popular in Spain that it was presented every year on the night of 1 November, the Day of the Dead. Many Spaniards, including Buñuel, knew all the verses by heart. One of the best-known passages involves the Guest Made of Stone, in which Don Juan invites the statue of the commander, Don Gonzalo de Ulloa, a man injured twice at the hands of Don Juan, who has both murdered him and seduced his daughter, the novitiate Doña Ines. The statue of the commander appears during the supper, inviting Don Juan to visit him in the pantheon of the cemetery.[7]

This peculiar – and very Hispanic – mixture of love, religion, and death had already inspired the sequence in *Viridiana* in which Fernando Rey is about to rape the drugged postulant. But in *The Discreet Charm* Buñuel makes explicit reference to Zorrilla's play in the episode entitled "Frustrated Supper and Theatrical Performance at the Colonel's Home." Here, the bourgeois protagonists and the bishop go to the colonel's home, where they are received by an ill-humored servant, who seats them at table and rudely serves them some rather odd-looking chicken that turns out to be made of rubber. At that moment, they hear three knocks like those that announce the start of a play. The curtain at the end of the room opens, and the group finds itself on stage, in front an audience that is whistling impatiently. A prompter clues in the bishop with words inspired by one of the scenes in *Don Juan Tenorio*: "And to prove your valor, you invited the ghost of the commander to dine with you."[8]

Buñuel valued Zorrilla's work: "I love the *Tenorio*. It's a masterpiece, a work of genius. . . . The *Tenorio* is one of the great achievements of the theater. If it weren't, people wouldn't have gone to see it all these years"[9] As he remarks in his memoirs, he had only directed two plays in his entire life – *El retablo de Maese Pedro* by de Falla, in 1926, and the *Tenorio*:

> The only other time I directed for the theatre was in 1960 in Mexico: Zorrilla's perennial *Don Juan Tenorio*, a beautifully constructed play which he wrote in a week. It ends in Paradise where Don Juan, who's been killed in a duel, finds that his

soul has been saved because of Doña Ines's love. The staging was very classical, a far cry from the satirical scenes from such classics we used to do at the Residencia.[10]

In the Residencia de Estudiantes, that famous dormitory-*cum*-cultural-center, Buñuel himself and Federico García Lorca (and Dali, after he entered the Residencia in September 1922) treated Zorrilla's text without much respect. In fact, the situation reflected in *The Discreet Charm* belongs to the fragment that Buñuel and Lorca chose to perform on All Saints' Day of 1920.[11] The filmmaker, who of course played the role of Don Juan, appeared in soccer shoes and carried a typewriter that he used for dispatching his abundant love letters.[12]

The actor Francisco Rabal, who knew about Buñuel's weakness for the *Tenorio*, suggested in the mid-1960s that he direct the play in Spain, but Buñuel was not anxious to be stuck for over a month in a Madrid theater. However, they did exchange a few letters about the possibility, and these show just how much the subject of Don Juan interested the filmmaker:

> I have been rereading all the Don Juan dramas, starting with the first one: Tirso (horrible), Molière (some decent lines), Goldoni (mediocre), Dumas (good, this is the father of Zorrilla's version, it premiered six years before his), Rostand (a stinker), Pushkin (blah).[13]

Buñuel told me once that what he most liked about Zorrilla's treatment of the Don Juan legend was the conflict between father and son. If we are to believe his *Memorias de un tiempo viejo* (Memories of Time Gone By), Zorrilla translated the terror he felt toward his own father into this form. The crux of the play, in this reading, is not love so much as the search for forgiveness, and this can be provided only by the imposing, stony bulk of the commander. Buñuel's choice of passages both for the performance in the Residencia de Estudiantes and for *The Discreet Charm* focuses on the father-son relationship. The reappearance of the statue at the beginning of *The Phantom of Liberty* also speaks to the paternal theme, although this time the motif is based on "El beso" (The Kiss) by another Spanish Romantic poet: Gustavo Adolfo Bécquer. The scene takes place in a church in Toledo during the Napoleonic invasion of Spain. A half-drunk French officer sees two stone effigies – an ancient, bearded knight and a beautiful, much younger woman – that guard the tombs. Having desecrated the sanctuary, the officer then kisses the image of the woman, but at that exact moment the knight lifts his stone gauntlet and whacks the man on the head. Once again, a ghost with paternal connotations comes between a suitor and his young intended.

It is hardly strange, then, that in *The Discreet Charm* the connection between Buñuel's father's ghost and Don Juan's should be reestablished. It happens in the episode known as "the Lieutenant's Dream." While the lieutenant is in a tea room recounting his dream, a flashback takes us to a period twenty years earlier when, as a child, he is getting ready to enter military school. The boy's father (he is designated by this generic name in the screenplay) warns him quite brusquely about the hard life and the rigorous discipline he will find there. Not much impressed by his father's speech, the boy starts playing in the hallway. Suddenly he glimpses his dead mother through a windowpane that opens onto the corridor. He calls her and then enters the room. It is abandoned, with the furniture covered up. The boy starts writing in lipstick on the mirror, "Mama, I love you . . ." when his mother's voice calls him from the armoire: "Hubert, my son. It's your mother. Don't be afraid." A gentle breeze blows out from the direction of the clothes that are hanging there. This scene brings to mind the beginning of *The Criminal Life of Archibaldo de la Cruz*, where the young Archibaldo tries on his mother's corset. It also recalls a real armoire where Buñuel used to play as a child (in fact, he has admitted that the bedroom is a copy of his parents' room).

As happens so often in the Buñuel films that turn on an oedipal conflict, the breeze becomes a storm. The mother confesses that the man he has just seen is not his father, and then she introduces him to the ghost of his real father: an attractive character, whose eye has been shot out in a duel with the putative father. The mother instructs the boy to poison the false father. He does so, and the man dies in the midst of terrible convulsions and impressive thunder. The ghosts of the real father and the mother watch him die without emotion.

Like the hallucination in his version of *Robinson Crusoe* (1952), this dream is loosely based on an experience Buñuel had the night after his father died:

> Suddenly I heard a loud noise in the dining room, as if a chair had been thrown against the wall. I spun around and there was my father, standing up, an angry look on his face, his arms outstretched. That hallucination – the only real one I've ever experienced – lasted no more than ten seconds. . . . The funeral took place the following day; and the day after that I slept in my father's bed. Just in case the ghost decided to reappear, I slipped a revolver – a handsome piece with my father's initials in gold and mother-of-pearl – under the pillow. (Needless to say, my sleep was thoroughly uneventful.)[14]

When Buñuel directed the *Tenorio* in Mexico, he reserved for himself the role of Don Juan's father. Many years earlier, a few days after his own father died, he put on his father's boots, opened his desk, and began smoking his cigars in an obvious effort to assume his role. There was a fifteen-year difference between Luis, the first born, and his little brother Alfonso. According to Max Aub, "Alfonso always said – and Luis used to laugh about it – that Luis was his father." "My mother was barely forty when I took over as head of the household."[15] It was not the only time the filmmaker emphasized his mother's youthfulness. In *The Phantom of Liberty* an adolescent tries to go to bed with his aunt, who is many years older than he but has the body of a young woman. By way of explanation, Buñuel invokes the image of his mother: "There are women of advanced age who have surprisingly firm and well-formed bodies. I never saw my mother nude, but when she went out in the street at a very advanced age, people would turn around to look at her: she carried herself like a young woman."[16]

SADE, THE MINISTER OF THE INTERIOR, AND
THE BLEEDING BRIGADIER

When he started work on a film, Buñuel often began
by establishing a framework of subliminal associations (more latent than explicit) that came from his own subconscious. These
images, which he drew from the repertory of obsessions that
made up his peculiar universe or from the residue of other projects, would transform whatever story the film ostensibly set out
to tell. Let's see how some of these elements work in *The Discreet
Charm*.

The first of them is Buñuel's use of the Marquis De Sade. Beginning with his second film, which closes with a reference to
The One Hundred and Twenty Days of Sodom, De Sade serves as a
constant point of reference, even a kind of ethical backbone, in
Buñuel's work. Except in *The Milky Way*, where he once again
contrasts the Marquis to Christ, these allusions are not explicit,
and as a result they have been too often overlooked in the criticism. They turn up in various forms: a gloss of *Philosophy in the
Bedroom* (in the sequence in *El* where Francisco tries to sew up
Gloria's orifices), the philosophy that motivates many of the
characters (e.g., Jaibo in *Los olvidados* and Shark in *Death in the
Garden*), and in a whole range of allusions to the *Dialogue between
a Priest and a Dying Man*.

The *Dialogue*, an early piece that De Sade wrote at the age of
forty-three when he had been incarcerated in the Castle of Vincennes for three years, is perhaps the most important single Sadian text in Buñuel's eyes. It enters his work in two ways: the
ideas (independent of the situation) and the situation (independent of the ideas). It is the dialectical structure of De Sade's arguments, for example, that inspires the discourse on free will in
Robinson Crusoe in which Crusoe and Friday argue about divine
omnipotence after reading the *Bible*. Buñuel's dialogue follows
Defoe's novel closely, but the film differs in its conception of
liberty, which is viewed here, as it is in De Sade, as a phantom.
De Sade wrote that if God is more powerful than man, He must
be the cause of all man's crimes. The conclusion is obvious, and

it illustrates the spirit that animates *The Milky Way*, which ends with Christ's declaration that he has come to bring the sword, rather than peace. As the dying man tells the priest in the *Dialogue*:

> Preacher, abandon your preconceptions. Be a man, be human, without fear and without hope. Put aside your gods and your religions. The only thing that has done is inspire men to take up the sword. The mere mention of all those horrors has made more blood run on the face of the earth than all the other wars and scourges put together.

The archetypal situation involving a priest and a dying man, in a Sadian context, first appears in Buñuel's filmography in *La hija del engaño* (Daughter of Deceit, 1951). Here, in a deathbed scene, an unfaithful wife faces her former husband, who refuses to forgive her. The dialogue between the priest and the dying man in *Death in the Garden* (1956) is a little more complicated since it has a specific function in the plot: it is used in a sequence that justifies Shark's escape from a prison where a wounded revolutionary lies dying. Basically, though, the scene comes down to Father Lizardi's effort to offer spiritual comfort to the dying man, and the man's absolute refusal to accept it.

The priest's failure is multiplied in *Nazarin* (1959). Here the priest-protagonist talks to the prostitute Andara and one of the thieves about doctrine, to no avail; Beatriz, who has become a follower of the priest, returns to her stupid and cruel lover, and, finally, in the plague sequence, in a genuine dialogue, a woman on the point of death rejects the heaven offered by the curate and, instead, demands the man she loves.

By the time this theme surfaces in *The Discreet Charm*, Buñuel has, then, already played numerous variations on it. In *The Discreet Charm*, the priest has been promoted to bishop and the dying person reduced to a self-confessed murderer. A peasant woman summons the worker-bishop to a deathbed. Before he enters the shack where the man lives, the peasant woman (played by Muni, an actress who became a kind of mascot or mouthpiece for Buñuel) spits at him: "I have no love for Jesus

Christ. I've hated him ever since I was a child. Do you want to know why? I have to deliver two bags of carrots. When I come back for you, I'll tell you why." Her comment introduces a Sadian note that is confirmed by what follows. The dying man confesses that he poisoned the bishop's parents while he was working as their gardener. Without much apparent reaction, the prelate gives him absolution and then, with great dignity, finishes him off with a rifle that he finds at hand. In an almost subliminal image that lasts only a few seconds, we see the dead man with his bloodied face. He looks like the crucified Christ, and the horror of the scene seems to embody the peasant woman's aversion to Christ. We never hear her explanation.[17]

The filmmaker applied de Sade's *Dialogue* to himself as well in an effort to exorcise the terror he felt about his own death. To irritate his old friend José Ignacio Mantecón, he invented a little scenario: "when I am about to die, let's say about twenty-four hours ahead of time, I'll have all my friends summoned, and I'll tell Jeanne to get a priest. And I'll confess and do everything like that just to bother Mantecón, who is the biggest atheist of all my friends." In a variation on this theme, he would plan to call the priest just to tell him he did not believe in God. In this way, he would practically reproduce De Sade's dialogue in his own life.[18]

In addition to the priest–dying man theme, another of Buñuel's favorite motifs reappears in *The Discreet Charm*: the minister of the interior. His area of influence is defined early on in *L'âge d'or*. In that film, the protagonists are enjoying an erotic encounter in a garden (a scene that will be taken up again in *The Discreet Charm*) when they are interrupted by a telephone call from the minister of the interior, who winds up committing suicide by "falling" onto the ceiling. The screenplay for *Ilegible, hijo de flauta* starts off in a similar vein. The protagonist has to redefine his identity after witnessing the mass suicide of the police corps: "he reaches the conclusion that he must let the subconscious emerge. . . . Perhaps in his mind he is considering the relationship between what the city police decided and the disappearance of the censor within his own psyche."[19]

In *The Discreet Charm*, the minister of the interior (Michel Piccoli) intervenes, also by telephone, to arrange for the release of three friends who have been arrested on narcotics charges. This scene involves the dream of the bleeding brigadier, thus making explicit the implied double meaning of the title, minister of the interior: an official who guarantees external, social control and the individual's superego who imposes control. The chief of police asks the minister to explain, and he does, but the noise of an airplane drowns out his words. The same thing happens when the chief communicates that information to the brigadier sergeant; the racket of a typewriter makes it impossible to hear.

The incident, Buñuel explains indirectly in his memoirs, is based on a real one which he refers to as "The Three Bombs," and which, he says, "sheds a curious light on the French police (not to mention police all over the world)." While he was staying at the Spanish Embassy in Paris during the Spanish Civil War, the filmmaker was present – but unable to intervene – when the Socialist prefect of police released a right-wing terrorist who had been setting bombs off with complete impunity. The man was released for "reasons of state."[20]

Finally, it is worth noting that the bleeding brigadier is inspired by the bleeding nun in Matthew G. Lewis's novel *The Monk* (1794), which is characterized by a highly stylized Spanish atmosphere along the lines of *The Manuscript Found in Saragossa*. Lewis's work was praised by De Sade and adapted by Buñuel and Carrière in 1968 (although it was actually filmed by Ado Kyrou). Late in his film career, Buñuel sketched out another version of the bleeding nun, mixing bloody ghosts (like the father in *The Discreet Charm*) with images of the *Rotten Bishop* (a work by the Spanish baroque painter Valdes Leal that inspired the rotting corpses in *L'âge d'or*) and it continues with Cardinal Tavera's tomb in *Tristana* and the remains of Carranza, the archbishop of Toledo, which are exhumed and burned in *The Milky Way*.

The old Hispanic imagery seems to fall short of the mark in conveying the obsessive horror and violence of Buñuel's last films. The first late variant on this imagery surfaces in the sequence about the execution of the pope in *The Milky Way*; the second, in the announcement heard on the loudspeakers at the end of *That Obscure Object of Desire* reporting on the condition of the bishop of Sienna, Monsignor Fiessole, who is in a coma due to an assassination attempt. But the clearest manifestation is the figure of the archbishop of Soldeville in *Swan Song*, the last screenplay Buñuel wrote with Carrière.[21]

In this project that was never filmed, Archbishop Soldevilla preaches against terrorism; his words provoke an armed band into assassinating him. His bloody ghost confronts the terrorist Norma in her cell. She is hallucinating because she is on a hunger strike: "The archbishop is dressed in his priestly robes, and he holds his staff in one hand. His bloodied body shows traces of the shots that were fired at him."

The Discreet Charm of the Bourgeoisie contains many other elements from the cultural background that nourished Buñuel, including Spanish tradition, his militant surrealism, and his personal life. The film includes a number of his most persistent dreams and even his recipe for a dry martini. Even the "discreet" of the title points to one of Buñuel's favorite authors, the Aragonese Jesuit Baltasar Gracián, who developed a very personal ethical and pragmatic system in *El discreto·* (The Discreet Man, 1646). *The Discreet Charm* shows, too, the need to recapitulate and revise some of the most important episodes of the surrealist adventure at a time when its postulates had become history, food for museums and official celebrations.

NOTES

1 Marie-Claude Taranger studies this trilogy from a very different perspective in her *Luis Buñuel: Le jeu et la loi* (Vincennes: Presses Universitaires de Vincennes, 1990). Her research is limited to the French bibliography.

2 Buñuel wrote this screenplay in collaboration with the poet Juan Larrea. They hoped to shoot the film in the United States, but it turned out to be too peculiar for the orthodox canons of Hollywood, and it was never filmed. Later there would be differences between Buñuel and Larrea. Larrea's version of "Ilegible, hijo de flauta" was published in 1979 in the Mexican magazine *Vuelta*. Buñuel gave me his version to include in the volume of his literary work that I edited.

3 In *Flashbacks in Film: Memory and History* (New York: Routledge, 1989), 226–227, Maureen Turim refers to Buñuel's use of this technique in *The Andalusian Dog* and *Belle de jour*, but she makes no reference to the complex use of flashbacks in Buñuel's Mexican phase (in films like *El: This Strange Passion* and *The Criminal Life of Archibaldo de la Cruz*), or in other films from his last French phase, like *The Discreet Charm*. For the use of dreams in this film, see Robert T. Eberwein's *Film and the Dream Screen: A Sleep and a Forgetting* (Princeton: Princeton University Press, 1984), 182–191. Like almost all essays that lie outside the area of Hispanic studies, these two volumes fail to make use of the bibliography in Spanish on Buñuel.

4 For Buñuel's career and the relevant documentation and bibliography, the reader may consult my books: *Luis Buñuel. Obra cinematográfica* (Madrid: Ediciones J. C., 1984), *Buñuel* (Madrid: Cátedra, 1991), and *El mundo de Luis Buñuel*.

5 Jean-Luc Godard, *Introducción a una verdadera historia del cine* (Madrid: Ediciones Alphaville, 1980), 1:217.

6 For the apocalyptic structure of *The Exterminating Angel* and its religious and sacrificial symbology, it is worth consulting Maurice de Gandillac, "Colloques de Cerisy-la-Salle," in *Le surréalisma*, ed. Ferdinand Alquié (Paris: Mouton, 1968), 427–430.

7 A French version of this legend, *Le souper chez le Commandeur* (1934) by Blaze de Bury, focuses on this dramatic situation.

8 For *The Discreet Charm*, I am using the French version of the screenplay, published in *Avant-Scène du Cinéma*, and the Spanish version, published in *Aymá* (Barcelona, 1973, 88–93). The dialogue whispered by the prompter continues: "And to make us believe he attended this banquet, you drugged us."

9 Max Aub, *Conversaciones con Buñuel* (Madrid: Aguilar, 1985), 130.

10 *My Last Sigh: The Autobiography of Luis Buñuel*, trans. Abigail Israel (New York: Knopf, 1983), 87. The filmmaker confessed that he had a hard time of it in this performance, in which he played Don Diego (Don Juan's father), because his hearing was bad and he didn't remember the text very well. The distress he suffered on the set (much like the bishop in *The Discreet Charm*) was the stuff of frequent nightmares: "I have to play a role in the theater, and I don't know my part. Anguish. It goes on for a long time. I see an enormous room with seats, a set, people are on the set, and I have to perform the part of X, and I don't know it" (Aub, *Conversaciones*, 163).

11 Buñuel gave me a copy of the original program in 1980.

12 They performed passages from acts 1 and 2 of the second part of the play, which they called "The Parthenon" and "The Last Knock."

Lorca played the sculptor. The variations they introduced into the original text have been studied and published by Antonio Sánchez Romeralo, "Un *Tenorio* de Buñuel ('Libreto' para una representación en la Resistencia de Estudiantes)," *La Terre* 3.10 (April–June 1989): 357–379.

13 Letter of 29 July 1967, quoted in Pedro Guerrero Ruiz, *Francisco Rabal, un actor de raza* (Murcia: Editoria Regional de Murcia, 1992), 174.

14 *My Last Sigh*, 77. In a later part of *My Last Sigh*, where he describes his dreams (a number of which he used in *The Discreet Charm*), he refers to a recurrent dream in which he returns to his native village of Calanda in order to insult and defy his father's ghost (93ff.). He describes all this in greater detail in Aub, *Conversaciones*, 41ff.

15 Aub, *Conversaciones*, 213, 77.

16 José de la Colina and Témás Pérez Turrent, *Objects of Desire: Conversations with Luis Buñuel*, ed. and trans. Paul Lenti (New York: Marsilio, 1992), 223.

17 Initially, the role of the dying man was to be played by Max Aub, who was working on a book about Buñuel that made the filmmaker nervous because of the way the writer was nosing about his private life (Moisés Pérez Coterillo, "Max Aub have de Buñuel," *Reseña* 57 [July – August 1972]: 53–55).

18 Aub, *Conversaciones*, 162.

19 Luis Buñuel, *Obra literaria*, ed. and introd. Augustín Sánchez Vidal (Zaragoza: Ediciones de Heraldo de Aragón, 1982), 215.

20 *My Last Sigh*, 161–162. The motif culminates in *The Phantom of Liberty*, in which two different actors – Julien Bertheau and Michel Piccoli – play the same character, the supreme chief of police. But in earlier films there are numerous policemen, police chiefs, or ministers of the interior who play a similar role, generally in conjunction with the church and the army, as in the inauguration in *L'âge d'or*, the wedding in *Archibaldo de la Cruz*, Chief Fasaro's dealings in *Cela s'appele l'aurore*, and the moral dilemma faced by the reformer Vázquez in *La fièvre monte à El Pao*.

21 Archbishop "Soldeville" is Cardinal Juan Soldevilla y Romero (1843–1923), assassinated on June 4, 1923, in Zaragoza by anarchists who shot up his car. Buñuel refers to the incident in *My Last Sigh*: "We heard that anarchists, led by Ascaso and Durruti, had assassinated Soldevilla Romero, the archbishop of Saragossa, an odious character who was thoroughly detested by everyone, including my uncle the canon. That evening at the Residencia, we drank to the damnation of his soul" (55).

FIGURE THREE

The recurring image of the six bourgeois characters on the road. Stills from *The Discreet Charm of the Bourgeoisie* shown in Figures 3–12 appear courtesy of Canal Plus Distribution.

FIGURE FOUR

Madame Sénéchal (Stéphane Audran) greets her unexpected dinner guests, who are headed by the Ambassador of Miranda (Fernando Rey).

FIGURE FIVE

The ambassador (Fernando Rey) demonstrates his rifle prowess to his partners in crime (Jean-Pierre Cassel, center, and Paul Frankeur, right).

FIGURE SIX

The ambassador (Fernando Rey) moves toward an adulterous embrace with his partner's wife, Simone Thévenot (Delphine Seyrig).

FIGURE SEVEN
The ambassador (Fernando Rey) is confronted by a young revolutionary (María Gabrielle Maione) from Miranda.

FIGURE EIGHT
The Sénéchals (Jean-Pierre Cassel and Stéphane Audran) evade their guests so that they can finish their lovemaking in the garden.

FIGURE NINE
The Sénéchals (Jean-Pierre Cassel, left, and Stéphane Audran, right) hire a bishop (Julien Bertheu) to be their gardener.

FIGURE TEN
In Sénéchal's dream the colonel's dinner party suddenly transforms into a theatrical performance in which the players do not know their lines.

FIGURE ELEVEN

The colonel's nightmarish dinner party becomes more violent in Thévenot's version of the dream.

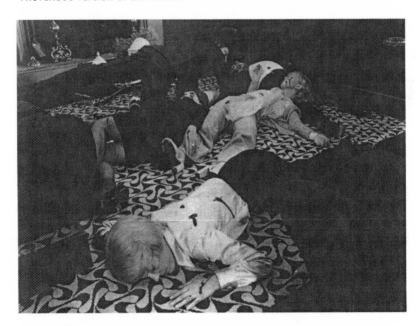

FIGURE TWELVE

In the final interrupted dinner party, the murdered guests all fall down like a pack of cards.

The Discreet Charm of the Postmodern: Negotiating the Great Divide with the Ultimate Modernist, Luis Buñuel

POSTMODERN AVANT LA LETTRE

The editor of this anthology suggested the title of this essay, and I accepted it gladly since Buñuel's work – so rooted in irony, humor, and ambiguity – lends itself perfectly well to mock all kinds of binary oppositions and divides. Furthermore, a film career that extends from the 1920s to the threshold of the 1980s is a privileged outpost for reflecting on the continuity-discontinuity between the two cultural slopes of our century: the modern and the postmodern. The surrealist game of "the one in the other" is inherent in Buñuel's work. Against its light, we can see him as classic avant-garde or ultimate modernist (with his talent for innovation, his coherent personal world view, and his unmistakable and highly valued signature), yet at the same time he is also a precursor of the postmodern. His first two movies, *Un chien andalou* (An Andalusian Dog, 1929) and *L'âge d'or* (The Golden Age, 1930), considered today as two peaks of the histor-ical avant-garde, contained more than one attack against mod-ernism. They repudiated the cult of technological modernization (with the Andalusian dog and the dead donkey replacing the airplane of the futurists) and the fetishization of the new, a trademark of the avant-garde.

From the beginning of his career Buñuel adopted the saying that in art "what is not tradition is plagiarism," and in his first two movies we find his innovative narrative experimentation fused with matrices of popular genres (such as melodrama and Hollywood comedy) and with other characteristics that are associated today with the postmodern: parody, intertextuality, and quotations. *L'âge d'or*, for example, has a rich network of intertextual relations with the Marquis de Sade's *120 Days of Sodom* and Emily Bronte's *Wuthering Heights*.

We move a step further into the undoing of the great divide when we turn to the films Buñuel made in the Mexican film industry during the 1940s and 1950s. On the one hand, as he worked within the popular genres of melodrama and comedy, he diluted himself as an auteur – a change that was demanded by the commercial system. Yet, at the same time he was recognized by the French critics of *Cahiers du cinéma* as one of the pillars not only of auteurist cinema but also of modernity. The face of Janus, with its unity of opposites, is the emblematic figure that Buñuel used to annul any Great Divide. This figure allowed him to remain the ultimate avant-garde modernist (without suffering the same destiny as so many of the other artists in that category who were absorbed by the market and the academy) and also to become one of those newly emerging European auteurs of the later modernist cinema of the 1950s and early 1960s (without falling into their excesses of self-referentiality and narcissism). Furthermore, by fusing popular forms with a rigorous, personal artistic practice and by returning to a cinema of storytelling that ironically revisited the past, Buñuel created an important place for himself within the postmodernist cinema of the 1970s and 1980s. With the international success of his Mexican movies such as *Los olvidados* (The Young and the Damned, 1950) and *Nazarin* (1958), Buñuel also challenged the alleged hierarchical boundaries between central and peripheral nations and their respective filmmaking practices – boundaries that were rooted in a European ethnocentrism and its devalorization of the cultural Other.

Buñuel continued to challenge these assumptions when he worked as an exile in France, making films in the post–May 1968 period. At a time when many other modernist filmmakers either became silent or kept repeating themselves, Buñuel's cinema experienced a new remarkable period of growth, which enabled him to flourish within the postmodern epoch. Nowhere was this "discreet charm of the postmodern" so pronounced as in *Le charme discret de la bourgeoisie* (The Discreet Charm of the Bourgeoisie, 1972).

A REVISITATION TO THE PAST WITH CELEBRATORY VENGEANCE

Buñuel's return to France, to the Europe of the Common Market and the consumer society of the 1960s and 1970s, has elements of the ironic revisitation of the past so characteristic of postmodernist art. After all, he had begun his filmmaking there in Paris in the 1920s. But in his case it was a revisitation not with nostalgia but with a celebratory vengeance. One should remember that his *L'âge d'or* was banned from the screens in Paris and that he himself was treated as a "meteque," a xenophobic term used to designate foreigners living in France.

In *The Discreet Charm* Buñuel zeroes in on Paris, the cultural capital of modern bourgeois civilization, whose epitaph he had sung in 1930 in *L'âge d'or* and that now, forty years later, in the midst of the consumer society still stands erect with its opulent "charm." Yet, as Buñuel's probing lens clearly shows, under its folds are hidden the wreck and ruins of the bourgeois society and culture. With the trope of entrapment in his Mexican film, *El ángel exterminador* (The Exterminating Angel, 1962), Buñuel already presented us with an allegory of the crushing of the bourgeoisie. In this sense, *The Discreet Charm* is the bourgeoisie's filmic postmortem, which helps account for the intertexts of the second part of *Don Juan Tenorio* (which takes place in the pantheon) and of Juan Rulfo's *Pedro Páramo*, a novel of "vivos muertos y de muertos vivos" (of death in life and the living dead).

Despite the glitter of the consumer society's not so "discreet charm," Paris, the capital of modernity in the 1920s and 1930s, is now in the 1970s an empty center. At least, that is how it appears in Buñuel's movie, which is attuned to the fact that in postmodernity the centers have lost their centrality. As if underlining this irony, the exiled Buñuel makes movies in Paris yet continues to live in Mexico with frequent visits to Spain. (The screenplay of *The Discreet Charm* was written in Madrid in the spring and summer of 1970.) By making films in France with the cultural baggage of the Spanish tradition, which was enriched by the diaspora of the exile and by his long stay in Mexico, Buñuel's work acquired two of the most valued dimensions of postmodernity: traveling culture and the recognition of otherness and diversity. The French lack of these dimensions is hilariously demonstrated in the sequence at the colonel's party, in which a whole set of guests corner the ambassador of Miranda with ignorant questions and prejudicial assumptions about his Latin American nation. From sequences like this and from the mise-en-scène of the film, we could infer that for Buñuel the Paris of the 1970s is a semisunk watchtower from which he looks out to reflect on the order-disorder of the contemporary world situation.

TOWARD A POSTMODERNISM OF RESISTANCE

Within the unity of opposites that prevails over all of Buñuel's cinema, his final phase connects with his first. This unity was favored by the neovanguardist bent of the postmodernist art of the 1970s, which (with the freedom granted him by his producer Serge Silberman) permitted him to update aspects of his surrealist phase with an ironic twist. We must keep in mind that the great historical changes and convulsions that occurred between the 1920s and 1970s rendered the most mordant elements of surrealism – love, revolutionary violence, and the shock effect – obsolete or inoperative. Far from having changed life, as was the declared aim of the movement, surrealism had become part of everyday existence. As Buñuel himself tells us, "Surrealism has passed on to life. Violence is everywhere." Building on this perception, we could say that in his last few films surrealism assumes the role of a contemporary *costumbrismo*, in which the semisacred principle of the surrealists, the unity of opposites, becomes repulsive in our daily lives. Thus, in his latter-day revisitation to surrealism, Buñuel exposes this unity of opposites: pleasure and horror, calm and violence, gratification and destruction, beauty and ugliness.

In the great artistic tradition of Spanish *costumbristas* – Cervantes, Velázquez, Goya, and Galdós – Buñuel's final films present a lucid diagnosis of our times in which violence is rampant. John Orr emphasizes this point when he writes: "In his 1970s films, Buñuel juxtaposes archaic notions of etiquette and honour to the nihilistic values of a consumer society of the present and of the future where casual sex, drugs and terrorism have become normalized as unremarkable features of everyday life."[1] Marking the difference between his films of the 1970s and those of his first phase when he considered "revolutionary violence" a weapon of liberation, Buñuel tells us that if art needs weapons, today's weapons are worth nothing and that to attack violence with violence is absurd. In *The Discreet Charm* and the movies that followed, Buñuel attacks violence by exposing its absurdity (as in the scene where the ambassador of Miranda uses a telescopic rifle to kill a little toy stuffed dog) or its horror (as in the sequence where the young Latin American female radical is kidnapped, a tragic prefiguring of the thousands of *desaparecidos* who would fall victim to the military dictatorships of Chile and Argentina only two or three years after the film's release).

The sociopolitical criticism in Buñuel's final films has much of the satire and black humor of his compatriot Goya. Though present in all of his works, this parallel is accentuated in his last three films. The intertext of Goya's painting, *The Shooting of the Moncloa*, is a leit motif in *The Phantom of Liberty*, where it expresses revulsion against our contemporary climate of generalized violence. Extending the parallel with the painter, we could say that in Buñuel's final series of French films that mock Cartesian rationality, the dream of reason (reasoning plus technology) produces monsters, which in many ways are like the ones seen in Goya's *Caprichos* and *Desastres*.

The metanarrative of revolution had disappeared from the historical and cultural horizons of the 1970s, rendering the surrealist motto of "art in the service of revolution" obsolete – a motto to which Buñuel had formerly subscribed. Nevertheless, he remained committed to art that was oppositional to established power and order, prefiguring the postmodernist resistance of the 1980s and 1990s. In a conversation with Mexican novelist Carlos Fuentes, Buñuel formulated his final position on the relationship between art and society:

> The artist is the eternal nonconformist. Thanks to the artist, power cannot say that everybody is in agreement with it. . . . When power feels totally justified and approved, it does not resist the fascist temptation. The small weapon of a book or film can still be useful to unmask that fascist potentiality hidden in the entrails of capitalism.[2]

COUNTERREVOLUTION AND REVOLT IN *THE DISCREET CHARM OF THE BOURGEOISIE*

Buñuel made the preceding declaration to Carlos Fuentes in Paris in the year of the May 1968 revolt, and in *The Discreet Charm* we find echoes of that debacle. It is more than coincidental that the film was made in 1972, the same year in which Herbert Marcuse published *Counterrevolution and Revolt*.[3] Referring to him within the context of May 1968, Buñuel declared: "I knew the works of Marcuse and I applauded them. I approved of all I heard about the consumer society and the need to change it before it was too late in the course of an arid and dangerous life." Then he adds, "May 1968 had marvelous moments, but by the end of a week, it returned to the prevailing so-called order, and the great fiesta (in which miraculously no blood was spilled) came to an end."[4]

The Discreet Charm was filmed in the climate of preventive counterrevolution then prevailing in the West and, according to Marcuse's analysis, with no changes in sight to alter the course of "an arid and dangerous life." Nevertheless, in the festive mood with which Buñuel attacks this course of events, we feel the embers of that aborted great "fiesta" of May 1968. Moreover, as he turns to surrealism's now intolerable unity of opposites as manifest in today's daily life, he brings to the screen many of the dangers, abuses, and horrors that Marcuse had described. In this sense, the title of his movie, *The Discreet Charm of the Bourgeoisie*, could very well allude to that climate of repressive tolerance theorized by Marcuse, or that fascist potentiality hidden in the entrails of capitalism, which Buñuel thought the contemporary artist should unmask. Marcuse similarly puts his reader on guard against attitudes and actions that indicate a "protofascist potential par excellence" in the American society of the 1970s. In describing how Buñuel reveals this fascist potential in *Le journal d'une femme de chambre* (Diary of a Chambermaid, 1963), *Belle de jour* (1966), and *Tristana* (1970), John Orr concludes, "Thus Buñuel's period films, his Nietzchean return, expose the deeply conservative face which often hides behind the liberal mask of Western culture, the fears and foibles of the bourgeoisie through which fascism briefly triumphed and on which the conservative spirit always thrives."[5]

In *The Discreet Charm* we find indications of this protofascist potential in several sequences, such as the kidnapping of the young Latin American woman and the torture of the young student demonstrator in the police headquarters, an image that illustrates Marcuse's statement, "Torture has become a normal instrument of interrogation around the world."[6]

Like Buñuel, Marcuse also called for artists to fight against the protofascist potential in our society. Yet, contrary to Marcuse and Sartre (who are possibly the last two ultimate modernists), Buñuel had lost all hope in the metanarrative of political or cultural revolution long before May 1968. In contrast to Buñuel's modest remarks on the oppositional function of art, the title of Marcuse's chapter, "Art and Revolution," sounds grandiloquent and dated. Nevertheless, despite the low key of their political reverberations, Buñuel's final films have a similar liberating agenda as the one proposed by Marcuse. Now that the radical, aggressive, antiart stance of his earlier films had disappeared, these later works accepted certain redeeming, liberating qualities in the artistic form: sensitivity, imagination, and a liberating cognitive power. As a result, *The Discreet Charm* contains a marked contrast between its repulsive content, which is full of nightmarish scenes saturated with a dystopic unity of opposites that paralyzes our society and leads it to chaos and apocalypse, and its beautiful, playful form, which provides "marvelous moments" that could be seen as an homage to the ephemeral "great fiesta" of May 1968 – a movement, like historical surrealism, that proposed the fusion of art and life. Buñuel, himself, acknowledged this shared vision through his choice of a slogan for the May revolt, "All power to imagination!"

POSTMODERNIST STRATEGIES

Contrary to the modernist Marcuse, who celebrated the classical form of bourgeois art, emphasizing the traditional qualities of order, proportion, and harmony while repudiating "elaborate anti-forms which are constituted by the mere atomization and fragmentation of traditional forms,"[7] Buñuel's final films demonstrate in a very playful and pleasurable way that form and antiform are not incompatible. Thus, he negotiated the Great Divide by freely combining a repertoire of classic, modern, and postmodern aesthetic qualities. This tactic alone would suffice to consider him a practitioner of postmodernist eclecticism.

A keen observer of the sociohistorical and cultural changes of our times, in his "French" films of the 1970s Buñuel showed he was attuned to some of the ideas of the French poststructuralist theorists, such as Foucault, Derrida, Deleuze, and Lyotard. In opening doors to experimental narrative fiction, he anticipated postmodernist filmmakers such as David Lynch and Pedro Almodóvar. He represented a cinematic equivalent to the narrative innovations of the new Latin American novel and of North American postmodern novelists like Barth, Pynchon, and Coover. Many of the strategies that critics such as David Lodge, Brian McHale, and Jim Collins attribute to postmodern fiction can already be found in Buñuel's last three films.

Specifically, in *The Discreet Charm*, a film that not incidentally won an Oscar, we find a Hollywood comedy of manners fused with a modernist film about time, a combination that is negotiated with a whole array of postmodernist narrative strategies. If we wanted to retain our belief in the modernist unity of his artistic vision, it would be possible to argue that some of these strategies were already present in his earliest films. Paradoxically, this line of argument might lead us to conclude that his artistic vision reached its zenith at the end of his career when it was enriched (rather than undermined) by postmodernism. Focusing on *The Discreet Charm*, such an argument might mobilize the following postmodernist characteristics as evidence.

1. *Middles without explicit beginnings or endings.* The film begins *in medias res* (in the middle of things) and ends not with the words, "The End," but with the puzzling, recurrent image of the disoriented group of bourgeois characters walking on a desolate road.

2. *Inclusiveness, indeterminacy, discontinuity.* This recurring image of the characters on the road, which jumps into the narration without any continuity or determinant meaning, could be emblematic of those characteristics present throughout the film.

3. *Randomness.* Not only is all narrative "causality" based on randomness in *Phantom of Liberty*, but many episodes in *The Discreet Charm* are also randomly motivated. The most striking example would be the summoning of the bishop-gardener to give

absolution to a dying man who just happens to be the gardener who murdered the bishop's parents.

4. *Contradiction.* The unity of contraries is present in the characters and actions of the film: the charming bourgeois drug dealers, and the bishop-gardener-killer. The already cited instance of the bishop killing the man he just absolved would be one of the most striking examples of the many contradictions in the film.

5. *Heterotopia, the incongruous.* As in dreams, the linking together of inappropriate combinations applies to characters (the bourgeois drug dealers, the pious priest turned killer) and to spaces (the bourgeois living room juxtaposed with the desolate highway, the restaurant converted into a funeral parlor, the colonel's dining room metamorphosed into a theatrical stage).

6. *Eclecticism, intertextuality, quotation.* One finds not only the mixing of narrative matrices (Hollywood comedy of manners and modernist narrative of time) but also intertextuality with specific works like *Pedro Páramo* and *Don Juan Tenorio*, and (within the theatrical dream) even a direct quotation from the latter play.

7. *Banality, the banal made extraordinary or the extraordinary made banal.* In the first case, we find the reading aloud of a menu, the recipe for how to make a perfect martini, and, most extraordinary, repeatedly being seated at a table for a meal that is never finished. In the second instance, we encounter matter-of-fact narrations of gothic dreams and a funeral service in a restaurant.

8. *Chinese-box, mise-en-abîme, trompe l'oeil constructions.* In this film we encounter a set of recurrent structures, each nested or embedded in each other like a series of Chinese boxes. The primary diegesis of the action, the desire of the bourgeois group to dine together, is constantly interrupted by actions that suppress the diegetic premise and redirect our attention to the framework of representations. Significantly the recurring interruptive image of the bourgeois characters on the deserted road (with which the movie ends) aptly demonstrates a characteristic of many post-

modernist fictions – the loss of the fiction's ontological horizon. By constructing trompe l'oeil illusions and by encouraging readers to mistake an embedded secondary world for the primary diegesis, *The Discreet Charm* pushes these postmodernist narrative strategies to their limits. In its use of interlocking dreams, the last part of the film moves us from one deception to another until we can no longer distinguish dreams from ordinary reality and we are left wondering whether the whole diegesis is merely a dream of the "honest" ambassador of Miranda who is purging himself of the fears and insecurities that have been displaced onto him by ethnocentric Frenchmen.

9. *Allegory.* In postmodernist art and literature there is a resurgence of allegory, although, as Brian McHale argues, its meanings are elusive and equivocal.[8] From the movie's title (which illustrates the surrealist tactic of establishing secret relations between a work's title and content), we can infer some ontological reflection between the world of the film and that of the bourgeoisie at a particular historical moment, late monopoly capitalism, when this class has lost control over society. Hence the allegorical resonance suggests this film is a postmortem for the bourgeoisie.

NEGOTIATING THE GREAT (AND MULTIPLE) DIVIDE: A RHIZOMATIC GOTHIC LABYRINTH, CHRONOTOPES, INTERTEXTS, FRAGMENTS, DREAMS, CARNAVAL, AND APOCALYPSES

In tune with the zeitgeist of the postmodern, Buñuel's final films have the kind of marked mannerism that Umberto Eco defines not as a simple aesthetic but as an approach to life: the discovery that the world has no fixed center, a realization that he associates with postmodernism and with the spatial model of the labyrinth.[9] We can see the labyrinth as the encompassing narrative figure of *The Discreet Charm* and its hybrid textuality: a labyrinth of the rhizomatic modality described by Deleuze and Guattari, without center, periphery, or exit.[10]

In *The Discreet Charm* this kind of labyrinth is evoked by the endless doors and windows (which the characters repeatedly cross while ending up at the same place where they began), by the circular reversibility of the story (in which characters continually return to cross the same threshold of the same bourgeois home, to sit at the same table to a meal that is constantly interrupted, and to walk down the same empty road without direction or destination), and by a sound track (containing the recurrent, dissonant ringing of the door bell and weird ominous sounds on the deserted road that emphasize disorientation and the many dead ends of the story).

Similarly, the Chinese box, tromp l'oeil, and mise-en-abîme structures contribute to the figure of the labyrinth, giving this tragicomedy of "discreet (and deadly) charm" a gothic architecture. The episode of the bleeding brigadier could be seen as the cipher of several gothic turns in the film. Ever since the final sequence of *L'âge d'or* (where a decadent Christlike marquis and his sadistic friends exit a ruinous castle after torturing local teens), gothic architecture has recurred in Buñuel's films, perhaps most notably in *El* (This Strange Passion, 1952) and *Abismos de pasión* (also called *Cumbres borrascosas* and *Wuthering Heights*, 1953). According to Peter Brook, the gothic castle – with its drawbridges, spiral staircase, and dungeons – is an architectural approximation to the Freudian model of the mind,[11] a symbolic role that it apparently played in the avant-garde and modernist films of Buñuel. But the postmodernist gothic labyrinth of *The Discreet Charm* lacks even that symbolic exit from the fantasies and nightmares of this dead class, the bourgeoisie. Significantly, the gothic reappeared in the American postmodernist cinema of the 1980s, especially in a film like David Lynch's *Blue Velvet*, in which the Buñuelian presence is manifest.

In the recurrent image of the desolate road of apocalyptic auguries, Buñuel closes the circle of one of the great chronotopes of world literature: the open road as a place of encounters, a motif that has great resonance in *Don Quixote* and in the picaresque novel. In contrast to *Don Quixote* where (as Bakhtin pointed out) the hero takes to the road to encounter all of Spain, in *The Discreet Charm* the bourgeois players fail to meet even their own shadows. With this image Buñuel seals the way traversed by the evolution-involution of modernity from the sixteenth century to the present.

Another chronotope of nineteenth-century literary modernity, the bourgeois living room, which was so important to the realist novel, also plays a crucial role in *The Discreet Charm*: staging the swan song of modernity. If in the realist novel the bourgeois living room was a microcosm of the complex relations between private intrigues and public socioeconomic matters (a mark of a society undergoing changes theorized as modern development and progress), in *The Discreet Charm* the living room completely lacks those dimensions. Devoid of all notions of progress, this space where time repeats itself and where its occupants talk nonsense, this space leads without transition, to the desolate road, where its former occupants senselessly walk forward going nowhere.

The magnificent labyrinth that is *The Discreet Charm*, with its carnavalesque and apocalyptic resonances, can be seen as an *ignis fatuus* of Western civilization. Hence, the amplitude of intertextual echoes of this tradition that we find throughout the movie functions as a lifesaver amid the historical vacuum. In this movie the pleasure of the text is linked to the horror of the context. The death, which is so pervasive in the film from its opening sequence onward, could refer to "the death of the author" theorized by Roland Barthes; indeed, we find a film that corresponds to the Barthesian definition of a text as a multidimensional space in which a variety of texts blend and clash, a tissue of quotations drawn, not from a single all-powerful auteur, but from innumerable centers of culture.

In the first sequence the ambassador's black car, more than an instrument of space-time progression associated with the modern metropolis and cinema, ominously resembles Charon's boat that carries spirits to the world of the dead. Very early in the story, we find echoes of the medieval dance of death (the dancing circle of dignitaries, bishop, bourgeoisie, gardeners, chauffeur, and maids) and of the Calderonian *Life Is a Dream* and *El gran teatro del mundo*, incarnated within a society of spectacle and simulacrum. The dinner with the colonel flows into the dinner with the statue of the *comendador* from Zorilla's *Don Juan Tenorio*, and throughout the movie we are in the world of the dead from *Pedro Páramo*.

Likewise, we find logical Cartesian reason presiding over the actions and events but linked to the Cervantine "la razón de la sin razón" and to the already mentioned conception of reason that produced the monsters of Goya. We also find a variety of combined narrative matrices, ranging from a Cervantine use of embedded stories and loose ends (we never find out what happens to the pious bishop-gardener after he avenges the murder of his parents or to the young *guerrillera* after she is kidnapped), to a modernist use of fragments (with a postmodern twist), to a fully postmodern rhizomatic structure. Without understanding the postmodern dimension of this hybrid structure, film reviewer John Simon accused Buñuel of creating a work in which "anything goes." Apparently unaware that this motto would become a password of creative freedom within the poetics of postmodernism, he declared: "The latest Buñuel film is a haphazard concatenation of waking and dream sequences in which anything goes, and which would make just as much, or just as little, sense if they were put in any other disorder."[12]

In using different modalities of narrative fragments, Buñuel continues to demolish the narrative totality of the nineteenth-century novel, a deconstruction that was initiated by modernist and avant-garde movements. However, in contrast to the avant-garde, the fragment does not have a value in itself for Buñuel; they are merely connecting paths that lead into a labyrinth with no center or periphery and with a single exit: apocalyptic destruction.

John Orr outlines a twin structure of feelings for "neomodern" filmmakers (whom we could also call "prepostmoderns"): the tragicomedy and the cool apocalypse. Linking these structures to a cinema that explores "the pervasive undercurrents of despair and paralysis in an age of rational technology threatened by extinction," he claims they "[put] into images the emotional sub-text of an unarticulated climate of fear." Among the film-makers who fit this description, he includes Resnais, Godard, Antonioni, Welles, Coppola, Tarkovsky, reserving a special role for Buñuel: "Here one of the most powerful texts is Buñuel's aptly named *The Discreet Charm of the Bourgeoisie*."[13] Indeed, his last three films end with images that evoke an impending sense of apocalypse. At the end of his final film, *That Obscure Object of Desire*, an apocalyptic explosion literally engulfs the whole screen. Set within a commercial arcade, the scene shows the consumer society of spectacle and simulacrum suddenly bursting into flames. *The Discreet Charm* could be seen as the dress rehearsal for that impending destiny, heightening the carnavalesque spirit with which Buñuel celebrates the apocalypse.

Hence the intertextuality with *Don Juan*, a play that begins in carnival and ends in a pantheon. In Buñuel the phantasmagoric dimension of Zorrilla's play has a dreamlike aspect, which leads the story to a level where life, dream, and death are intermingled. For example, the phantasmal apparition of the ghost of the *comendador*, who in the play comes to invite Don Juan to a dinner in his pantheon, corresponds to the reappearance of the colonel, who comes to invite the bourgeois friends to dinner at his house, which has an eerie feeling of a pantheon. He enters into the dining room the same way that Don Gonzalo does in the play: he "passes through the door without opening it and without making any noise." Although the uncanny feeling of the colonel's entrance (like the intertextuality with the play in the scene that follows) deeply disorients spectators who are not aware of the allusions to the Zorrilla play, it is finally explained when we discover that everything is a dream within a dream. Nevertheless, for the informed spectator everything in the film – from the opening sequence of the wake in the restaurant through these unconsummated dinners – has the taste of the funerary dinner from the play. In the final scene, where the richly decorated table of the bourgeois dinner party is swept away by gunfire, the same kind of transformation occurs, again evoking lines from Zorrilla: "Instead of the wreath that folds the table cloth in a manner of banners, of its flowers and luxurious services, snakes, bones, and fire. On top of this table appeared a dish with ashes, a cup of fire, and an hourglass."[14]

This table could be an emblem of how this carnavelesque movie by Buñuel (like the carnavalesque literature studied by Bakhtin) – with its compact matrix of death, laughter, drinking, and sexual indecency – celebrates the doomed apocalypse of modernity, but with an ironic and redeeming postmodernist twist. For, in Buñuel's final works from the 1970s, as in so many mythic cosmogonies, destruction heralds a new dawn. The end is a new beginning: there is no Great Divide in the cinema of Luis Buñuel.

NOTES

1 John Orr, *Cinema and Modernity* (Cambridge: Polity Press, 1993), 29.
2 Buñuel as quoted by Carlos Fuentes, *Casa con dos puertas* (México: Joaquín Mortiz, 1970), 214.
3 Herbert Marcuse, *Counterrevolution and Revolt* (Boston: Beacon Press, 1972).
4 Luis Buñuel, *Mi último suspiro*, trans. Ana María de la Fuente (Barcelona: Plaza y Janés, 1982), 122–123.
5 Orr, *Cinema and Modernity*, 28.
6 Marcuse, *Counterrevolution*, 1.
7 Ibid., 94.
8 Brian MacHale, *Postmodernist Fiction* (New York: Methuen, 1987), 140–147.
9 Umberto Eco/Stefano Rosso, "A Correspondence on Postmodernism," in *Zeitgeist in Babel: The Postmodernist Controversy*, ed. Inbergorg Hoestercy (Bloomington: Indiana University Press, 1991), 244.
10 Gilles Deleuze and Felix Guattari, *Rhizome: Introduction* (Paris: Les Editions de Minuit, 1976).
11 Peter Brook, *The Melodramatic Imagination* (New Haven: Yale University Press, 1976), 19.
12 John Simon, "The Discreet Charm of the Bourgeoisie: Why Is the Co-Eatus Always Interruptus?" in *The World of Luis Buñuel*, ed. Joan

Mellen (New York: Oxford University Press, 1978), 367–368. This essay is also included in the appendix within this volume.

13 Orr, *Cinema and Modernity*, 14–34, 23, 27.

14 José Zorrilla, *Don Juan Tenorio* (Madrid: Cátedra, 1979), 220.

Retheorizing Buñuel

MARVIN D'LUGO

Buñuel in the Cathedral of Culture: Reterritorializing the Film Auteur

In the summer and autumn of 1996, as part of the commemoration of the centenary of the birth of cinema, the Spanish Centro de Arte Reina Sofía presented a unique retrospective of the life and films of Luis Buñuel. Entitled "Buñuel! The Look of the Century" (¿Buñuel! la mirada del siglo), the show claimed for Buñuel special status as the emblematic figure of Spain's hundred years of cinema history. The Aragonese director's life had begun with the century and his fifty-year career spanned both the silent and sound periods, including landmark works in French surrealism and even an Oscar for best foreign film in 1972.

"Buñuel, the Look of the Century" was inspired by an earlier retrospective of the director's works organized in 1994 by the Kunst-und Ausstellungshalle in Bonn. Whereas the German show was designed as homage to one of the most internationally revered figures of world cinema, the objective of the Reina Sofía exhibition was much more ambitious and complex. Buñuel seemed at first a natural choice for the official Spanish celebration of a century of cinema in that it recognized the most universally praised of Spanish filmmakers. To add a distinctive national luster to the occasion, the king of Spain and the president

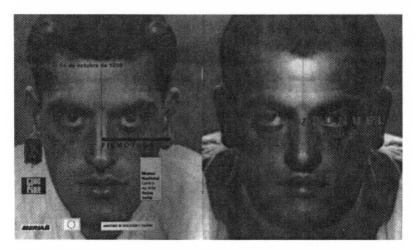

FIGURE THIRTEEN
The catalog for *¡BUÑUEL! La mirada del siglo*.

of Mexico were made the honorary sponsors of the show. Reflecting Buñuel's dual cultural identities, a Spaniard by birth and
a naturalized citizen of Mexico, this binational sponsorship,
however, only drew attention to the artificiality of the entire
enterprise of the exhibition. For those who were already familiar
with the director's life and work, it was clear that the museum
show was more than a simple retrospective of the filmmaker's
life and films. Buñuel had been transformed into the site of a
series of cultural scenarios that said much more about the status
of the cinematic institution in the age of globalized cultural production than about the man or the director. Let us look at the
way some of these scenarios are interwoven into the conception
and presentation of "Buñuel, the Look of the Century."

The official opening of the Madrid exhibition began with the
ceremonial beating of forty drums brought from Buñuel's native
village of Calanda, recreating part of that village's traditional
Holy Week ritual. In his memoirs, *My Last Sigh*, Buñuel described
the hypnotic effect of these drum rolls upon listeners as "a secret
rhythm in the outside world [which] produces a real physical
shiver that defies the rational mind."[1] Because of the very som-

ber and haunting nature of the drums, Buñuel included them on the sound track of two of his films, once at the ending of *L'âge d'or* and again in *Nazarín*. Over time, the drum rolls became so identified with Buñuel that they formed a kind of biofilmographic signature.

The eerie reverberations of the drums in the cavernous halls of the Reina Sofía museum contribute to the impression of the massive scale of the show, which includes some five hundred paintings, drawings, sculptures, documents, books, photographs, and correspondence by and to Buñuel, as well as the screening of sequences from all of his thirty-seven films. Here, as with the staging of the drum rolls, the filmmaker's life and work are conflated in ways that reinforce for visitors the implicit message of an intimate relation between aesthetic causality and the director's biography. The Buñuel of the Reina Sofía show thus comes to be seen as an artist whose creative output is aligned simultaneously with both the history of cinema and Spanish culture.

The physical dimensions of the exhibition are indeed impressive, not only for what they include of Buñuel's life and work, but for the sheer scale of their layout, covering more than ten immense rooms of the museum's first floor. This includes an auditorium in which is shown a continuous program of clips from Buñuel's films, including a newly restored version of *Tierra sin pan* and a synchronized sound version of *Un chien andalou*. At various other sites within the museum, visitors may view clips from specific films as well as montages of photographs from Buñuel's life and times. This amalgam of film images and related memorabilia could not be better designed to produce the effect of Buñuel as an almost bigger-than-life figure whose "aura," both visual and auditory, surrounds visitors as they pass from room to room. The physical scale of the show, in fact, goes hand in hand with the exhibition's goal, suggested in its title, of imbuing Buñuel with an Olympian status and, playing with one of the most prominent visual-narrative tropes of his film work, the glance (*la mirada del siglo*), positioning us to imagine Buñuel looking down from on high at the century of cinema.

II

In a number of ways, this grandiose presentation seems at odds with the values inherent in Buñuel's cinema. One Madrid reviewer, Jorge Barriuso, writing in *El país*, called the display a "cathedral for Buñuel" and wondered what Buñuel would have thought of the show.[2] For the master of surrealist cinema, for whom the pretensions of high culture and bourgeois tastes were the target of much of his derisive humor, the idea of film as art, and of the filmmaker, especially himself, as its author, might well sound like one of the intellectual pretensions Buñuel loved to ridicule.[3] As well, for the director of *Viridiana*, whose most often quoted epigram is "Thank God I'm an atheist," his placement in a cathedral, even, paradoxically, a cathedral of culture, smacks of the kind of ironic reversal so characteristic of his own filmic narratives.

In broader terms, Barriuso's reference to the exhibition as a cathedral of culture underscores the shift in aesthetic logic in which cinema has become art. Recall Walter Benjamin on "The Work of Art in the Age of Mechanical Reproduction" in which film, by its emphasis on technology and its potential for infinite reproducibility of images, was described as "shriveling" the aura of pictorial art.[4] In commemorating the centenary of cinema, the Buñuel show reminds us that we are situated within a new cultural landscape in which film has repositioned audiences in often surprising ways. Just as, according to Benjamin, the motion picture displaced painting and photography as privileged forms of realistic representation, so television and the new technologies in video and satellite transmissions have, in turn, displaced film, endowing it with a nostalgic status as art object with the filmmaker transformed from artisan to artist.

In part, Buñuel's placement in this museum of culture has been the result of the efforts of a later generation of filmmakers, the French New Wave, to wrest the motion picture away from the pretensions of one literary tendency, the "tradition of quality," and to enhance the status of cinema by likening the film-

maker to a literary author and his work to that of art.[5] The paradoxical result of this aggrandizement of cinema that has brought
Buñuel to the attention of new generations of film viewers is that
it has been achieved precisely through the transformation of his
condition of provocateur-saboteur of cultural pretensions into
the very object of adulation. This is indeed an ironic coda to the
work of a director who throughout his adult life gravitated toward those characters and situations that expressed marginality
and resistance to bourgeois values and gave meaning to the ad-
jective Buñuelian to describe certain disquieting and often violent images that shattered the conformism and complacency of
audiences.

His surrealist work, perhaps the most universally revered stage
of his creative career, was marked by a vehement disdain for the
bourgeois tastes and culture of his day. One need only recall the
scandalous first narrative sequence in *L'âge d'or* in which Lya Lys
and Gaston Modot passionately revel in the mud as their moans
of sexual ecstasy disrupt the gathering of dignitaries and officials.
The eruption of instinctual reality calculated to deflate the pretensions of proper social behavior is a cardinal motif that recurs
in myriad forms throughout nearly all of Buñuel's films.

Along with this disdain for bourgeois decorum came Buñuel's
insistent identification with popular forms of cultural expression, not simply as the culture of the masses, but moreover as
the expression of an unaffected taste of the people. His Mexican
films often embraced the basest forms of Mexican popular cinema, the *churro* – that is, quickly and cheaply made films for easy
domestic consumption. Even the four films Buñuel directed for
Filmófono in Spain before the Civil War were all based on popular cultural genres, especially the *sainete*. Buñuel's objective was
clearly to address mass audiences through a popular medium
with one of his implicit themes being the disparagement of in-
flated cultural posturings. Yet, appropriated into the museum
exhibition, that popular cinema has been metamorphosed into
the Buñuelian "art" that seems, at best, ill-placed within the
space of the museum.

III

At the root of the Buñuelian authorial event, one may discern an even more surprising phenomenon: the official and quasi-official adoration of the film author by agents and institutions aligned with certain conceptions of the nation-state. Such an alignment immobilizes the figure of the seemingly peripatetic Buñuel within the boundaries of the nation. To some degree this identification of Buñuel with national cultures is inevitable since much of his most memorable film work was rooted in critiques of specific cultural practices identified with national stereotypes. But more than merely underscoring what some spectators and critics might call the "Spanishness" of Buñuel's work, the Reina Sofía show makes clear that it is official Spain, the Spanish state, the king, who is sponsoring Buñuel, a figure whose relation to official culture was always, at best, tangential. Although Buñuel had been commissioned by the Spanish government in 1932 to make *Tierra sin pan*, it was also a subsequent Republican government that eventually banned the film. Despite efforts by the Franco regime and later post-Franco governments to adopt him, Buñuel was a figure who characteristically shunned identification with the cause of patriotic national cultures, whether Spanish, French, or Mexican. With the exception of his support of the Spanish Republic during the Civil War and his subsequent anti-Francoism, his politics was consistently antinationalistic and international.

What seems especially noteworthy about this new national rendering of Buñuel for the museum show is not so much that it is politically inaccurate, but that this inaccuracy reveals the common reality of most alignments of cinematic authorship with nationality, namely their condition of constructedness. The "repatriation" of Buñuel by the agents of national culture must inevitably imply, if not a falsification of identity, then certainly a potential permutability of the film auteur. The instances of the Franco regime's initial embrace, then disavowal, of affiliation with *Viridiana*, the mistaken claim that Buñuel's *Discreet Charm of the Bourgeoisie* was the first Spanish film to win an Oscar, and the fanciful attribution as examples of French cinema of a series of Buñuel's "Mexican films" spoken in French and starring prominent French actors such as Simone Signoret and Gerard Phillipe are all variations on the dynamics of the shifting set of signifiers that shape the nation-author linkage.

Seen in a more positive light, this tendency to link freely Buñuel's name with various national cinemas might productively be understood as part of a process of "reterritorialization." In effect, the author is appropriated as a strategy through which the affective boundaries of the nation are redrawn. In this manner Buñuel has often been used to express the universal values of French and Mexican cinema. In a contrary move, he has even been made the object of a form of regional boosterism. Described by one critic as representing a tradition in Aragonese cinema, Buñuel, along with other notable filmmakers born in the region, such as Florían Rey, Segundo de Chomón, Carlos Saura, and José Luis Borau, is cast as part of a distinctive microregional cinematic tradition.[6]

Through the Reina Sofía show, however, Buñuel becomes emblematic of a more universal projection of Spanishness that seeks to transcend the geographic insularity of its national boundaries. This Spanish articulation of Buñuel, however, is constructed around the work of a filmmaker who claimed to have made only four of his thirty-seven films in his native country, two of which were officially banned for decades. This is also a director who made twenty films in Mexico, and nine others in France.

The "Mexican" Buñuel is, in his own way, equally problematic. The twenty films he shot there between 1947 and 1965 contain a variety of reworkings of material from his earlier Spanish and French periods. Along with these are two English-language "American" films shot in Mexico, *Robinson Crusoe*, starring Dan O'Herlihy, and *The Young One*, featuring Zachary Scott and actually set in the United States, as well as the previously mentioned trilogy of French films shot in Mexico. Despite these qualifications, Buñuel's Mexican films constitute quantitatively the largest single phase of his creative career. Yet in the Reina Sofía show, the Mexican Buñuel is relegated to a single pair of rooms in which only the memorabilia of his various successes are on display, and in which he even is forced to share billing with his Mexican cinematographer, Gabriel Figueroa.

Such spatial configurations of Buñuel's life and times are, of course, not intended to represent an accurate portrayal of the filmmaker's career. Rather, the continuity of the museum spaces and the itinerary upon which museum visitors embark as they visit the exhibition provide a spatial geographic coherence to Buñuel's life and work, just as that life and work provide a simple comprehensible "biography" of Spain's contributions to world cinema.

IV

What the image of the cathedral of culture built around Buñuel tells us is not so much that the authentic Buñuel has been deformed or violated, but rather that the filmmaker has been appropriated as a cultural product and incorporated into a strategy of resistance to the globalized media culture. The agents of this resistant nation-based culture employ a variety of means to construct and project certain images of culturally specific national identity in defense of their own national media space and in competition for world markets. The struggle for the survival of Hispanic cinemas, almost always perceived as marginal and exotic within the context of the dominant international film culture, has led to an intensification of what Thomas Elsaesser has called in the context of recent German cinema, a "cultural mode of production"[7] – that is, a formulation of state-subsidized film production around the packaging of the works of directors whose artistic vision, though clearly idiosyncratic and highly personal, is used to represent a national culture in its projection, primarily to international markets.

The logic of that cultural mode of production, understood here as the production of cultural objects for international consumption, goes far to explain the peculiar logic of the Reina Sofía exhibition. At its source, first of all, we find the authorial canonization of the filmmaker as author, a process essential to creating the impression of a unified chain of products all understood as the result of a single and unique conceptual talent. Indeed, the very idiosyncrasy of Buñuel's vision becomes a way of explaining the uniqueness of the Spanish culture that "produced" him. From here we note the alignment of the film work with the biographical author, a process of substitutability wherein the life of the filmmaker confers "biographical unity" to an otherwise fragmented filmography. The biographical film author is subsequently used to give metaphorical unity to the national culture, thus insuring the easy linkage of culture with film product. Biography, in effect, proves an easily comprehensible way of portraying an otherwise fragmentary and uneven cultural or institutional history. The physical display of the exhibition effects a remapping or reterritorialization as it literally reshapes the spaces of the filmmaker's life and works to coincide with the projection of the nation upon the world.

Finally, the aggrandizement of the entire project in the name of the state and in the place of the museum works to update cinema itself as high Spanish art, a point that is underscored by the positioning of the Buñuel exhibit within the symbolic spaces of the museum. On the floor directly above the huge Buñuel exhibit stands the elaborate permanent exhibition of Picasso's *Guernica*, commemorating a tragic moment in the bloody Civil War, perhaps the last major period when Spain occupied sustained international attention. Only a short walk from the Reina Sofía Museum, lies the Prado, with its enshrinement of the other great visual masters Spain has given the world: Velázquez, Murillo, and Goya. Appropriately placed in the museum, "Buñuel, the Look of the Century" further updates that constructed history of Spanish cultural contributions to Western visual culture by incorporating the history of cinematic representation within the history of Spanish culture rather than, as the innocent visitor to the museum might have imagined, the other way around.

NOTES

1 Luis Buñuel, *My Last Sigh*, trans. Abigail Israel (New York: Vintage Books, 1983), 20.
2 "Una catedral para Luis Buñuel," *El País, Babelia*, July 13, 1996, 2.
3 Buñuel, *My Last Sigh*, 222.
4 Walter Benjamin, "The Work of Art in the Age of Mechanical Reproduction," in *Illuminations*, ed. and introd. Hannah Arendt (New York: Schocken Books, 1969), 231.
5 The literature on auteurism is abundant and reflects the evolving polemical discussions of the nature and importance of this concept to the study of film. For an overview of the elaborate debates around film authorship, see John Caughie, ed., *Theories of Authorship* (London: Routledge & Kegan Paul, 1981); see especially pp. 35–47 for excerpts of the original positions taken by François Truffaut and other New Wave filmmakers and critics in the film journal, *Cahiers du cinéma*. Other important critical positions are presented by Andrew Sarris in "Notes on the Auteur Theory in 1962," *Film Culture*, no. 27 (Winter 1962–1963): 6–7; and Stephen Heath, "Comments on the 'Idea of Authorship,' " *Screen* 14, no. 3 (Autumn 1973): 86–91.

   For more recent discussion of authorship in relation to questions of gender, see Kaja Silverman, "The Female Authorial Voice," in *The Acoustic Mirror: The Female Voice in Psychoanalysis and Cinema*, (Bloomington: Indiana University Press, 1988), 193–212; for discussion of authorship in the context of Third World cinema, see Roy Armes, *Third World Film Making and the West* (Berkeley: University of California Press, 1987), 80–85; for discussion of the publicity marketing of contemporary film authors, see Timothy Corrigan, "The Commerce of Auteurism," in his *A Cinema without Walls: Movies and Culture after Viet Nam* (New Brunswick, N.J.: Rutgers University Press, 1991), 101–136.
6 See Agustín Sánchez Vidal's studies of prominent Aragonese filmmakers: *Borau* (Zaragoza: Caja de Ahorros de la Inmaculada, 1990); *El cine de Carlos Saura* (Zaragoza: Caja de Ahorros de la Inmaculada, 1988); *El cine de Segundo de Chomón* (Zaragoza: Caja de Ahorros de la Inmaculada, 1992); *Luis Buñuel. Obra cinematográfica* (Madrid: Ediciones J. C., 1984).
7 Thomas Elsaesser, *New German Cinema* (New Brunswick, N.J.: Rutgers University Press, 1988), 40–44.

HARMONY H. WU

Unraveling Entanglements of Sex, Narrative, Sound, and Gender: The Discreet Charm of *Belle de jour*

¿Por qué no he de contar, yo también, mi vida? A él no le gustaría nada . . . en su libro Luis no dice nada de su familia, o casi nada. Tengo la certeza de que se pondría furioso con mi libro, así era él.

Why can't I, too, tell my life story? He wouldn't like it one bit . . . in his book, Luis said nothing about his family, or almost nothing. I am certain that he would be furious with my book; that's the way he was.

    Jeanne Rucar de Buñuel[1]

THE PERSONAL NARRATIVE

Jeanne Rucar de Buñuel, wife of the great film director Luis Buñuel, published her memoirs, *Memorias de una mujer sin piano* (Memories of a woman without a piano), seven years after her husband's death (Figure 14). In them, she relates a personal side of Buñuel that we could never know from his films, or from his own autobiography published toward the end of his life. Luis

FIGURE FOURTEEN
Jeanne Rucar de Buñuel. Courtesy of José Luis Borau.

Buñuel was bitterly jealous and jealously irrational. He kept Jeanne out of all his public affairs. He kept her on a strict curfew of five o'clock in the evening. He made her stop gymnastics – a sport in which she won an Olympic bronze medal in 1924 – because, to him, it showed too much of her body. He willfully destroyed some of her treasured personal belongings. He made her stop playing piano, because her instructor was handsome.

How can we fit Jeanne – Mrs. Buñuel – into the picture of Luis Buñuel's cinematic oeuvre? How can we reconcile the public radical with the private reactionary patriarch revealed by his wife?

Susan Suleiman touches on this question of the place of surrealist wives in her book on avant-garde movements, *Subversive Intent*. Considering the role, symbolic and real, of women in surrealism, she looks at a Man Ray photograph taken in 1924 of the real wives of Philippe Soupault and André Breton seated with the surrealist group (sans Buñuel and Salvador Dalí, who were admitted to the group after *Un chien andalou* in 1929). She reads Mick Soupault's image as the "chaste, asexual wife-mother," while Simone Breton's provocative stare and bit of exposed leg suggest "the burning-eyed whore." Careful to note that she is reading only an image, not the real women themselves, Suleiman concludes that the photograph reveals "the degree to which the subject position of Surrealism, as it was elaborated at the inception of the movement, was male. The photograph also makes explicit . . . the problematic position of *actual women* who might wish to integrate themselves, as subjects, into the male script."[2]

This question of "actual women" and surrealist wives resonates particularly strongly with Jeanne Rucar de Buñuel, whose memoirs, interestingly enough, were published the same year as Suleiman's book. The coincidental historical convergence of these two books points to the crucial importance of considering the question that both authors, from different perspectives, ask: what is the position of a woman in surrealism, and by extension – the conceptual diving board of this article – what does the life of a surrealist wife add to our understanding of surrealist works, particularly their engagement with issues of gender?

Suleiman's remarks are suggestive as well for her metaphor of "the script," which is applied both to surrealist texts *and* to the real lives of the surrealists themselves. If life is a story, a script, Luis wrote Jeanne's part. Jeanne insists that although Luis was hard with her and at times she resented it keenly, she still loved him immeasurably. How should we understand these confessions about a famous subversive, now dead? In spite of her professions of love, it is difficult *not* to read these memoirs as an act of defiance, in his death, against the role Luis assigned to her in life. In writing her own story, the script from her perspective, she wrested a little control over her life with Luis Buñuel. Story – narrative – can be an instrument of control, or a strategy of resistance.

Rucar's memoirs directly compete with Buñuel's own autobiography, *My Last Sigh*: "in his book, Luis said nothing about his family." She is right – Buñuel devotes one whole paragraph to his meeting and marriage to Jeanne, in spite of the book's dedication, "To Jeanne . . . my wife, my companion."[3] *Una mujer sin piano* gives another version, a competing narrative that counters not only her husband's memoirs, filling in the holes in the story, but also that narrative he imposed on her in their long life together, where her world was limited to Luis, the children, and the home. She had been, to paraphrase Teresa de Lauretis, inscribed in a hero narrative, *in someone else's story*, not her own, making her a marker of positions, through which the hero, Buñuel, and *his* story move to their destination and accomplish meaning.[4] Rucar's assertion of her *own* narrative demonstrates quite suggestively and powerfully that narrative has the potential to unravel patriarchal authority.

Herein lies *my* strategy: how can we rethink the representations of gender in Buñuel's films *through* the operations of narrative? My interests lie *not* in trying to reread Buñuel's films with new "insights" into the man and thus his work gleaned from *Memorias de una mujer sin piano*, trying to uncover heretofore hidden meanings and references to Buñuel's private life through his wife's accounting of them. Rather, I will take as a point of departure and remembrance the lesson learned from Mrs. Buñuel of narrative's potential to disrupt patriarchal authority as I begin to think about some of Buñuel's films.

THE CINEMA-NARRATIVE

One of the central problematics for feminists thinking and writing about film has been how to find a place for women within a system dominated by patriarchy. In her groundbreaking 1975 essay "Visual Pleasure and Narrative Cinema," Laura Mulvey concluded that feminists must abandon narrative cinema, for it is based on a structure that ritually punishes and objectifies women. While her totalizing rejection of narrative cinema has been criticized by many feminists writing later, her formulation of the cinematic apparatus still informs much of the thinking and writing about film today. The two central arguments of the essay are, first, the assertion that the cinematic gaze is implicitly gendered male and, second, that narrative itself is phallically sadistic – "sadism demands a story" – and is also, like the gaze, gendered male.[5] The implication is stunning: the cinematic apparatus and the structure of narrative itself *always already* assume a patriarchal "vision" before any organization of the profilmic event or story takes place.[6]

Linda Williams historicizes the first of these assertions, showing how even in Eadweard Muybridge's supposedly scientific protocinematographic locomotion studies of humans and animals, the figure of the woman's body creates a *male* anxiety that provokes a disturbance in the texts, causing the deployment of different representational strategies for men and women.[7] Williams persuasively illustrates how the gendered gaze of the cinematic apparatus was ground, at the birth of cinema, in the very lens of the camera. Mulvey's second argument about the gendered nature of narrative structure itself as active-male is elaborated and extended by Teresa de Lauretis: "to say that narrative is the production of Oedipus is to say that each reader – male or female – is constrained and defined within the two positions of a sexual difference thus conceived: male-hero-human on the side of the subject; and female-obstacle-boundary-space on the other."[8] Narrative structure is such that the female is rendered passive, background almost, to the active quest of the male who moves through the obstacles presented by the feminine.

Judith Roof suggests that patriarchal heterosexuality is yet another mechanism reproduced in the structure of narrative. Arguing that narrative's operation is like that of ideology, where that which is constructed (culture, normative heterosexuality) presents itself as natural and innocent, Roof concludes that "interwound with one another, narrative and sexuality operate within the reproductive and/or productive, metaphorically heterosexual ideology that also underwrites the naturalized understanding of the shape and meaning of life."[9] Narrative reproduces not only patriarchy as Mulvey and de Lauretis suggest, but heterosexuality as well, so that even narratives that do not deal specifically with sexuality still *metaphorically* reproduce and situate this heterosexual ideology.

In this brief outline of some of the sexual and gendered implications of cinema-narrative, what is clear is that ideologically there is much at stake in the production of narratives. Structures of both narrative and cinema (both film language and hardware) work as just two of the "innumerable points" of the diffuse operations of power Foucault describes in *The History of Sexuality*, working to reproduce the existing normative social structure.[10] De Lauretis is quite clear about what is involved in these power operations:

> Subjectivity is engaged in the cogs of narrative and indeed constituted in the relation of narrative, meaning, and desire; so that the very work of narrative is the engagement of the subject in certain positionalities of meaning and desire. . . . [The] subject [is] engendered, we might say, precisely by the process of its engagement in the narrative genres.[11]

The gendering of both apparatus and narrative suggests that it is not simply a matter of generating "positive" feminine stories and "good representations" of women to construct a more feminist, less patriarchal cinema – indeed, these theories show that the question of "good" or "bad" representations is hardly the point. But, *how* precisely can feminists produce or find filmic texts that do not suppress the female within this double operation of patriarchal and heterosexual gaze and narrative? Is it even possible for a feminist discourse to be spoken from *inside* these powerful structures?[12]

Feminist theoretical responses to Mulvey's call for the total destruction of pleasure and narrative in the cinema have suggested that there are indeed alternatives, that feminists watching or making films have other strategies for squirming out of patriarchal narrative's grasps. Yet, despite the theoretical promise of these theories – from Mary Anne Doane to de Lauretis – there is a general dearth of examples of what these kinds of films would look like. I propose that Buñuel's films offer concrete and provocative models of how to construct a *pleasurable* mode of subversion of narrative and its patriarchal structures from inside those very structures.

INFINITE STORIES – UNTANGLING NARRATIVE

One of the last films of Buñuel's career, *The Discreet Charm of the Bourgeoisie* (1972) is an example in extremis of how internal subversion of narrative can function. This film illustrates the degree to which narrative form can provide, create, or even unsettle meanings, and so is a useful preface to a consideration of the explicit interactions of narrative *and* gender. The director's maturity and four-decade engagement with cinema had made him a mannerist, stretching and playing with the cinematic-narrative form with great ease and obvious pleasure. This mastery makes *The Discreet Charm* a provocative vantage point from which to look back at *Belle de jour*, which explicitly pairs sex and narrative. *The Discreet Charm* may not be *about* gender, but it is definitely about narrative.

The simple brilliance of the film is its simultaneous lack of and excess of plot. On the surface, there is not much happening – there seems to be no objective, no clear goal, at least not one that fits our conception of a "proper" subject for a feature film: a group of bourgeois friends can't seem to have an uninterrupted meal together. Mainstream movie critic Roger Ebert writes that "the movie isn't about anything in particular, I suppose. . . . Buñuel seems to have finally done away with plot and dedicated himself to filmmaking on the level of pure personal fantasy."[13]

Yet, at the same time, embedded in the main simple "story line" are multiple mininarratives, told in the form of dreams and flashbacks. Each operates independently of the rest, each has an internal structure of suspense, drama building, and climax, yet all are intertwined through associative imagery and similar thematics (ghosts, secrets, unfinished business). For a film "without a story," *The Discreet Charm* in many ways is actually an *excess* of story – everyone, from a lonely lieutenant in a tea room to the commissioner of the police department, has a narrative to tell.

Part of the playing against/within narrative in *The Discreet Charm* is the suturing of the spectator into these stories, but then deferring any conclusion. Nearly all the stories are dropped abruptly at the height of their climaxes, at the height of our interest and curiosity: the lieutenant succinctly concludes, after relating the fascinating oedipal ghost story of his mother's beyond-the-grave desire that he kill his false father, "A few days later I was off to military school where an exciting life was in store for me"; the commissioner awakes from his dream just as the vengeful, bloody ghost of the murdered sergeant appears. This frustration and deferral of narrative desire happens in the "real" waking world of the bourgeois friends, too: the promise of international intrigue with Acosta's cocaine smuggling is a red herring of a plot line that is never followed through. And crucial "information" about that intrigue is routinely and comically obliterated by diegetic industrial noise on the soundtrack: a plane flying overhead denies us access to the reason why the bourgeois friends must be released from jail. In *The Discreet Charm*, Buñuel delights in whipping up our narrative desires and then withholding the goods.

Part of the "excess" of the story is the extreme fluidity – the seeming naturalness – of the continuity between the otherwise disconnected episodes. The links between the dreams-flashbacks are, cinematically speaking, highly structured. For example, the colonel's dinner party dream is deliberately constructed to link up in an ultratight transition with the preceding scene. The colonel invites the friends to his house for dinner a week later and states his address: "17 rue du Parc." The scene cuts from the Sénéchals' living room to the number plate "17" on the colonel's apartment building *as* the colonel says the number. The camera then swish-pans to the street sign, "Rue du Parc" *as* the colonel says that. The transition from the invitation in the Sénéchals' living room to the dinner party one week later couldn't be more clearly mapped out: the visual and aural cues work literally "in synch" to tell us that we have traveled forward one week in time and are at the designated place. We have no reason to assume otherwise. The language of cinematic convention locks us into the logical next step of the narrative – from dinner invitation to dinner itself. The editing is motivated and subordinated to the demands of the narrative (get them to the colonel's for dinner).

Retrospectively, however, we discover that not only is the dinner party set in a theater, not in the colonel's house (the guests have unwittingly assembled as part of a play) but that the whole procedure of going to the party, sitting down, and watching the curtain rise was really just a dream. Sénéchal awakes with a start, cutting off the dinner-theater dream just as he can't remember his lines; he and Mrs. Sénéchal then head for the dinner party for real. Once there, the narrative focus switches to Ambassador Acosta, who is accosted by various of the colonel's guests about barbaric conditions in his homeland, Miranda. Driven to defend his country's honor, Acosta draws a pistol and shoots the colonel. At this point, *Thévenot* awakes from his dream – *he* has dreamed that Acosta shot the colonel *and* that Sénéchal was dreaming that they were eating dinner on stage!

In two moves, Buñuel undermines the reliability of the whole meaning-making system of both his film and conventions of film and narrative language in general. He undercuts our understanding of those events and, thus, our ability to rely in good faith on the cues that led us to that false understanding. However, the main point here lies in the fact that the film simultaneously relies on our understanding of the conventions in order to subvert them. From inside this mise-en-abîme of dreams and dreamers we must ask, as spectators, What and who are real? Is the whole film a dream? Whose? Buñuel's? Mr. Foucauld's, the (possibly) hallucinating insomniac of Buñuel's next and last film, *The Phantom of Liberty*? The ripples of Thévenot's statement "I dreamed Sénéchal dreamed . . ." pulse outward infinitely; the structure of narrative implodes.

In *The Discreet Charm* we find a narrative that fulfills Suleiman's call for a feminist fiction, which, as she sees it exemplified in Angela Carter's novel *The Passion of New Eve* (1977), is:

> a new kind of writing even while apparently remaining within the bounds of a certain "traditional" narrative logic. . . . [Instead of] refusing linear narrative . . . Carter multiplies the possibilities of linear narrative and of "story," producing a dizzying accumulation that undermines the narrative logic by its very excessiveness . . . suggest[ing] a direction for postmodern feminist fiction, based on parody and the multiplication of narrative possibilities rather than on their outright refusal.[14]

The Discreet Charm – released five years earlier than the publication of Carter's novel – fits this descriptive bill in almost every way. But in Suleiman's earlier chapter on the surrealists, she states in no uncertain terms that the project and the worlds of the (male) surrealists were steeped in misogyny.[15] Buñuel fits *this* bill – known surrealist, alleged misogynist. Can *The Discreet Charm of the Bourgeoisie* be *like* a radical feminist text, even with a purported patriarchal author? For that matter, *can* a film that doesn't explicitly engage in gender concerns be like a radical feminist text at all?

I'll take the latter of these questions and defer, like the narrative conclusions of the film's dreams, the other for the time being. As is probably already clear from the opening discussion about narrative structure, the very act of *dismantling* (as opposed to rejecting) narrative involves a dismantling of the patriarchal structures that are locked within the cogs of narrative: because they are so tightly wound, unraveling one undoes the other. If indeed *The Discreet Charm* offers on the level of form a filmic example of the kind of "writing" Suleiman holds up as a model for feminist fiction, it is but a small conceptual leap to conclude that there are feminist interests at work here – what if Jeanne had never written her memoirs? Another question is thus raised – in our poststructural, postmodern moment where readers are writers and authors are dead: just how much of a role, if any, does the author have in determining the ideological or political valence of a text? I'll defer again for now.

But it must be noted that *The Discreet Charm of the Bourgeoisie* is not without suggestively progressive representations of gender. Alice Sénéchal's insistent lust just as the guests arrive shows a woman subject with sexual agency whose mad desire flouts convention and bourgeois manners: Alice demands that her husband climb out the window with her for a quickie in the garden while the guests are left inside to amuse themselves with the ins and outs of martini etiquette. Florence – Simone Thévenot's vaguely petulant sibling – is a woman whose appetite for earthly pleasures (food and especially alcohol) displays a bodily sensuality that visibly unsettles the others' discreet charms. When she starts "reading" Raphael through numerology and astrology, we know she's a flower child trapped in bourgeois company.

In spite of these refreshing women characters (who have a strong antecedent – remember Lya Lys in *her* garden), *The Discreet Charm* is not really a film *about* the characters or their subjectivity. The continual deferral and hyperprogression of narrative limits how "close" we get to them. After all, Florence's astrology bit comes in a scene that is, again, retroactively revealed to be a dream. And dreams function quite differently here than conventionally – that Thévenot dreams that Sénéchal dreamed that Sénéchal forgets his line on stage (a version of a generic anxiety dream) unveils *nothing* about Thévenot's character and less about Sénéchal's. Switch the characters around (Sénéchal dreams Thévenot dreamed he forgot his lines) and nothing changes. The simple point is that *The Discreet Charm* is not concerned with the complexity of the characters as subjects, either masculine or feminine.

I have suggested the feminist value of narrative *subversion* (rather than rejection) and raised the troubling problem of the author through *The Discreet Charm of the Bourgeoisie*. To illustrate more fully the power of tinkering with sexual ideology through narrative and to further complicate the author question, I turn now to narrative subversion exploited in specific relation to issues of gender, sexuality, and women's social roles: *Belle de jour* (1967). This tale of a Parisian woman whose desires cannot be met at home dovetail with the picture painted in Rucar's *Una mujer sin piano*: both concern housewives who are trapped; both foreground narrative processes as a means of subverting their oppressions.

I choose to look at *Belle de jour*, as opposed to *El: This Strange Passion*, the Buñuel film that immediately comes to mind in hearing Jeanne's story, because the narrative focus is on the oppressed woman, rather than on the extraordinary oppressions of the man (in *El*, Don Francisco, whom Buñuel readily admits is modeled after himself). *Belle de jour*'s successful rerelease, presented by Martin Scorsese, in 1995 makes a reconsideration of *Belle de jour* through feminist lenses even more timely. One might ask why was *Belle de jour* the Buñuel film to rerelease instead of, say, *Nazarín* or *Viridiana*? The answer seems clear – *Belle de jour* offers the dual and still pertinent attractions of perverse sex and Catherine Deneuve's visage, making this and further investigations into the film's gender operations all the more pressing. I argue, of course, that there is more to the film than its seductive content. Indeed, *Belle de jour*'s complexity and apparent timelessness seem to depend ultimately *not* on its controversial content and thematics but rather precisely on the intersection of this content with the film's transgression of the rules of patriarchal narrative and cinema.

THE SEX NARRATIVE

But first, an accounting of the narrative content is required, for the subject matter of *Belle de jour* already manifestly presents several potential problems for a feminist understanding

of the text. The story concerns Séverine Serizy (Catherine Deneuve), a proper bourgeois housewife, whose violently masochistic sexual fantasies can find no expression in her marriage with
romantic and doting doctor husband Pierre (Jean Sorel) and thus
drive her to seek erotic fulfillment in a brothel. Her fantasy sex
life involves being whipped, tied up, raped, and generally assum-
ing a passive position where the man takes a "firm hand" and
must authoritatively tell her what to do.

The film's opening squarely situates us in Séverine's desires
and subjectivity. A horse-drawn coach carries the lovely Séverine
and handsome Pierre through a wooded path covered with autumn leaves. They whisper loving sweet-nothings, until quite
suddenly, an argument interrupts the picture-perfection of their
relationship. Pierre orders the two coachmen to stop the carriage
and bodily drags Séverine screaming and kicking through the
woods and ties her to a tree. Ripping off her clothes, he commands the coachmen to whip her and then to have their way
with her. As one of them begins to caress her (still tied to the
tree), Séverine's expression in close-up changes from one of protest to pleasure.

One of the great tricks of the film is that this scene, telescop-
ing *The Discreet Charm of the Bourgeoisie*, with a sudden cut to
another close-up of Séverine's face but in a different mise-en-
scène, is retroactively shown to be her erotic fantasy as she set-
tles down to sleep in their bourgeois bedroom. This sexual violence was not forced on her, but rather a fantasy created and
sustained in her own imagination, precisely the point we must
stop and consider.

Peter Evans is helpful in disengaging the content from sim-
plistic discussions about "good" or "bad" representations of
women, demonstrating that the issue is much more complicated
than passing judgment on whether Séverine's desires are in line
with feminist thinking:

> For a radical feminist, to whom eroticized female display is
> regarded as irrevocably linked to male coercion and violence,
> the film would always be beyond the pale, a further example
> of women's exploitation through stereotype. [But] for a liber-

tarian feminist, to whom the liberation and exploration of female sexuality are regarded as more important than restraint of the male's, it would probably be seen as having the potential not only for interrogating sexuality in general but also . . . for exploring extreme situations and behaviour, transgressing realism, and extending the frontiers of consciousness.[16]

His own analysis proceeds with a detailed discussion of the motivations of Séverine's perverse desires, seeking an explanation for her seemingly regressive fantasies in Freudian theories of frigidity and Séverine's history of childhood sexual abuse.

But, while Evans succeeds in nuancing a feminist reading of the film, his discussion remains problematic within the terms that he himself lays out. Though seeking to reclaim Séverine's fantasies as viable expressions of desire, he only ends up recodifying these desires as irredeemably rooted in perversity by inordinately stressing the childhood sexual encounter: "For various reasons, including *above all* the trauma caused by sexual abuse in childhood, Séverine has become *sexually retarded*, unable to engage in sexual activity in a way that does not reproduce the power relations of that incident."[17]

This emphasis is partly due to Evans's working through the novel by Joseph Kessel, where Séverine's past is given more narrative time and consideration. However, Buñuel's screen version only barely alludes to the event, and just once in very brief flashback. In stressing the "perversity" of Séverine's sexual condition, Evans inadvertently validates so-called normal woman's sexuality under patriarchy, evacuating from Séverine's behavior the potential critique of that "normative" sexuality from which she so apparently deviates. In this reading, Séverine's desires are simply an unfortunate aberration within patriarchal heterosexuality.

Without dwelling too long on the issue, I would suggest that there is in fact *nothing* perverse about Séverine's daydreams and desires. Rather, the dream narratives and her fulfillment of them in the brothel are carrying to the *logical extreme* the nature of woman's sexuality under patriarchy – controlled by male desire, passive. This does not mean that we should thus either unquestionably accept this portrait of female sexuality *or* that we should simply assume that Séverine's desires and pleasures are regressive: Tania Modleski has demonstrated how the seemingly masochistic fantasy of being sexually taken by force can harbor, paradoxically, desire for power and revenge.[18] To interpret such fantasies as Séverine's as revealing all women's "true" desire to be raped is to engage in vulgarly reductive and misogynist Freudianisms. In the logic of "normal" female sexuality within patriarchy, what is "perverse" about Séverine is that she gets *pleasure* in a system that tends to erase woman's pleasure out of the sexual equation. So if *Belle de jour* does not provide a vision of a feminist *alternative* to female sexuality under patriarchy, the film does release a desiring mechanism from within the system that could potentially disrupt the whole order (which, in microcosm, does happen by the film's end, as we shall see).

Even the brothel is an institutionalized avenue of those sexual desires that are irrecuperable in the bourgeois system of sexuality – only under patriarchy brothels exist as covertly acceptable institutions for *men* to seek sexual release in ways social conventions of marriage and monogamy do not allow, certainly not for women to seek *their* pleasure. So again, Séverine's use of the system for her own pleasurable ends suggests a path of subversion from inside the system. It is perfectly Buñuelian: the mechanisms of repression that create the eruption of desire are threatened by the very desire they created (think of Gaston Modot's destructive rage in *L'âge d'or* when he literally tosses society's symbols out the window after social convention finally succeeds in frustrating a sexual union with Lya Lys).

Gaylyn Studlar also helps in recasting this narrative in a more complex light. Through Gilles Deleuze's *Masochism: An Interpretation of Coldness and Cruelty* (1971), Studlar refigures the conception of masochism from the Freudian model in which masochism is always considered the flip side of sadism where the two are locked into *one* mutually reinforcing dynamic, and necessarily a response to the fear of castration by the father.[19] By reconnecting masochism with Leopold von Masoch's *Venus in Furs*, Deleuze shows that the masochist ritually and willingly (re)submits to the controlling *mother*. In this reconception, masochism is removed from a position of powerlessness – the masochist seeks to be controlled and, in so doing, asserts power. Inside the masochistic scenario, the *masochist*, here Séverine, controls the (sexual) narrative.

This excursion through Deleuze and Studlar suggests that on the level of story, *Belle de jour* represents a departure from the patriarchal structure of narrative where the subject is figured as male-hero-agent. Through flaunting the status of women within the scenario, exaggerating their position within the narrative and patriarchy – which is precisely what is at work in Séverine's erotic adventures both as sexual masochist *and* as virginal-asexual wife who won't have sex (or children) with Pierre because she perceives it would ruin the preciousness of their marital union – the flip side, the feminine side, of the patriarchal narrative becomes the focus. For Séverine to eke pleasure out of patriarchal sexuality through the amplification of its inherent masochism and passivity is "to enact the contradiction of female desire, and of women as social subjects,"[20] putting into practice de Lauretis's call to feminist action both against and within male-oedipal narratives. Indeed, Séverine is the embodiment of that contradiction of women as social subjects we saw earlier in the surrealist wives of Man Ray's photograph, merging into one conflicted body-subjectivity the chaste-asexual wife and burning-eyed whore.

UNRAVELING THE NARRATIVE

Although it is now clear that the narrative *content* works to undermine patriarchal authority, *Belle de jour* is even more subversive on the level of form, where it works to release heterosexuality's patriarchal hold on the gaze and narrative.

An understanding of the film turns on an understanding of *Belle de jour*'s digressions from reality into fantasy and reverie.

Part of the "game" of watching the film is the frustration in trying to sort out the "real" from fantasy. But, once Séverine's fantasy life starts taking on real dimensions within the bedrooms of chez Anaïs, it becomes increasingly difficult to filter out dream from reality. This reading practice is finally revealed to be entirely futile. Paul Sandro explains:

> [The uncertainties of the ending of the film] not only . . . make the "outcome" of the story ambiguous, but . . . disrupt retrospectively the solidarity *of the entire narrative system* by discrediting the dichotomy upon which its logic had been established. Every segment that had been distinguished previously from dream is now cut loose, dispersed; attempts to recover narrative meaning lead, through a network of internal contradictions, to its self-cancelation.[21]

Sandro goes on to show how this troubles the viewer's own subjectivity, implicated as she or he is "in the cogs of narrative." But the point here is to suggest that these slip zones opened up by this uncertainty in reading remove yet another nail in the patriarchal structure of narrative. This "cutting loose" of categorizations produces an indeterminacy that completely subverts a narrative logic that is dependent on tight temporal causality; for the contradictions and self-cancellations cannot be rationally explained away into a neat, ordered fictional universe.

But the particular subversiveness of *Belle de jour* is that, like *The Discreet Charm* and unlike *Un chien andalou*, it plays against narrative conventions by playing within them. The "real" scenes of Séverine in her apartment are acoustically marked by the ticking and chiming of clocks, hyperbolically underscoring the alleged "reality" with "real" progression of time. The obsession with time not only represents the highly structured world of the bourgeoisie, as Evans rightly suggests,[22] but also the tightly structured progression of time in conventional *narrative*. The acoustically omnipresent time markers chart almost hysterically the unfolding of the textual space that is supposed to be marked as "real." Thus the time markers become an ironic sign of the false distinction between "fantasy" and "reality," a separation finally made untenable by the film's conclusion. By using this obsessive logicality and sequentiality to suggest the tight structure of a conventional, readable narrative, Buñuel makes the *un*readability of the ending all the more shocking and unsettling.

The indeterminacy of this ending is not, as Pauline Kael suggested, sloppy filmmaking.[23] Rather, it is a specific strategy of subversion of the conventional narrative structure. Unlike the classical narrative, which suppresses other possibilities of the events unfolding, thereby naturalizing its choices and progression as the only possible combination and path, Buñuel projects some of the alternative endings into the very diegesis (Séverine stops dreaming, Séverine dreams, Pierre is paralyzed and emotionally broken, Pierre is healthy and happy, they are in Paris, they are in the woods . . .). This projection of alternatives unsettles the fixity of the entire narrative and reveals it to be not a complete entity but a site of construction.

THE SOUND OF SUBVERSION

The importance of the soundtrack in the hermeneutics of the film cannot be understated. Just as obsessively as the diegetic spaces of the "real" events are marked with aural cues, so are the fantasies. The insistent jingle of carriage bells marks the opening scene with the coach. Cow bells and the stampede of hooves brand the soundtrack in the first fantasy that follows Séverine's initiation in the brothel. Sound provides the bridge from the real diegesis to Séverine's subjective states; the attentive viewer *must* also be an attentive listener.

The two flashbacks to Séverine's childhood are indicated through sound, so it is not only fantasy but also memory – supposedly diegetically real, only past, time – that is coded by acoustic signs. But while the sounds mark distinctions between real and subjective space, they also simultaneously work to break those distinctions down. As Séverine approaches Anaïs's apartment door, the fetishistic close-ups of Séverine's fashionable patent leather shoes (a Buñuel "trademark") making their climb up the carpeted stairs are interrupted aurally by a male voice reciting in Latin, and visually with a reaction shot of Séverine's face. She turns to her right, as if to hear the voice better, as if the source were in the stairwell with her. The following shot of the priest in the church – in a clearly different mise-en-scène – *appears* through shot structure as if it were in the same diegetic space-time as Séverine approaching Mme. Anaïs's brothel. If Séverine had not turned, had not *reacted* visually to an aural cue, the reader of the film text would understand that these are two spaces unconnected except through Séverine's subjectivity. Buñuel uses here the convention of the "voice-off" – the voice of someone off-screen – to collapse (in a series of two shots and one voice) real time-space and subjective time-space into one continuous plane.

The same technique is used in the other flashback, where Séverine recalls the plumber's sexual overtures in her childhood. As she stares blankly into space, a female voice calls from off-screen, "Séverine! Séverine!" She doesn't look toward the presumable source this time; there is a direct cut from her blank face to the close-up of young Séverine's legs, which tracks up her body to show the plumber kissing her. The voice continues calling, but the source of the voice is never shown.

The use of the voice-off to shift the diegesis into subjective spaces has profound implications. Mary Ann Doane shows that the sound register can serve as a privileged site of interiority[24] – Buñuel's use of it to get inside Séverine's fantasies-memories is consistent with this description. But the voice-off as cinematic tool is itself significant. In a lengthy discussion, Doane shows how the voice-off is conventionally used to *extend* the perceived limits of the screen-diegetic space, reassuring the spectators that the world does indeed extend beyond the limits of the frame.[25] Voice-off works as an assurance of completeness and unity of the diegesis.

For the voice-off to be successful in this regard however, the *source* of the voice, the speaker, must eventually be shown as

speaking, to reconnect the implied body and space with the ordered universe of the story. Neither of these instances of the
voice-off does this in *Belle de jour*. In the plumber flashback, the
voice of the mother exists both in the present reality and Séverine's past as an aural perception *only*. In the communion service,
the source of the voice-off, the priest, *is* shown, but Séverine's
turn of the head, as if to look at the speaker within her present
space, undercuts the reassurance of the time-space continuity,
which is supposedly restored when the voice is "returned" to the
body of the priest, falsely conflating two separate times and
spaces. By alternately withholding and subverting the assurances
of the voice-off operation, the created and impossible space of
the film text (and of Séverine's subjectivity) is exposed, revealing
everything to be constructed rather than organically whole, na-
kedly betraying the truth of cinematic "lack," which all conventional rules of filmmaking obsessively seek to conceal.

Buñuel pushes the potentialities of the soundtrack even farther. In the sequence with the bulls named "Remorse" and "Ex-
piation," Séverine fantasizes she is tied to a barn and wearing a
virginal white dress. Husson and Pierre hurl epithets and mud at
her. The scene is visually broken down by elliptical jump cuts of
merely a few frames (channeling Godard's *Breathless*, to which
Buñuel also makes explicit reference through gangster-lover Mar-
cel and the sale of the New York *Herald Tribune*). The jump cuts
foreground the subjective nature of the sequence; here, fantasy
space is *visually* coded, too. But in addition to this new visual
marker of interiority, Husson's, Pierre's, and Séverine's voices are
not synchronized with their mouths. In fact, Séverine's does not
appear to be speaking at all – though her voice is heard repeating
"I love you, Pierre!" her mouth remains resolutely shut. This is
underscored by the movement of her head from side to side as
her face is splattered with the mud: not only is her mouth
closed, but our visual attention is drawn to that fact as her head
lolls and as we watch splatters of dirt cover her face.

The effect of these disruptions at the dual levels of sound and
image is intense. Doane argues that the synchronized voice pro-

vides the image of the fantasmatic body on screen with a sense of wholeness and unity.[26] Nonsynchronous voice unhinges this illusion of organic unity, threatening to expose the lack that underlies all of cinema. Coupled with the jump cuts' visual disruption of the screen body's wholeness, this sequence violently rips the spectator out of any sutured relationship with the film world, coldly exposing the cinematic constructedness of the text, which has (so far) unfolded with visual pleasure and stable aural signifiers. That this occurs in fantasy does not negate the effect; even if the viewer is able to dismiss this disruption of continuity and organic unity as "just a dream," we are, at this point, within Séverine's unconscious. The disruptions must be explained away then as manifestations *of Séverine's subjectivity*, with which we are identifying. Indeed, the implications of this second option are even more profound, for the stability of her very subjectivity is radically thrown into question.

Kaja Silverman explains the gender implications of this violation of synchronization in *The Acoustic Mirror* where she argues that in classical Hollywood narratives the rules of synchronization are more rigorously imposed on female characters than on males.[27] A complex system through sound is enacted on the female voice and body to align her deeply within the diegesis, in order to "[isolate] her definitively from the site of textual production."[28] To cut loose the body from the voice – especially the woman's body and voice – is to remove one of the crucial linchpins in the structure of conventional cinematic narrative: "the female voice [is] a stress point in the functioning of the entire cinematic apparatus."[29] Suddenly, the viewer's always fictional but always *supposed* mastery over the text is unraveled; the whole text is revealed as a discursive construction, enunciated from a site somewhere other than oneself. The full phallic (viewing) subject supposedly reaffirmed through film narratives and cinematic systems of synchronization and suture is unveiled in *Belle de jour* as lacking. This narrative breakdown into impossible spaces is connected with those impossible, contradictory positions imposed on female subjects by the patriarchy: as simulta-

neous virgin-wife-mother-whore. The exaggerated split of Séverine's subjectivity is mirrored by the fractured narrative structure.

Buñuel's sound design deconstructs the conventional film
narrative in another more basic sense as well. In this film of
previously unmatched visual beauty for Buñuel (luxurious color,
gorgeous cinematography by Sacha Vierny, the beautiful, flaw-
lessly costumed and carefully made-up Deneuve, and beaucoup
bourgeois bijoux to fill the mise-en-scène with visual interest),
the richness and textual importance of the soundtrack challenge
the visual as the primary place for the production of meaning
and thereby undermine the authority of the cinematic male
gaze. According to Amy Lawrence, the feminized soundtrack is
usually "assigned the role of the perpetually supportive 'acoustic
mirror' that *reenforces* [*sic*] the primacy of the image and the male
gaze,"[30] but here in *Belle de jour* it undermines the visual to an
astounding degree.[31] Buñuel always claimed credit for sound design in his films even when deaf in his later years – allowing us
to assign him conceptual control if not actual authorship of the
sound track. Here he uses that control to brilliantly showcase the
aural as a site for resistance against the primacy of the sadistic,
phallic gaze.

UNMASKING MASOCHISM AND MASQUERADE

In the preceding discussions, the specter of spectatorship has continually resurfaced. In returning to one of the gen-
erative questions of this essay – how do we write about film-
narrative as feminists? – it is worthwhile to consider how to
receive film narratives as feminists. This very subject has taken up
much of feminist writing on cinema in the aftermath of Mulvey's "Visual Pleasure" article, and, intriguingly, some of the
most innovative theories on spectatorship have dealt specifically
with masochism. This confluence of masochism in both receiving strategies in feminist film writing and narrative content in

Belle de jour raises certain pressing problems in the ways spectatorship has been theorized.

Mary Ann Doane proposes women should "masquerade" as
spectators to gain the distance from screen representations of
women that is necessary to form criticisms of them. The masquerade involves flaunting the constructedness of femininity,
presumably getting a woman out of the trap of having to either
"masculinize" herself to identify with the hero (following Mulvey on *Duel in the Sun*) or accept a masochist position with her
passive female screen counterparts (subjected, as they are, to the
sadistic male gaze and relegated to narrative background).[32] Gaylyn Studlar, on the other hand, suggests that masochism *is* and
should be the model of cinematic spectatorship. She argues that
masochism is not entrapping of women; on the contrary, it represents the exaltation of the powerful oral mother (instead of the
Mulveyian idea that cinema is based on the castration complex
and its attendant overvaluation of the phallus and women's
lack).[33]

To consider the appropriateness of applying these approaches
to *Belle de jour*, we can examine a key sequence that is overlaid
with structures of looking, masochism, and sadism and that
helps decode the position *the film* constructs for the audience.
Newly working at the brothel, Séverine is called upon to service
Victor, the "famous gynecologist." Victor goes through his suit-
case in the bathroom, literally trying on different hats to decide
what role to play in the sexual masquerade he anticipates with
Séverine in *her* role as Belle de jour (this emphasis on *deciding*
makes us aware, again, of the different choices operative in constructing the narrative, as in the final sequence). Séverine, however, cannot adequately play the controlling, cruel woman to Dr.
Victor's groveling masochistic servant (suggesting masquerade
also functions on the level of class); quickly unsatisfied with Séverine's performance, Victor trades in Belle de jour for the more
practiced – and lower-class – Charlotte, selecting, as it were, just
another item on the menu or paradigm. Anaïs commands Sév-

erine to watch them through a peephole from the adjacent room. Séverine, hidden, watches and says to Anaïs with disgust, "How could anyone sink so low?"

Séverine at the peephole is a clear reflection on the structures of seeing and looking in the film narrative, and the self-reflexive moment invites critical interrogation of the viewer's position in relation to *Belle de jour*. Séverine's resultant disgust at what she sees has been interpreted as disgust with Victor's masochism, which in turn seems to reflect back onto herself and her own masochistic tendencies.[34] However, Séverine, in being put at the peephole, has taken the position of a voyeur, like spectators in a theater – a sadistic position with its requirement of distance and implications of investigation. Her discomfort at the keyhole could be read, then, not as a rejection of the display of masochism, but discomfort with having to masquerade as sadist. Séverine at the peephole is a spectacular display of a masochistic voyeur watching with discomfort a masochist. This quite literally describes *our* place as spectators of the film text – and the very position Buñuel has constructed for us to inhabit.

What I am suggesting here is that through all the gaps and discontinuities in the narrative and filmic structure, and for all the ways that Buñuel has made the narrative structure obvious to us, the spectator cannot deny that there is a discursive agent, an enunciator of the text, that exists outside the spectator's own subjectivity. The illusionary sense of power usually bestowed on film spectators in which we conceive ourselves as the site of the production of meaning through the erasure of all marks of enunciation is completely undercut in *Belle de jour*. In revealing the film as a created construct, Buñuel *publicizes* that we are at the mercy of his text – and he explicitly shows us his hand in this when he makes an iconic cameo appearance during Séverine's meeting with the duke, not coincidentally the very sequence where the cues of fantasy and reality begin to irreparably erode and bleed together. The spectator becomes aligned with Séverine *as* a masochist, for to watch or listen to the film is to accept the condition of being spoken for, a condition literally made visible in the peephole sequence. In watching the film, we are like Séverine watching at the peephole, and in watching her play out *her* masochist role, we must become aware of our *own* masochism, submitted as we are to the mercies of Buñuel and the text.

Here we encounter a limitation in the feminist theories of spectatorship, and perhaps not surprisingly, we find it colliding with the question of the author. If there is a distinct discursive agent (Buñuel), how does Doane's suggestion of masquerading as spectator help in dislodging the discourse? Buñuel shows how powerless we are; our viewing position is as masochist. But unlike Victor, we cannot control the discourse; we can only accept the terms of Buñuel's "game" or walk out of the theater. This suggests that it is not enough to be aware of the discursive site; the enunciator still produces specific meanings and subject positions for both characters and spectators, troubling Barthesian theories of readers as writers and the free play of meaning in a text.

Trying to apply Studlar's model to *Belle de jour* poses even more difficult problems. Studlar proposes the masochist viewing model as one that opens up the potential for *male* spectators to identify with the powerful oral mother figure such as Dietrich in von Sternberg films. Central to this argument is the need for the spectator's loss of ego boundary – to fall into a kind of "magical thinking" where "the spectator becomes the passive receiving object who is also subject."[35] But what happens when the masochism is manifest rather than latent, when the female figure is explicitly posed as a masochist herself? Or when the conditions of the limits and contingencies of the oral universe recreated by the dream screen are *highlighted* through the kinds of reflexivity and self-awareness in *Belle de jour*? When there is no "oral mother" character to identify with, does the submission to the oral mother get displaced onto the enunciator – Buñuel? And what does this in turn suggest about Buñuel's *own* gender masquerade – especially given our knowledge of his fondness for it in real life (Figure 15)?[36]

Belle de jour suggests that a recuperation of the masochist po-

FIGURE FIFTEEN
Luis Buñuel, in nun drag, rests his arm on the shoulder of Jeanne
Rucar, who is seated next to her sister, accompanied by Juan
Vicens masquerading as a monk. Courtesy of José Luis Borau.

sition and a strategy of masquerade are not adequate enough
when a text is so highly structured and such a specific place for
the viewer is so adamantly insisted upon. Through problematic
texts (and auteurs) like this, there needs to be more theorizing of
spectatorship and feminism and a reconsideration of masquerade and masochism.

CONCLUSION: COMPETING NARRATIVES

In this essay, I have attempted to show that the texts of Buñuel are privileged sites for feminist investigations of how to subvert gendered narrative and interrogate cinematic spectatorship. But I began with another narrative – Jeanne Rucar de Buñuel's. For all of *Belle de jour*'s piercing attacks against patriarchy's hold on female sexuality and its deconstruction of the maleness of narrative, much like Thévenot or Séverine waking up from a dream, Jeanne's story retroactively and very seriously problematizes the text. How can a man so arcane in his gender politics in the home possibly produce texts in which we can find provocative explorations of feminine conditions and desires? *Can* we accept *any* of Buñuel's narratives, knowing that behind them looms the more insidious, controlling, and very "male" enunciator, as Suleiman shows the surrealists to have been, as Jeanne tells us Luis was? Is it indeed possible to completely divorce the text from its author – to celebrate the author's death?

The answer, to me, is quite plainly no. To celebrate the death of Luis, as author, requires that we also do the same to Jeanne, and *both* of their personal narratives are too important and real: on both sides of the story, there is too much to forget. They are historically situated subjects, and *both* of their unique – and conflicting – voices affect our understanding of the films. If we are looking for the portrayal of the contradiction of historical women – and can we add men, too? – as social subjects in narratives, a wise place to begin would be with the historical author. If we are looking for the flip sides of patriarchal narratives to be written and heard, we have this in Jeanne's story. However, knowing Jeanne's story, we should not then write off Luis's oeuvre. As I showed with *The Discreet Charm of the Bourgeoisie*, the kinds of cinematic and narrative experimentation – regardless of gender as subject – that Buñuel played with throughout his career do hold considerable promise for unraveling the patriarchal ideology entangled in those structures. Like the Marquis de Sade, whom Angela Carter declares a misogynist and who also, almost paradoxically, admitted a position for women as sexual sub-jects,[37] Buñuel – a follower of the philosophies of de Sade – pro-vides us in Séverine with complex investigations into the mech-anisms of feminine desire in patriarchy, and in *The Discreet Charm*'s mise-en-abîme of dreamers, a model for writing against the ideological status quo from within. These are just two of his over thirty films. We cannot close ourselves off to the possibili-ties embedded in these works.

But, at the same time, we also must not invest overmuch au-thority in his voice, which is by turns conservatively patriarchal and radically subversive. We need to make a space for the voices of the surrealist wives – real and fictional – as well as our own as readers. These historical and fictional narratives interweave with the narrative of surrealism and the narrative of Luis Buñuel, and only in that complex matrix can we find the depth of our desires *and* oppressions, and their infuriating, exhilarating intersection.

NOTES

1 Jeanne Rucar de Buñuel, *Memorias de una mujer sin piano*, with Marisol Martín del Campo (Madrid: Alianza Editorial, 1990), 157. The trans-lation is mine.
2 Susan Suleiman, *Subversive Intent: Gender, Politics and the Avant-Garde* (Cambridge, Mass.: Harvard University Press, 1990), 24 (emphasis added).
3 Luis Buñuel, *My Last Sigh*, trans. Abigail Israel (New York: Vintage Books, 1983). The paragraph about Jeanne falls on pages 85–86. Cu-riously, her name is consistently misspelled.
4 Teresa de Lauretis, "Desire in Narrative," in *Alice Doesn't: Feminism, Semiotics, Cinema* (Bloomington: Indiana University Press, 1984), 109. The actual passage reads: "Medusa and the Sphinx, like the other ancient monsters, have survived inscribed in hero narratives, in someone else's story, not their own; so they are figures or markers of positions – places and topoi – through which the hero and his story move to their destination and to accomplish meaning."
5 Laura Mulvey, "Visual Pleasure and Narrative Cinema," in *The Sexual Subject: A Screen Reader in Sexuality* (New York: Routledge, 1992), 22–34.
6 Steve Neale, "Masculinity as Spectacle," and Richard Dyer, "Don't

Look Now: The Male Pin-Up," in *The Sexual Subject*, specifically deal with the maleness of the cinematic gaze.

7 Linda Williams, *Hard Core: Power, Pleasure, and the "Frenzy of the Visible"* (Berkeley: University of California Press, 1989), 36.

8 De Lauretis, "Desire in Narrative," 121.

9 Judith Roof, *Come as You Are: Sexuality and Narrative* (New York: Columbia University Press, 1996), xxvii.

10 Michel Foucault, *The History of Sexuality: An Introduction*, vol. 1, trans. Robert Hurley (New York: Vintage Books, 1990), 93–97.

11 De Lauretis, "Desire in Narrative," 106.

12 The last question is the raison d'être of de Lauretis's writing, and the answer she gives is a resounding yes. This essay will bracket de Lauretis's "oedipus with a vengeance" as a general strategy and focus on the specific resistances as manifested in an actual text.

13 Roger Ebert, review of *The Discreet Charm of the Bourgeoisie*, *Cinemania* (Microsoft Corporation, 1996) available at http://cinemania.msn.com.

14 Suleiman, *Subversive Intent*, 137–139.

15 Ibid., 11–32.

16 Peter Evans, *The Films of Luis Buñuel: Subjectivity and Desire* (Oxford: Clarendon Press, 1995), 152.

17 Ibid., 168 (emphasis added).

18 Tania Modleski, *Loving with a Vengeance: Mass-Produced Fantasies for Women* (New York: Routledge, 1990), 39–48.

19 Gaylyn Studlar, "Masochism and the Perverse Pleasures of the Cinema," in *Film Theory and Criticism: Introductory Readings*, ed. Gerald Mast, Marshall Cohen, and Leo Braudy, 4th ed. (New York: Oxford University Press, 1992), 773.

20 De Lauretis, "Desire in Narrative," 156.

21 Paul Sandro, *Diversions of Pleasure: Luis Buñuel and the Crises of Desire* (Columbus: Ohio State University Press, 1987), 134 (emphasis added).

22 Evans, *The Films of Luis Buñuel*, 159.

23 Pauline Kael, "Saintliness," *New Yorker*, February 15, 1969, 109.

24 Mary Ann Doane, "The Voice in the Cinema: The Articulation of Body and Space," in *Movies and Methods*, vol. 2: *An Anthology*, ed. Bill Nichols (Berkeley: University of California Press, 1985), 572.

25 Ibid., 571.

26 Ibid., 567.

27 Kaja Silverman, *The Acoustic Mirror: The Female Voice in Psychoanalysis and Cinema* (Bloomington: Indiana University Press, 1988), 47.

28 Ibid., 69.

29 Ibid., 63.

30 Amy Lawrence, *Echo and Narcissus: Women's Voices in Classical Hollywood Cinema* (Berkeley: University of California Press, 1991), 111.

31 That this castration, as it were, of sight could be read as a devaluation of *feminine* sight, insofar as it is Séverine's point of view and subjectivity, is a valid argument. However, given the subversive nature of Séverine's desire within the system, I doubt that she and the meaning of the text can be fully recuperated back into a normative patriarchal scenario.

32 Mary Ann Doane, "Film and the Masquerade: Theorizing the Female Spectator," in *The Sexual Subject: A Screen Reader*, 227–243.

33 Studlar, "Masochism," 773–790.

34 Margot S. Kernan, Review of *Belle de jour*, *Film Quarterly* 23 (Fall 1969): 40.

35 Studlar, "Masochism," 785.

36 Buñuel writes in his autobiography: "In those days, the Closerie des Lilas was still only a café. I used to go there frequently, as well as to the Bal Bullier next door. We always went in disguise. I remember dressing up one night as a nun, in an elaborate and wholly authentic costume. I even put on false eyelashes and lipstick. As we were walking down the boulevard Montparnasse, with Juan Vicens dressed as a monk, we saw two policemen coming toward us. I began to tremble under my headdress; in Spain, a joke like that could get us five years in jail" (*My Last Sigh*, 83–84). Rucar's memoirs contain a charming photograph of Luis and Vicens in these costumes, with Jeanne and sister Georgette seated between them. Rucar also relates that Luis and friends would often ride the buses dressed as priests, attempting to first dupe and then surprise other passengers (36–37).

37 Angela Carter, *The Sadeian Woman and the Ideology of Pornography* (New York: Pantheon Books, 1978). See the "Polemical Preface," 3–37.

JAMES TOBIAS

Buñuel's Net Work:
The Detour Trilogy

In 1957 Roland Barthes identified the silent work of bourgeois ideologies by isolating them as images that are inverted from the historical course of events, configured for representational abuse: "The flight from the name 'bourgeois' is not therefore an illusory, accidental, secondary, natural or insignificant phenomenon: it is the bourgeois ideology itself, the process through which the bourgeoisie transforms the reality of the world into an image of the world, History into Nature. And this image has a remarkable feature: it is upside down."[1]

Polish video artist Zbigniew Rybcynski's 1984 *The Discreet Charm of the Diplomacy* goes Barthes's formulation one better. Rybcynski, known for his video repurposing of images from the works of film directors ranging from Eisenstein to Méliès, reworks Luis Buñuel's *The Discreet Charm of the Bourgeoisie* into a political critique of a gathering of the crème de la crème of the American diplomatic corps in an elegant reception for the Soviet ambassador, but adds an element that intensifies the parodic reuse of Buñuel's 1972 film: upside-down, noisy farm animals and pets parade across the underside of the dining table behind which the dignitaries are standing. If the video's title and setting have already called up Buñuel's famous interruption of a bourgeois feast, the animals seems to have wandered out of *Susana*—and found their way north to Washington, D.C. After surreptitiously offering diplomatic handouts to the excluded and unruly animals below, the bearded U.S. representative finally gets sucked under the table and turned upside down in a mimicry of Fernando Rey's attempt to avoid assassination in the last sequence of Buñuel's film. Caught in a change of sides, the dignitary finally pulls down a bottle of champagne from the table, and crawls out of the frame to celebrate.

At once pointing up Buñuel's signature strategy of reusing and repeating elements and themes from his own films while relocating Buñuel's own cinematic operations quite literally within his own video art, Rybcynski doesn't just manage to redirect the viewer's experience of Buñuel's radical experiments in cinematic form toward his own project of reinterpreting the great films for newly arising conditions. Rybcynski also projects an incisive media critique that challenges the U.S. administration's indulgence of attempts to stifle a movement that would radically alter the nature and balance of political power in Poland. Rybcynski's gain is Buñuel's gain. The video artist recombines the film director's elements and settings, leveraging Buñuel's more complex cinematic broadsides in order to align electronic art with forces of social transformation in a time of political resistance. That recombination also injects Buñuel's oeuvre into new domains, reactivating it in the world of cut-and-paste media.

A more hyperrealistic repurposing of Buñuel can be found in other, perhaps surprising places: for example, in an urn on a dining table. In *The Discreet Charm*, Fernando Rey as the ambassador of Miranda keeps a handgun in a porcelain urn in his apartment as a defense against attempts on his life by left-wing terrorists. After Delphine Seyrig as Simone Thévenot casually appears out of Rafael's bedroom when her husband comes to call, the Thévenots' departure is followed by the entrance of a terrorist against whom Rafael will brandish the gun from the urn. This container, or one remarkably similar to it, reappears on Delphine Seyrig's dining room table in Chantal Akerman's *Jeanne Dielman,*

23 Quai de Commerce, 1080 Bruxelles (1975). The urn is where Seyrig, as bourgeois homemaker and widow Jeanne, periodically deposits the money that she earns from her afternoon work as a prostitute. If Rybcynski obviously and intentionally forges links with Buñuel, perhaps it is not intentional but only inevitable that links would appear in the work of Akerman as she takes up a personal critique of bourgeois femininity and contests the conventions of narrative form in the cinema. As the drug-dealing ambassador in *The Discreet Charm* keeps a gun in his pot, so the reserved housewife who has inherited the bourgeois household keeps the proceeds from prostitution in hers.[2]

But is *The Discreet Charm of the Bourgeoisie* really a farcical critique of a class culture? Whereas for Barthes the bourgeoisie functions as a "joint-stock company," for Buñuel in *The Discreet Charm* it is a gang of drug dealers devoted to fine liquor and sumptuous meals, which the narrative movement of the film never allows them to enjoy. With conflicting desires for each other, at war with other gangs, threatened by terrorists, and operating in limited alliances with the state, the army, and the Catholic Church, their lavish feasts are always interrupted by real-world threats or dream digressions. In Barthes's terms, the film might be seen as an explicitly political act of speech that calls bourgeois cinematic ideology by name. But Buñuel does more than challenge the status of bourgeois ownership, political order, and ideology by calling attention to them. His late films, like his earliest, work against some of the most fundamental conventions of mainstream narrative film. Buñuel finds conflict where Barthes sees only the diffusion of bourgeois ideals by force:

> The whole of France is steeped in this anonymous ideology: our press, our films, our theatre, our pulp literature, our rituals, our Justice, our diplomacy, our conversations, our remarks about the weather, a murder trial, a touching wedding, the cooking we dream of, the garments we wear, everything, in everyday life, is dependent on the representation which the bourgeoisie *has and makes us have* of the relations between man and the world.[3]

For Barthes in 1957, left-wing myth is powerless, clumsy, and borrowed, and if authentic, then threadbare. In defining itself in relation to the oppressed, leftist myth cannot avail itself of the luxury of metalanguage, and cannot lie: "lying is a richness, lying presupposes property, truths, and forms to spare."[4] Barthes undertakes his semiology as an attempt at deconstructing dominant discourses in mass culture to reveal the operative modes in which they are elaborated and to point out the elisions which mask the sources of those ideologies, their codes, and their goals. In the filmic medium, however, Buñuel continues cinematic strategies less deconstructive than mystifyingly constructive. Barthes will aim to produce an amplified, annotated counterdiscourse that can lay bare those operations of ideology which constrain the oppressed to a transitive form of speech (which at its best can only express truth) and to forgo the excesses of property, wealth, and lies. In *S/Z*, Barthes will articulate a network of codes from which the voice of a text is woven, and which gives its reading a particular "grain." Buñuel will not offer a critical vocabulary for the deconstruction of lying ideology. Instead, he will demonstrate by example the rich reappropriatability of pleasures through a never-ending struggle for a personal and experiential ethic in the mass cultures of the industrial and the informatic.

Perhaps, as Jean-Louis Commoli argues in "Machines of the Visible," "modern travel, exploration, and colonizations" have produced an extension of the representable with the effect that "the whole world becomes visible at the same time as it becomes appropriatable."[5] Commoli claims that social forces mobilize technologies, making them crucial instruments in producing ideological subjects. He observes an inversion at work in the cinema: it is found within a Deleuzian "social machine" which is "driven by representation," not by historical forces tending toward scientific knowledge or progress.[6] Barthes's "unwritten norms of interrelationships" are revised as Commoli presupposes a "set of apparatuses of representation" operating through not only ideologies but relational behaviors including "balances of power, confrontations, manoeuvres of seduction, strategies of defense, marking of differences or affiliations."[7] For Commoli, so long as social order is at work, a real world mise-en-scène precedes any cinematic reproduction of it on film. Since that precinematic mise-en-scène ultimately is sourced from spectators and utilized by creators of cinematic works to render the visible, the cinema has wise, not imbecilic, spectators who willingly expect to be fooled in order to enjoy the possibilities for varying identifications with cinematic representations. Commoli's visual culture activates appropriation and identification to find power wielded by spectators who swing back and forth from "criticism to fascination."[8] Through a body of films that starts as an avantgarde "call to crime," then trends to subtler subversion in various commercial cinemas, and finally turns the international feature film inside out with *Discreet Charm,* Buñuel not only anticipates and illustrates Commoli's formulation but also provides correctives to the shortcomings in his argument.

Engaging cinema's hypnotic power that often delivers experiences and feelings otherwise unattainable, Buñuel's *Discreet Charm* projects both the dreamy lives of privileged consumers and the starker lives of the less privileged where violence is not simply a distant threat that can be kept at bay. The casual luxuries of the bourgeoisie, most of what constitutes their discreet charm, are available for appropriation by pleasure-seeking spectators who are produced in the networks of cinematic creation and dissemination, yet they must acknowledge the violent effects that these pleasures are revealed to be linked to. In this process of exchange, we become both critical of and fascinated by our relationship to narrative film itself, complicit with it through collusion and resistance as we are with the discourses or institutions it represents.

But it is not self-quotation, intertextual references, and explicitly political subject matter that make *The Discreet Charm* and the other late films different from Buñuel's previous commercial films; it is rather an escalation in the use of the outrageous, irrecuperable narrative devices that mark each of these films with an iconic distinction. As *The Discreet Charm* wanders on, unable to resolve the deferred consumption of the feast, we detour periodically through a pivotal image in which the main characters are framed walking along a deserted country road. Buñuel refuses to ascribe any particular meaning to this recurring scene, but points out that an ideological condemnation aimed *solely* at the bourgeoisie as a class devoted to a dying ideology, going nowhere, is not exactly what he had in mind: "I don't believe that it's just the bourgeoisie that are on the brink of extinction. In many places, the proletariat is becoming less revolutionary and bit by bit more bourgeois."[9] As Augustín Sánchez-Vidal points out elsewhere in this volume, in his memoirs Buñuel retroactively groups this film into a "trilogy, or rather a triptych"[10] of journeys with the preceding *Milky Way* and the later *Phantom of Liberty*. Taken as an image of the ever resistant privileged bourgeoisie or of the ever restless audiences of film, this sequence structures the film's cycle of increasing incoherence that replaces the usual diegetic movement toward closure and release. The image of the meandering bourgeoisie also positions this film as an exploration of mass audience identification with the moving image, one located between the spatiotemporal pilgrimage through Catholic heresies in *The Milky Way* and the discursive journey through a careening array of narrative geographies in *The Phantom of Liberty*.

Using this detour scene as a pointer to Buñuel's increasingly radical experiments with the mobility of identificatory pleasures, I will appropriate the figure of the trilogy as a template to configure his last three films as a closely linked succession of narratives that continue, revise, or reject earlier themes or strategies from his oeuvre. By setting these three detours together – the meandering identification in *The Discreet Charm*, the exposition of the cinematic network in *Phantom*, and the flagrant disruption of continuity and transparency of the global film narrative in *That Obscure Object of Desire* – we emphasize Buñuel's unceasing and evolving effort to project cinematic pleasures while radicalizing cinematic narrative. Later, artists like Rybcynski and Akerman would lay claim to this effort of formal innovation and remake it by combining it with political or social engagement.

While it may seem disingenuous to utilize the critical strategies of, say, Commoli to read Buñuel, a filmmaker who helped create the conditions of the cinematic "apparatus" which Commoli describes, perhaps it will be less so if we consider Buñuel not simply as a surrealist or one of the "Generation of 27," but as one of many creators and critics who have taken up the challenges to knowing and doing posed by the nineteenth century's "three masters of suspicion" – Marx, Nietzsche, and Freud. Buñuel may be considered a masterful "agent of construction" in our own century. In this essay I will bring together for consideration a brief sampling of the works of three twentieth-century agents of construction: Buñuel, Michel Foucault, and Marvin Minsky. I will outline Buñuel's films beginning with *The Discreet Charm of the Bourgeoisie* as a critical aesthetic practice in the light of our era's articulation of technologies of representation and movement in the form of the network. If I concentrate less on a Barthesian conception of intertextual networks woven from reducible textual codes in favor of strategic networks never too interested in coherence as such and designed to proliferate through interacting with real persons, that is only to reveal a bias that our century's agents of construction have taken as a given: as our bodies are mobilized to bear meaning, it is the effects that transform them that count.

WANDERING IDENTIFICATION IN *THE DISCREET CHARM OF THE BOURGEOISIE*

I've suggested that the scene of the main characters tramping down a country road helps call attention to the work of identification that dynamically occurs between audience, work, and creators. This "detour" scene is not simply plopped down in random spots in the middle of the film, but works strategically with and against the more conventional constructed sequences to reveal the work of the audience in the production of meaning within the film. But how? The reasons have to do with an explicit if tortuous relationship with "the real world" found in the director's last three "surrealist" films that is hardly, if at all, identifiable in the early films made when he was a "sectarian" of the surrealist movement.[11]

The detour scene points up the conventions of narrative continuity through its interruption of the more conventionally structured sequences of the film. By naming filmic narrative conventions in this way, the film accomplishes two simultaneous operations. First, the spectator is moved into a position where he or she can see through the frames of dominant discourses. Then this new configuration of knowledge is pushed into further ambiguity, which the spectator experiences as paradox. Buñuel designed specific strategies for accomplishing these effects: As Marsha Kinder has pointed out, *The Discreet Charm* constantly encourages us to form expectations and then avoids fulfilling them through shifts that pit sound against image, characters against their own lines, and clothes against bodies to indicate, for example, the censorship of political discourse but, more generally, the denaturalization of cinematic conventions. "As a result, despite the emphasis on repetition, it is always impossible to predict what will happen next."[12] Also, Buñuel expects the audience to pay attention not only to how he depicts a given situation but how he undermines our usual ways of contextualizing it. Gaps and exclusions are constructed in such a way as to invite audience speculation that will supply ambiguous meaning. What is in the bag that Mateo carries in *That Obscure Object*? Buñuel doesn't know, but, for example, Linda Williams can still be persuasive in finding the bag open to interpretation and filling it with excrement.[13] If Buñuel's productions seem to resist analysis, perhaps that is because much of the time he allows us to decide what he is saying.

For this reason the detour scene where the main cast is seen walking down a deserted country road becomes a crucial innovation in Buñuel's bag of tricks. In this film, it breaks up the continuity of the localized "dream" logic that develops over the course of the film, and thus helps to "name" the techniques of mise-en-scène and montage within the sequences it punctuates. In differentiating this technique of interruption from techniques of continuity, it effectively names itself as well, and in fact is reappropriated by the film as it plays out. As it is repeated throughout the film, the detour scene becomes a figure which stands for the narrative contradiction occuring on multiple levels of the film.

The scene of the cast on the country road recurs three times, its final projection ending the film. The detour recalls a previous device employed in *Belle de jour*, the carriage with its jingling bells that ambiguously begins and ends that film, but importantly, in *The Discreet Charm*, the detour occurs first only to punctuate an initial cycle of episodes, through the story of the interrupted feast. This first demonstration is then replayed twice more to provide post hoc structure to additional cycles.

The second cycle of episodes introduces dreams of minor characters as explicit digressions that return to the main path, but it ends with a main character, Thévenot, not sure whether he has dreamed a dream of his own or of his partner in crime, Sénéchal. These dreams are now only identifiable after they have appeared, in what Eberwein calls "the retroactive mode."[14] We cannot judge where they begin until we receive an explicit wake-up call that announces that they have ended. This second cycle introduces an instability in the narrative flow, which to some degree is foreclosed by the reoccurrence of the detour that occurs again to end these episodes. Simultaneously, however, the fact that characters seem to be dreaming each other's dreams also poses the question of whether the preceding cycle has been a set of intersubjective dreams collectively dreamed by the cast as they detour toward an unknown destination: the next cycle in the film.

The third cycle places the intersubjectivity of the dreaming parties in a broadening spiral that effaces the boundaries between the threatening dreams of minor cast members. Preceding Rafael's final dream of a gangland assassination of the cast (as they finally are able to enjoy a feast at the Sénéchals') is the dream of a police commissioner who has arrested the cast for drug smuggling. The police commissioner's dream starts in a sequence in which the cast has been arrested and jailed, through the legend of the bloody brigadier (the ghost of a torturer who returns to the precinct jail each 14 June). The dream extends into the office of the commissioner himself as he wakes up to a telephone call from the minster of the interior commanding him, for reasons that are obscured in the noise from international airline traffic, to release the bourgeois prisoners. But as the return of the cast to the Sénéchals' home for dinner is ultimately revealed to be an execution nightmare from which Rafael awakens, it is quite possible that the arrest of the cast was also simply a nightmare that *didn't end*. That episode too can be fully subsumed within the dream of Rafael, if we choose to use the "grammar"[15] (Figure 16) that the film develops in order to interpret even a cut into a new scene as the retroactive revelation of a dream.

The dream of identification, however violent, between the members of the bourgeoisie is thus extended as far as their strategic opponents in the third cycle, before it also detours toward destinations unknown. The detour scene does not function as an ostensible beginning-as-ending as the carriage scene does in *Belle de jour*. But this detour is also quite far from Buñuel's frequent "detournement,"[16] or strategic redefinition of meaning through the recall and recombination of images and elements.

The repetition of the detour stresses both the appropriation of the real-world mise-en-scène which precedes the film and the work of identification on the part of the audience. In the naturalistic scene of the detour, a crowd of characters which is completely out of place moves toward an uncertain destination, what could be a better description of an audience looking for coherence and closure in the ideological playground of the cinema. Linda Williams suggests a key shift in Buñuel from a use of predominantly metaphoric figures in *Un chien andalou* toward techniques of metonymic displacement in *L'age d'or*, which are

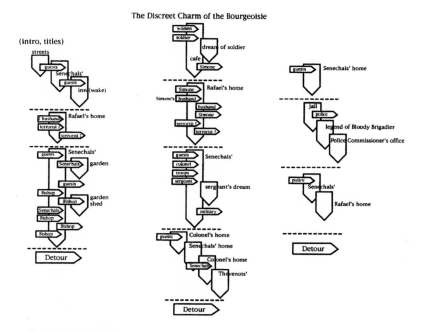

The Discreet Charm of the Bourgeoisie

FIGURE SIXTEEN

We learn to read the cuts into new sequences (dotted line) ambiguously. If we read forward, they signify a jump to a new sequence. But we learn that they can be read backward as well,
indicating a dream within a dream.

refined in the displaced narrative of *The Phantom of Liberty*. Both
techniques, she argues, are balanced to some degree in the finale
of *That Obscure Object of Desire*.[17] But the repeating detour of *The
Discreet Charm* evinces not a simple reuse of early techniques but
an invention of new ones. The detour can work both as a metaphor for the cast's wanderings, but it can also metonymically
continue the dreamlike digression of the film into a disconnected narrative that demands that we suspend our conclusions
about who in the movie is dreaming what. To accept both of
these readings is to acquire an ambiguous rhetoric that leads us
to find a point of entry into the film from the work the audience
performs on it. If we accept the detour as part of this film, and I
think that inevitably we must, we might most simply accept its

apparent *isolation* from the rest of the film, as well as its *structuring* of the film. We notice our identification with those in the cast; they are no longer a glamorous party of revelers above all law but merely a set of all too human bodies traveling an uncertain path.[18]

Cinematic duration is evident here in the most material way. Without any establishing shot or any continuity with preceding or following scenes, we identify en masse with the cast of members simply because their bodies move as ours might. The absence of subjective points of view emphasizes the individual subjectivity that is denied to the characters in the rest of the film, and that is denied to us. They fall behind, they adjust their shoes, they catch up to the rest, they slowly outpace the others. Time passes. They blur into end titles as we are left with the sound of their footsteps, the wind, and the lonely call of a raven. The detour works as a placeholder for audience identification because the film locates the spectator in a cinematic network whose paradoxes have become apparent. Finally, the detour leads us out of *The Discreet Charm* and, after a brief digression on the discourses of the network, I will follow where it seems to point us: toward *The Phantom of Liberty*.

DISCOURSES ON AND OF THE NETWORK

Rather than put the figure of the network at the service of interpretation, I'm more interested in how the network figure has been used in a variety of discourses that evolved concurrently with Buñuel's work; not merely in the context of literary interpretation, where Barthes's *S/Z* would be a prime example,[19] but in the broader discursive contexts of cognition and power.

Originally referring to communication links established over a geographical space as in a broadcast network, "network" as a structuring motif has come to replace "circuit" in much of our thinking about complex elements of a biological nature, allowing us to speak of "neurotransmitters," "receptors," "input," and

"output." "Thought" and "soul" can be placed in a neural chain
of command somewhere farther down the line than "retina" or
"visual cortex."[20] With the rise of cybernetic telecommunications, network has also come to mean the elements and links
that carry data within and between computers,[21] leading to the
use of the figure as a processing paradigm wherein networks
function in a description of the knowledge and actions that produce, for example, intelligible speech.[22] The connectionists of
the 1980s built "massively parallel" computers that would ena-
ble "intelligent machines" and modeled schemes for the acqui-
sition, storage, and processing of data as operations upon items
existing in networks, this time configured after a neurological
model.[23] Marvin Minsky's polemic, *Society of Mind*, combines social, technical, and neurological senses of the network figure to
argue that our brains are *societies* of elements assisting each other
in a technical collaboration that results in effects that we call
emotion and intelligence.[24]

"Network" can thus describe any structure that includes elements that communicate to each other in one sense or another.
What constitutes an element and what constitutes a link become
defining qualities with great implications. With the garrulous
networks whose cumulative effect is intelligence in a "society of
mind," Minsky proposes an understanding of "the strangest
mysteries of mind." Minsky reproduces his concept of networked agents by making each page in the book an independent
section that links to the others, and which are organized into
sections that handle a specific function: memory, emotion, and
so on. Each page in the book itself is an element in a potential
network of rationality that waits for the user to read, activate
links, and begin to bring the network into being. On a macro-
level, the book reprises the work of the networked agents he
describes as the builders of consciousness. The book sets out an
agenda for a cognitivist enterprise that will finally build mind
out of brain by positing "agents" that communicate with each
other in different sorts of groups, acting hierarchically, that per-
ceive the world, make it into sense, and move the body into

action. "Agents" are the "particles" that theories of artificial intelligence need to become robust and productive. And at the level of the book, the reader becomes an agent that can help Minsky to implement the society of mind.

In Minsky, the network figure becomes internal to a machine in the same way as it is internal to a human; human intelligence turns out to be that of a "wonderful machine," and the mind falls into line as the rational (and rationalized) output of a neurological brain. Mind is explained by this cognitive networking in the same way that biology has successfully explained "life."[25] In the bargain, we have a model for our social world as well. Minsky understands liberty, that is, "freedom of will," to be an imaginary construction, a *phantom* if you will, that is necessary for sanity and social order:

Consider how our social lives depend upon the notion of *responsibility* and how little that idea would mean without our belief that personal actions are voluntary. Without that belief, no praise or shame could accrue to actions that were caused by Cause, nor could we assign any credit or blame to deeds that came about by Chance. What could we make our children learn if neither they nor we perceived some fault or virtue anywhere? We also use the idea of freedom of will to justify our judgments about good and evil. . . . But if we suspected that such choices were not made freely, but by the interference of some hidden agency, we might very well resent that interference. Then we might become impelled to wreck the precious value-schemes that underlie our personalities or become depressed about the futility of a predestination tempered only by uncertainty. Such thoughts must be suppressed. No matter that the physical world provides no room for freedom of will: that concept is essential to our models of the mental realm. Too much of our psychology is based on it for us to ever give it up. We're *virtually forced* to maintain that belief, even though we know it's false – except, of course, when we're inspired to find the flaws in all our beliefs, whatever may be the consequence to cheerfulness and mental peace.[26]

I quote this passage at length in order for the implications of network, knowledge, element, and link to become clear and their relation to power unmistakable. Minsky posits the mechanical as but a well-understood version of the human, and designs a cognitive science that finds networked agents internal to the brain, a science that will explain the mind just as other sciences – physics, biology, chemistry – have explained the external world. In this virtual world in Minsky's mind's eye (which he proposes as a program for the world of industry and research that will take many years to implement), communicating agents are unique but can possess multiple links and be hierarchicized in complex ways, while free will is a ghost of an idea that motivates children to learn and virtuous citizens to refrain from evil. To question freedom of will in the name of self-knowledge is to risk the loss of "cheerfulness"! Not much to give up, in fact, if you are an agitating filmmaker out for a hearty laugh in a less than perfect world where mystery is more of a criterion for hope than is mechanization. As to what Minsky's phantom of liberty might mean in a world where so-called intelligent agents haunt our digital networks, I will defer this question in the interest of making my way back to cinema.

The various networks that Minsky and other technologists are implementing are only one sort among many conceivable networks. These technical networks have the benefit of delivering data, but the drawback of having little ability to explain themselves. They are far from intelligent. These resource-oriented networks have topologies that are only coherent as long as elements remain unique in name so that they may be successfully addressed in a link. There is an analytical engine at work in all of them: link is different from element, and elements must be unique so that links may be multiple but delivery of data is guaranteed. In a resource-oriented network, the world gets processed to deliver knowledge that is then constructed in the process of delivery.

The networks that Michel Foucault describes in *The History of*

Sexuality are not resource-oriented but power-oriented networks. Foucault's networks make no apology for wanting to be intelligent but not being able to manage the task. For Foucault, power operates in networks of "institutional devices" and "discursive strategies." For example, sexuality is produced in these networks; sexual repression *may* occur but only does so in a multiplication of discourse on sex. Repression does not reduce or confine sexuality but helps to multiply it in new forms.[27]

Power-oriented networks might deploy or utilize the sorts of resource-oriented networks described here, as well as institutions such as schools, hospitals, psychologists' offices, confession cabinets, or other sites. But Foucault's networks of power cannot be reduced to networks of resources and operate fundamentally differently. An element in a power network may have more than one name, and delivery of knowledge as an effect of power is never guaranteed and not always predictable. Foucault finds power at work in the family producing "multiple, fragmentary, and mobile sexualities."[28] Sex can be transformed from what we might think of as a "link" between singular and "elemental" bodies[29] into "that which had to be confessed": power gives many names to sex, and the difference between element and link begins to blur. It is for this reason that Foucault goes to great lengths to define how power operates, what its effects are, and consequently how it can be discerned in action.

Buñuel, on the other hand, structures narrative in a complex network of effects. The effect-oriented network works as a depiction of a power network; for elements are no longer unique and links are no longer distinct from elements. But Buñuel shows that when it is only the reading of the work that makes power real, networks of power can be represented in disconcerting ways that call into question the presumed coherence of those networks' operations. Networks of effects can have links that are disjunctive as well as conjunctive; reversal, juxtaposition, doubling, and opposition and other operations work as well as input and output in producing knowledge. Resource networks, then, operate in terms of input and output between linked elements

to fabricate and supply knowledge. Power networks multiply elemental identities to produce truth. Effect networks link multiplied elements through disjunctive operations to question the
truth of knowledge. Minsky's book is a network of effects that
aims at convincing the reader of his program for the mechanization of consciousness in resource networks; Foucault's book is
a network of effects for identifying and understanding power
networks; *The Discreet Charm, The Phantom,* and *That Obscure Object of Desire* are individually and collectively a network of effects
for causing a power failure.

PERFORMATIVE DOUBLES IN THE PHANTOM OF LIBERTY

Whereas *The Discreet Charm* performed cyclical revi-
sions on one narrative, what I will call the narrative network is
the primary mode of cinematic operation in *The Phantom of Liberty.*[30] Dozens of characters involved in particular configurations
representing real-world power networks constitute narrative networks that Buñuel introduces successively throughout the film,
but which he quickly leaves *in potentio* as one set of elements
and links leads to the next.

Beginning by posing Goya's *El 3 de Mayo de 1808 en Madrid*
(depicting the execution of Spanish resistance fighters by the
invading Napoleonic forces) behind titles that introduce the film
and then explain that it will dramatize the novel that inspired
Goya's painting, the action proceeds by dramatizing the painting instead and then hovers briefly over the desecration of the
tomb of a miraculously preserved virgin saint before shifting
into modern-day France with the retroactive locating of the female voice which has taken over the narration in the body of a
maid. She sits in a park with an acquaintance who, as she calmly
continues knitting, must explain the meaning of "paraphernali-
a" in the novel the maid is reading. In short form, questions of
identity are set at play with doubts cast on authorial enunciation. As the maid struggles with concepts of female ownership

with which she is unfamiliar, her friend continues knitting, and the action moves to a suspicious person who gives the maid's charge, Veronique Foucauld, pornographic postcards, which she will carry home to her parents who will use them to arouse each other's passions before firing the maid for lax supervision. That night the Foucaulds frigidly retire to bed where Mr. Foucauld will receive a real letter in an unreal dream, but we "wake up" in a doctor's office where the events are being recounted. A nurse interrupts the consultation to ask for time off, and the camera follows her as she drives to an inn where all manner of debauchery will be screened in each of several rooms, through which the narrative moves us, and from which it will again escape (Figure 17).

The characters' moves in these narrative networks crosslinking film, painting, literature, history, sexuality, transportation, labor, leisure, and child rearing prove fragmentary and contradictory, revealing the fragmentary and contradictory nature of the power networks that Buñuel is setting up as extratextual referents. And our own identification with each character, each network, also is limited to a fragmented and contradictory experience, as the story moves through many narrative networks just as a data packet moves through a digital network. In total, the experience we have depends more on impossibility than verisimilitude, and that quality has helped to inspire a range of divergent responses to the work.[31]

The pseudorandom transitions between situations in *The Phantom* thus build on the work of wandering identification we have performed in *The Discreet Charm*. In their rapid and unpredictable deflections of the narrative, these techniques now can name that earlier detour through their difference from it. A wandering through a site of cinematic reproduction turns here to an exposition on the cinematic network per se. *The Phantom's* narrative networks make use of a critical notion of power networks that define individuals at the site of the reception of the messages that the networks carry. Aligning Buñuel with Michel Foucault, we can best understand *The Phantom of Liberty* as a special

effect made visible where narrative technologies produce knowing viewers in the power network that cinema is. In this film,
one particular path out of many potential paths is taken across
narrative networks that Buñuel screens as a critic of the political
and social structures that continue to rule the twentieth century.
In a world where we imagine networks of power articulating possibilities of identification and movement, Buñuel constructs a
personal vision of those networks of power in order to expose
them as such.

Take the example cited earlier of a Buñuelian family as portrayed as a family narrative linked to other narratives. The family
network as such is implied by the characters, their relationships
to each other, and the situation within which they are found.
But the family narrative may be surprised to find that the family
network structure that it seems to depend on is somehow dra-
matically or comically hinged on the narrative movement of a
character belonging to a different network, the maid, for example, whose relation to the family is one of class and labor. These
links are enabled and can become critical, since characters
having roles in different networks can lead to multiple networks
that depend on one character. Buñuel, like Foucault, intertwines
functional structure and motivating content, ultimately portraying power as utilizing both and pretending to require neither. A
shift in one may produce a shift in the other.

Foucault's *The History of Sexuality* reads almost as a primer for
getting at the subtle and surreal dynamics of the film. Foucault
explains the nature of the family network vis-à-vis sexuality in
the nineteenth century:

> Was the nineteenth-century family really a monogamic and
> conjugal cell? Perhaps to a certain extent. But it was also a
> network of pleasures and powers linked together at multiple
> points and according to transformable relationships. The sep-
> aration of grown-ups and children, the polarity established be-
> tween the parents' bedroom and that of the children (it be-
> came routine in the course of the century when working-class
> housing construction was undertaken), the relative segregation

Buñuel's *The Phantom of Liberty*

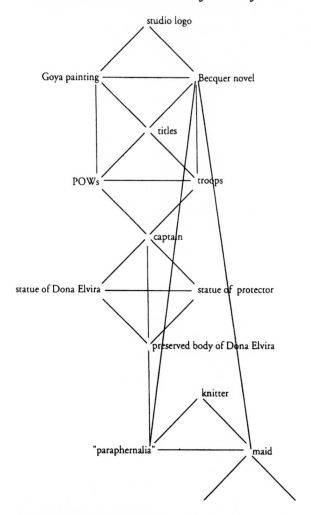

FIGURE SEVENTEEN

A networked view of the film. "Paraphernalia" (elements) and "vehicles" (links) appear as effects in a basic configuration that awaits viewers. Viewers help define meanings and add new links. Each link is of three types: elements or events, which interact in frame, or soundtrack; editing and synchronization suggest they interact; we speculate that they must be related in order to explain what we don't understand. Narrative networks continue to

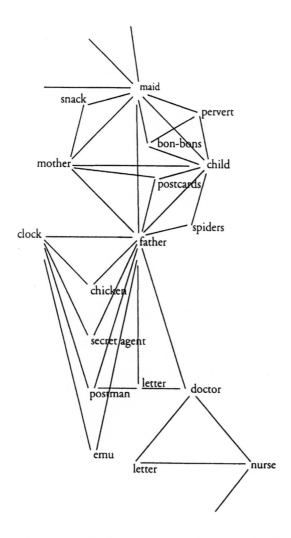

complexify. Multiple triangulations and forward thrust appear as the situations deepen and the pace increases. Who is the focus, and why? Is there a subject, or subjectivity?

of boys and girls, the strict instructions as to the care of nurs-
ing infants (maternal breast-feeding, hygiene), the attention
focused on infantile sexuality, the supposed dangers of mastur-
bation, the importance attached to puberty, the methods of
surveillance suggested to parents, the exhortations, secrets,
and fears, the presence – both valued and feared – of servants:
all this made the family, even when brought down to its smallest dimensions, a complicated network, saturated with multiple, fragmentary, and mobile sexualities.[32]

Buñuel's Foucauld family is perverse in exactly these ways.[33] Foucault outlines five features of power in its deployment of sexuality. Let's consider two of them in relation to Buñuel's countering
of that deployment.

The first concerns "the negative relation": "Where sex and
pleasure are concerned, power can 'do' nothing but say no to
them; what it produces, if anything, is absences and gaps; it
overlooks elements, introduces discontinuities, separates what is
joined, and marks off boundaries. Its effects take the general
form of limit and lack." Rather than a negative structuring, Buñuel portrays positive yet indeterminate relations. When the little girl is shown the "dirty" postcards in the park, she knowingly
chuckles along with the pervert, humoring him. The pervert's
success continues in that the postcards are enjoyed by everyone
in the Foucauld family. Sexual power relations are defused from
the bottom up, as the pervert fails to exert sexual power over the
child, and the parents are seduced by the pervert.

The last feature of power that Foucault outlines is the uniformity of the apparatus. "Whether one attributes it to the form of
the prince who formulates rights, of the father who forbids, of
the censor who enforces silence, or of the master who states the
law, in any case one schematizes power in a juridical form, and
one defines its effects as obedience. Confronted by a power that
is law, the subject who is constituted as a subject – who is 'subjected' – is he who obeys." Not only is the sex as it is visualized
in Buñuel fascinating, it is also often patently ridiculous. By par-

odying the ways in which people obey the rule of power over sex, Buñuel makes it hard to reproduce the sexualities he brings to the screen. Further, sex here is plural, existing in a set of networks that you see but will not likely ever experience. Try as you might, it would be exceedingly hard to obey the Buñuelian communication of sex as it wanders all over France in *The Phantom*.[34] But a related point needs to be made: at the level of the film as a whole, Buñuel utilizes techniques of movement through representation and identification pointedly distinct from those of *The Discreet Charm*, destabilizing the uniformity of his own apparatus.

Erotic desire and oppressive political systems are indeed directly linked in this film, but they are also indirectly linked through institutions of labor. One key link is Muni, the wonderful character actor who is so overworked by Buñuel in his last three films as peasant (*Discreet Charm*), maid (*Phantom*), and concierge (*Obscure Object*). Pointing to the themes of tyranny and convention, Kinder notes that it is the maid who leads us out of a situation where a military officer is going to rape a dead woman into one where two women discuss property rights and women's place in differing cultures. This shift happens through a female voice-over, which, at the same time as it challenges the dominant convention of giving the narrating voice-over to a male figure, leads into a serious discussion of property and law. The transition here effectively challenges gender conventions and class knowledge, Kinder points out, shifting us into the present day by "introduc[ing] a class discourse about punishment, power, and property": the maid, the hesitating "voice" of our story, is fired for not watching her charge closely enough.

Kinder reads the film as a collection of competing stories built out of coordinated arrays of elements[35] that are able to mirror our world of competing discourses and institutions. Perhaps that mirroring relationship can be characterized by observing the kinds of operations that Buñuel is performing in linking both disparate erotic and political narratives at the same time as he shows them to be conventions. How is it that paradigms can be switched in the way Buñuel allows? More accurately, how is it that *we* can make the switches that Buñuel sets up?

Elements in networks of effect belong to more than one network at once; they have multiple names. The links that Buñuel sets up are made through our recognizing *double* figures such as the two police commissioners who unite to repress student demonstrators at the close of the film or *multiple* figures, such as Muni's working-class roles across a number of films. Or we recognize a *reversal* when, later in the film, a defecating party stands in for a dinner party. Buñuel is not just reversing terms; he did not, for example, show a vomiting party. He is reversing terms that sustain physical feelings of disgust at the same time as they expose the feelings and customs associated with our most fundamental architectural discourses. Or we might recognize a crucial *juxtaposition* such as monks seated before a sadomasochistic scene. Or we might see an orchestrated *opposition*, such as the doctor denying the authenticity of the letter that the dream postman has left Mr. Foucauld, followed by his granting the nurse a leave by virtue of the letter from her father. These narrative actions are the disjunctive operations by which Buñuel's network of effects so smoothly accomplishes its work.

Each plot twist that moves us from perversion to perversion is entirely legible in terms of the cinematic language that it is phrased in so that the transitions between episodes are indistinguishable from the episodes themselves. For example, the nurse's entrance into the consulting room first constitutes an interruption to a conversation, and the camera doesn't seem to emphasize her, only to include her as the newest element at work in the story. Smoothly, the camera moves around to find her central, framed to give full expression to her concern for her father and her need to take time off. We end up following her, and do not return to Mr. Foucauld. There is no moment when she is suddenly established as the narrative focus and Mr. Foucauld becomes insubstantial; her story has already begun by the time we have shifted our allegiances to her. That story begins not with the cut that finds her driving through the rain, but with the door in the doctor's office through which she demurely entered. Because of the way we read movement within the frame, and of the ways the script concentrates on overdetermined elements belonging to multiple networks, two "stories" can co-occur for a certain duration of time. As we begin a new one, Buñuel is careful to allow the old one to linger by using continuity to make the shift between episodes instead of strong cuts or other cinematic statements of severance. Instead of seeing the shift between Mr. Foucauld, the doctor, and the nurse as a line formed between two successive episodes then, it is more productive to see them as overlapping or continuous narrative networks that share complex elements of time, character, setting. The camera is not cutting between two episodes: it is panning between the visible effects of two, or more, narrative networks.

In this way, what I call the "impossible narrative" becomes a requirement, if one is even to pose the question of portraying power in film fiction. Without apparent contradiction, the necessary yet invisible relations of power to power will not become visible, and so cannot become cinematic. In *The Phantom of Liberty*, each time Buñuel shows one networked structure hinged to another in a narrative movement, he does so with a twist that in the same moment makes it clear both that the structure is apparently the double of a real-world power structure external to the narrative, *and* that the external structure that it doubles is, in some sense, twisted. Undoing the double effectively becomes the imaginary undoing of the original. Still, the double can only resemble the original to the degree that you share Buñuel's cultural background or can read his frames. The undoing of the double, ultimately, is your job. Buñuel's job is to make your work a pleasure. You become involved in what may be termed a syndicalism of narrative work, but in Buñuel's anarchosyndicalist vision, you labor to produce *The Phantom of Liberty*.

A critical work as well as a narrative plaything, *The Phantom of Liberty* projects the viewer as a willing participant in the elaboration of power, but at the same time as it puts the viewer in the spotlight, it offers the chance of escape back into the dark, irreducible mysteries beyond power's blaze. In a vivid example of the fact that a work that seems narrative may not only elucidate a critique of power but work to devoid power of itself, *The Phantom* requires a disjunctive reading of power networks both interior and exterior to cinema. Buñuel's spectator is created recognizing those power networks which not only produce cinema but which cinematic narrative reproduces. As viewing actions, the contradictions through which *The Phantom* is structured make those networks discernible, and allow the viewer produced at their articulation to take pleasure at their expense. The film shimmers with ambiguity.

We are left with many possibilities for rendering the film coherent as we trip down the primrose path where *The Phantom* leads us. Not the least of these possibilities is that in an originary experience of the film, we viewers are only a phantom of Buñuel's imagination. This possibility becomes conceivable to us, yet patently impossible. Of course, we exist, but how can we otherwise explain our experience of the hermetic nature of Buñuel's passionate meaning making? After all, somehow we are making *some* sense of this nonsense. Contrariwise, we can also imagine that Buñuel has only produced this work to satisfy the actions that we will take upon it. In this reading, *he* becomes the phantom, and if we imagine him at all, we imagine him only as an originary excuse that relieves us of taking full responsibility for the implications that the film sets forth. And yet, the film's contradictions demand a response: what of our phantom, liberty? Buñuel's "net work" posits both a creative, historically existing author, and a creative viewing subject, each of whom exists at cross-purposes to each other in a work that is not entirely reducible in terms of either figure's perspective.

THE THIRD TERM: THAT OBSCURE OBJECT OF DESIRE

Buñuel's knitter, or her twin, the lacemaker, is a sign of the power networks that he interrupts in addition to being a signifier of narrative coherence-in-complexity. Finally, she performs as a signature identifying his body of work.[36] She appears in *The Phantom* as the listener who clarifies meaning, and in *That Obscure Object* as the emblem of an oeuvre that is mended only to explode again. In the detour trilogy, her networking weaves Muni throughout, mobilizes Milena Vukotic in the roles of nurse, maid, and mother, and brings Julien Bertheau from gardener-bishop, to a double police commissioner, to Mateo's cousin Foucade in *That Obscure Object*.[37] Fernando Rey disappears from the trilogy in *The Phantom*, only to surface again as frustrated Mateo. The woven bag of the young terrorist of *The Discreet Charm*[38] now reappears in the hands of Concepcion, who is the clear sign of mimetic repetition in *That Obscure Object*.

Narrative authority is placed with Mateo as he tells his story to a group of first-class passengers on a train, echoing our preoccupation with the narrative privilege granted the bourgeoisie in *The Discreet Charm*. The network exposition of *The Phantom* is recalled as Mateo indicates the story's unfolding detours through Europe, even as he is driven from Spain by Concepcion. Although those two earlier themes are here compressed into one, it is the figure of Concepcion, rather than a new grammar of montage, that destabilizes the innovations of the previous films. She appears in the form of two very different actresses, neither of whom imitates the performance of the other. Concepcion becomes Conchita and vice versa in an unverifiable and unpredictable pattern, which may be aligned with the random acts of terrorist groups that finally join forces to blow up the film before Mateo ever possesses Concepcion. The two actresses' collaboration to steer the film toward detonation suggests a lesbian plot that, in Judith Butler's words, "pursues disruptive repetition within compulsory heterosexuality."[39]

Mateo's narration attempts to confine Concepcion's repetitive excess in either a sadistic or masochistic position, which he will alternate with her. Meanwhile, the double Concepcion leads Mateo to the ground zero of a terrorist explosion where both disappear in a cloud of smoke and flame. As told to a judge, a psychoanalyst, and a mother and daughter in his compartment,

Mateo's adjudicated, well-balanced, family version of the heterosexual narrative (in which Concepcion is drenched with water,
repeatedly subjected to attempts of seduction and rape, sold by
her mother, publicly shamed, and finally beaten) challenges the
viewer to misrecognize the obvious cinematic error within the
frame. Only once we have done that can we also forget that this
error turns Mateo and other "stable" characters into differentiated iterations of their earlier performances. Mateo's claim on
narrative control is undone by a conspiracy of "sexuality *against*
identity, even against gender, and of letting that which cannot
fully appear in any performance persist in its disruptive promise."[40]

CONCLUSIONS

While international terrorists explode the final scene
of *That Obscure Object* to occlude any sole claim by heterosexuality on passion or pleasure, Buñuel seems pleased to report in
his memoirs that a group of possibly homosexual terrorists
bombed the Ridge Theatre in San Francisco in October 1977
where the film was being shown.[41] This unexpected violence in
the network coheres with the near circularity of the soundtrack
of *The Phantom*: we hear student protesters shouting "Long live
our chains!" as gunfire suggests massive political repression, echoing the haunting sounds that begin the film.[42] That political
violence plays against, in turn, the gangland execution from
which Rafael awakens as *The Discreet Charm* ends. In the power
network of cinema, how do we understand the aftermath of Buñuel's network of detours which so relentlessly works on the
world before the film to change the ways we see the world after
it? Once we find ourselves awake in this cinema of hallucina-
tions, confusions, dreams, and provocations, we are free to make
them meaningful in ways that Buñuel could not have predicted.
But we cannot make them meaningful in ways that restore the
power networks that Buñuel is exposing to an unchallenged position, unless we literally forget what we have seen or refuse to

interpret it. The usual relationship of surveillance and subject formation has been reversed: power has become visible, and we are safe in the dark to appraise its effects.

NOTES

1 Roland Barthes, *Mythologies* (New York: Hill and Wang, 1972; original French version 1952, revised 1957), 141.
2 Akerman, as Godard said of Buñuel, has always been interested in innovation on the level of cinematic form, but also has consistently created work that is designed to operate in the social field as a foil and challenge to mainstream narrative film. Although Akerman's strategies of challenging mainstream narrative conventions are hardly reminiscent of Buñuel's, a few tendencies are visible in both: an emphasis on social rituals as both sources of pleasure and identity, a continuing interest in bodily actions and habits, the construction of unusual acoustic spaces that amplify or transform the visual space of the narrative, and even an insistence on narrative, albeit in forms that require new actions on the part of the audience.
3 Barthes, *Mythologies*, 140.
4 Ibid., 148.
5 Jean-Louis Commoli, "Machines of the Visible," in *The Cinematic Apparatus*, ed. Teresa de Lauretis and Steven Heath (Milwaukee: University of Wisconsin Press, 1980), 123.
6 As commentators have pointed out, Commoli fails to explore gender or sexual difference, or to make any significant accounting of cinema as an audiovisual medium, apart from a brief discussion of the "fetishization" of the speaking subject with "the coming of sound" only to suggest that it does not matter much; ibid., 132.
7 Ibid., 121.
8 Ibid., 139.
9 José de la Colina and Tomas Perez Turrent, *Objects of Desire* (New York: Marsilio Publishers, 1992), 210.
10 Luis Buñuel, *My Last Sigh* (New York: Vintage, 1983), 249.
11 In response to José de la Colina's statement to the effect that Buñuel would never have made fun of *l'amour fou* in his early works, Buñuel replies: "Then I was a member of the Surrealist group, a group that was very ideologically compact, one in which I was a sectarian. . . . Now I have as much freedom as I want and, if it occurs to me, I can blaspheme against *l'amour fou*. Sometimes it's vivifying to blaspheme against that which one believes." De la Colina and Turrent,

Objects of Desire, 176. Still, Buñuel allows himself to pontificate on the subject of the world's problems in various ways. About the police instructor's speech in *The Phantom of Liberty* on environmental pollution, Buñuel says: "Is it too much talk and too little cinema? I don't care: I had that on my mind and I put it in 'at the slightest provocation.'" (220). By speaking through a character that is neither sympathetic nor reliable, Buñuel "blasphemes" against his own directorial authority.

12 Marsha Kinder, *Blood Cinema: The Reconstruction of National Identity in Spain* (Berkeley: University of California Press; 1993), 327.

13 Linda Williams, *Figures of Desire* (Berkeley: University of California Press, 1981), 200. Cf. also Williams's later problematizing of her earlier reading as positing "an ultimately static statement of meaning that it has been the work of the Buñuelian cinema to perpetually evade." In Rudolf E. Kuenzli, *Dada and Surrealist Film* (Cambridge, Mass.: MIT Press, 1996), 205. Williams here provides a useful overview of the differing interpretations that subsequent schools of critical thought have produced out of Buñuel's films. While I agree with Williams regarding the difficulties in "sewing up" the meanings of Buñuel's work, in my view that is not only because Buñuel constantly works to develop techniques of "evasion" but also because he expects us to fabricate meanings for his productions.

14 Roger Eberwein, *Film and the Dream Screen* (Princeton: Princeton University Press, 1984), 140–141.

15 "Grammar" is one of the features that *The Discreet Charm* shares with *The Milky Way* and *The Phantom of Liberty*, according to Buñuel, cf. Buñuel, *My Last Sigh*, 249. While he doesn't specify what that "grammar" actually is, one narrative technique all films share is the misattribution of characters and dreams.

16 The term *detournement* is defined as a technique of reverse discourse by situationists Debord and Wolman, anthologized in Ken Knabb, *Situationist International Anthology* (Berkeley: Bureau of Public Secrets, 1981), 8–14. I use the term here to suggest the situationists' debt to the dadaists and surrealists, as well as to point out that Buñuel's own technique went on to evolve beyond what, at least, the early situationist writings propose as effective strategies of demystification.

17 Williams, *Figures of Desire*, 215,217.

18 Buñuel's technique of letting the bodies of the actors carry more of the load of cinematic communication reflects a substantial change of style over the years. Note the increasing access to highly skilled actors from around the time of *Diary of a Chambermaid*, particularly Jeanne Moreau in the latter film. Cf. Bunuel, *My Last Sigh*, 241:

"Jeanne is a marvelous actress, and I kept my direction to a minimum, content for the most part just to follow her with the camera." Also, note the tracking shots that remain invisible despite their complexity, cf. de la Colina and Turrent, *Objects of Desire*, 214–215: "The camera must move slowly without the viewer noticing. But I don't overplan these movements; it has something to do with instinct and practice."

19 Roland Barthes, *S/Z*, trans. Richard Miller (New York: Hill and Wang, 1974), 18–21. In *S/Z*, Barthes makes one of the clearest attempts to place the figure at the service of interpretation by elaborating five codes of denotation and connotation, which, he says, all lexia fall into. The voices of a text are woven as these codes are networked to produce pluralities of meaning in a definitely segmentable literary topos, which produces texts that are imperfectly reversible. Barthes's use of the network figure relies on a propositional segmentation of verbal elements, which is more appropriate for the construction of verbal subjectivities than cinematic ones. Buñuel's films in general and the three I am taking up here in particular demand a fuller accounting than *S/Z* can provide. They call for an analysis that can handle texts that are not definitely segmentable, and which might have sections which demand reading backward as well.

20 David H. Hubel, *Eye, Brain and Vision* (New York: Scientific American Library, 1988), 24. Hubel describes "circuits" of brain cells and organizes them as networked structures in his diagrams. The network diagrams illustrate actions of "neurotransmitters," "receptors," "input," "output." The figure shown echoes Marvin Minsky's positing of networks of communicating agents that produce effects we understand as "intelligence," "emotion": somewhere after the perceptual processing is finished, "memory," "thought," and "soul" begin.

21 See Carl Malamud, *Stacks: Interoperability in Today's Computer Networks* (New York: Prentice Hall, 1992), 198, for an example of an extended star topology designed for a broadband public network. The figure impresses with its elegance, reminding us of the highly representational nature of the real-world networks that process knowledge. The more mundane World Wide Web is a metanetwork enabled by a widely agreed upon specification for the transfer of data between computers of different types over a plurality of redundant links (the Internet) that, in the United States at least, was designed as a military communications medium that would ensure the transmission of sensitive information in the event of a nuclear war. Networks with redundant links are "fault-tolerant" and resistant to systemic failure.

22 Jonathan Slocum, ed., *Machine Translation System* (Cambridge: Cambridge University Press, 1985), 76. In the system described here, the network figure is intended to model knowledge of language, not the neural processes themselves. Knowledge is held in a network form that is processed via rules of grammar into linguistic surface structures. Elements are linked by specific names that related those elements in a propositional equation, which must describe the real-world nature of the referent of the word in question.

23 Garrison W. Cottrell, *A Connectionist Approach to Word Sense Disambiguation* (San Mateo, Calif: Morgan Kaufman Publishers, 1989), 28. Cottrell offers a connectionist approach that sets out an explicit metaphor between neural processing and the machine processing of language. In contrast to the semantic network in Figure 16, ambiguous terms are eliminated by "training" wherein the network "learns" how to suppress certain elements given that a more sensible parsing is desired. Feedback "teaches" the network when to activate links and when to suppress them in which circumstances.

24 Marvin Minsky, *The Society of Mind* (New York: Simon and Schuster, 1986), 17, 168. Minsky arranges "agents" in "societies" which are pictured as networks of linked elements. He does not use the word network, because he is arguing implicitly that networks are societies. Thus, instead of societies being networked, we have networks being socialized. Minsky also seeks to understand humans as "wonderful machines," but cautions that "machine" has negative connotations that we are better off forgetting. His argument is designed to make us think of machines as potentially social and intelligent.

25 Ibid., 19.

26 Ibid., 307, emphasis added.

27 Michel Foucault, *The History of Sexuality: An Introduction* (New York: Vintage, 1978), 30: "Speaking about children's sex, inducing educators, physicians, administrators, and parents to speak of it, or speaking of it, or speaking to them about it, causing children themselves to talk about it, and enclosing them in a web of discourses which sometimes address them, sometimes speak about them, or impose canonical bits of knowledge on them, or use them as a basis for constructing a science that is beyond their grasp – all this together enables us to link an intensification of the interventions of power to a multiplication of discourse. The sex of children and adolescents has become, since the eighteenth century, an important area of contention around which innumerable institutional devices and discursive strategies have been deployed."

28 Ibid., 46.

29 Ibid., 61: "In Greece, truth and sex were linked, in the form of ped-
agogy, by the transmission of a precious knowledge from one body
to another; sex served as a medium for initiations into learning. For
us, it is in the confession that truth and sex are joined, through the
obligatory and exhaustive expression of an individual secret. But
this time it is truth that serves as a medium for sex and its manifestations."

30 Buñuel describes this film as his "most surrealist film," and one of
his personal favorites. Francisco Aranda, *Luis Buñuel: A Critical Biography*, trans. and ed. David Robinson (New York: Da Capo Press,
1976), 249; and Buñuel, *My Last Sigh*, 249.

31 In an early review, Marsha Kinder notes the near circularity brought
about by the film's conclusion. She observes that the sounds of gunfire and scenes of violent repression that begin the film are echoed
in the final scenes, and that the soundtrack cues the "circular framework" since the visuals do not depict the same scenes: the film ends
with scenes of animals in a zoo presumably seeing gunfire directed
at student demonstrators in France, while it opened with Goya's *The
Third of May*, which depicts the execution by firing squad of Spanish
patriots in Toledo during the Napoleonic Wars. Marsha Kinder, "The
Tyranny of Convention in *The Phantom of Liberty*," *Film Quarterly*
(Summer 1975): 25. In a later critical study Susan Suleiman considers
the continually displaced narrative as radically linear. Susan Suleiman, "Freedom and Necessity: Narrative Structure in *The Phantom of
Liberty*," *Quarterly Review of Film Studies* vol. 3, no. 3 (Summer 1978):
289. Suleiman also considers Kinder's positing of a thematics of the
"tyranny of convention" to be "too tragic": "I would hesitate to
affirm [Kinder's thematics of tyranny] so strongly; the humor of the
film, although it can be read as very bitter, can also be read as detached" (295). Still later, Linda Williams finds the film a surrealist
statement on the oppositional structuring of law and desire, but
considers Suleiman's reading overly formalistic, while disallowing
Kinder's reading of the film as a moral statement by Buñuel, as the
surrealists were not likely to take moral positions in their art.

32 Foucault, *History of Sexuality*, 46.

33 In fact, Buñuel seems to be playing a joke on Michel Foucault, by
naming the father of this family after him, causing him to see a
variety of strange visions, which seem imaginary and yet have real
effects, and then having a doctor tell him to go see a psychoanalyst
if he wants to talk about dreams. Part of Foucault's project in the
History of Sexuality was to see psychoanalysis as one of the ways that
sexuality is produced through confession. *The History of Sexuality* was

originally published in French in 1976, while *The Phantom of Liberty* was released in 1974.

34 Foucault, *History of Sexuality*, 83–85.

35 Kinder, *Blood Cinema*, 332. Extending the idea of paradigmatic variation that Suleiman has used to establish a "radical linearity" in the film, Kinder finds an "array of paradigms" in the film and indicates how Buñuel uses them: "There are several instances in the film where the array of paradigms is actually dramatized in a visual figure. . . . The best example occurs in the inn, which has a long tradition as a reflexive stopping point (or chapter break) in Spanish narratives that can be traced back to *Don Quixote* and picaresque fiction. Here the several rooms off the hallway provide a perfect visualization of the mini stories that compete for control over the narrative."

36 Her figure reminds us of Madame DeFarge in Dickens's *A Tale of Two Cities*, who not only is a recurring figure in the unwinding of Dickens's narrative but finally turns out to be a subversive figure working to overthrow the French monarchy. Linda Williams recognizes the lacemaker in *That Obscure Object* as a link back to *Un chien andalou*, where she is appropriated from Vermeer's famous painting on the open page of a book. Williams, *Figures of Desire*, 207.

37 If we take Mateo as a self-blaspheming distortion of Buñuel himself, we can read the conversations between Mateo and his cousin Foucade as yet another invocation of Buñuel's punning "collaboration" with Michel Foucault, countering Jean Luc Godard's satirization of the vogue for Foucault's *Discipline and Punish* in *La Chinoise*, and Godard's attack on Foucault's historical critique of Marxism in *The Order of Things*. In the latter regard, see David Halperin, *Saint Foucault* (New York: Oxford University Press, 1995), 154.

38 Even her identification as terrorist in *Discreet Charm* is indeterminate: as Rafael opens her bag he first finds a head of lettuce – is she perhaps a housewife or domestic with a romantic obsession for Rafael? Perhaps she also carries a gun out of reasoned fear or unreasonable paranoia. The conflation of domestic and terrorist is taken up again in *That Obscure Object*.

39 Judith Butler, "Imitation and Gender Insubordination," in *Inside/Out*, ed. Diane Fuss (New York: Routledge, 1991), 28.

40 Ibid., 29. Buñuel rarely takes up homosexuality per se, but in a related vein does often suggest his own transvestitism (*Viridiana*, for example) and enjoyment of disguise across status or gender. However much Buñuel doesn't articulate homosexuality per se, he also avoids placing the homosexual as a "bad copy." For example, in *The Discreet Charm* there is a moment when in the foreground two pot-

smoking soldiers with their backs to the camera stand arm in arm and fondly gaze at each other in profile; beyond them, sister-in-law Florence gazes at both of them in fascination. The scene projects indistinguishable homosexuality and homosociality as a fantasy for the young woman of the 1970s, even as it suggests that France, for example, might not go to the lengths that the U.S. administration continues to in order to construct gays in the military through a network of exclusionary and silencing discourses.

41 Buñuel, *My Last Sigh*, 250.
42 De la Colina and Turrent, *Objects of Desire*, 218. Buñuel suggests that he avoided visual closure in this film because "if it closes itself into a circle, it's not liberty, it's death."

Appendixes

Vintage Reviews

THE DISCREET CHARM OF THE BOURGEOISIE

Director: Luis Buñuel. Script: Buñuel and Jean-Claude Carriere. Photography: Edmond Richard.

STEPHEN KOVÁCS

On the night of December 4, 1930, members of the League of Patriots and the Anti-Jewish League interrupted the projection of a new movie by hurling rocks and inkwells at the screen of Studio 28, the leading avant-garde movie theater of Paris. After this patriotic display they rushed into the lobby to tear up the paintings of the young artists who had chosen to exhibit there. Among them were some of the leading painters of the day, men like Joan Miró, Max Ernst, Man Ray, Salvador Dali. Curiously enough, the authorities were not so much intent on punishing the demonstrators as they were on imposing restrictions on the film itself. First, they merely demanded the removal of its explicitly sacrilegious passages, but when the outcry in the daily papers became too loud, they decided to ban the movie altogether. Indeed, the newspapers were right: the movie's anticlericalism was perhaps its least offensive feature. The movie was an all-out attack on bourgeois society, showing its very foundations being shaken simply by the violent love of a man and a woman. In the movie we see them roll around in the mud, their frenetic screams of delight disrupting the proceedings of a state ceremony conducted by high officials nearby. Separated from his love, the man lets loose his fury on a blind man and a dog by kicking them aside. The passion of the women is so strong that the toilet paper ignites when she sits on the john. Yes, such a movie was unfit for public consumption. The ban that the fascist disrupters succeeded in imposing on the film was not lifted until the end of the Nazi occupation of France. Even now, Luis Buñuel's *L'Age d'Or* (*The Golden Age*) is unknown in America to all but avid archivists of the cinema.

A lot of pictures have flickered on the screen since that memorable night in Studio 28. Yet over the years Buñuel's surrealistic vision and his concern with human nature in what is definitely not the best of all possible worlds have remained constant. To that his latest movie, *The Discreet Charm of the Bourgeoisie*, bears witness.

Buñuel has said that be bases his movies on a single image or idea that grabs hold of him. *Viridiana* developed from his vision of an old man holding in his arms a young girl unable to resist him because she is under the influence of drugs. *Simon of the Desert* grew out of the image of a saint withdrawing from the world by living on top of a column – the story of Simon the Anchorite who did just that somewhere in Asia Minor in the fourth century. *The Exterminating Angel* was based upon the idea that a group of fashionable people gathered together are unable to leave the premises. And the central problem of *The Discreet Charm of the Bourgeoisie* is that a group of people who are trying to get together for dinner are prevented from doing so by an extraordinary series of unforeseen circumstances. Buñuel himself has remarked upon the close relationship between these last two films. He sees them both as surrealistic creations – that is, movies based on a surrealistic premise as distinguished from the realistic vein of *Tristana* and the theological nature of *The Milky Way*.

The movie begins with two couples driving up to an elegant house in the Paris suburbs for the intended dinner. They are most cordially welcomed by the hostess, but they soon find out that their dinner invitation was for the following day. They graciously invite their hostess to accompany them to dinner and so the five of them drive to a nearby restaurant. They are allowed to enter after some mysterious hesitation on the part of the woman who opens the locked door. Although they find it somewhat unusual to be the only customers, they proceed to order from the elegant menu. Muffled sobs bring the women to their feet and into an adjacent room to investigate. The body of the owner is laid out on the funeral bier surrounded by the mourning family. The customers are informed that he passed away that very afternoon so there simply has not been enough time to remove his body. The women are intent on leaving, but now the previously hesitant waiter insists that the guests stay, assuring them of an excellent dinner. The waiter's warm assurances only serve to accentuate the black humor of the situation.

Gradually the plot is unfolded, but it really does not develop very far. That the three friends in question are the ambassador of a Latin American republic and his two partners in an international heroin ring is of little consequence: no gut-searing chase scenes here à la *French Connection*, no glimpse into the machinations of the Corsican mafia. Instead, the film becomes a series of loosely joined episodes, vaguely related to the initial impulse of the film. Buñuel's latest idea does not lend itself to a dense elaboration as was possible with his idea of people confined by an unknown force in *The Exterminating Angel*. In fact, his premise is its polar opposite – the problem of getting together instead of trying to separate. The loose structure of the film is inherent in that initial idea.

When an academic speaks of lack of structure, you can be sure that he is trying to pan a work. Years of apprenticeship at brightly lit stalls brings out a compulsive need to put a framework around everything. But Buñuel was forged on the anvil of anarchist Spain, only to be thrown into the cauldron of Parisian surrealism. "Today I feel happy because I achieved a certain physical victory over myself. But I would be just as happy if I had not shot the film. I am a little bit of a nihilist, I don't care much about what I do." Buñuel's anarchic spirit emerges in full force in this movie. It does so in spite of the fact (or is it because?) he has worked on it on and off for the last two and a half years, ever since he finished *Tristana*. Indeed, the film's lack of rigorous structure carries out the disparate spirit of the working premise.

Buñuel's very first film tried to create such apparent incoherence.

Un Chien Andalou was an attempt to express in a film the spontaneous illogic which the Surrealists had tried to embody on canvas and in verse. Yet they also knew that their fervent search for chaos would reveal a new, hitherto virtually unexplored realm of experience, the terrains of the unconscious. Echoing Freud, they drew deeply from their dream life in order to confront man with the frightening disorder that lurked in the shadows of his mind. Thus Buñuel, working with Dali, joined a number of dream images, systematically removing anything that they thought might have a symbolic meaning, and in this way arrived at *Un Chien Andalou*.

If all of this seems to be talking around Buñuel's latest film it is because the movie refuses to be put inside any kind of framework. After the initial premise is all too clearly stated Buñuel plunges into the dreamworld of his characters. Since they are unable to fulfill the most ordinary of social obligations their human drama is revealed through an ingenious display of their internal explosions. The Ambassador of Miranda, for example, dreams of being held up by bandits at dinner and escaping their machine gun fire by ducking underneath the table. He is noticed because, out of sheer gluttony, he reaches up with his hand to grab a piece of meat lying on a plate. As he is about to be shot, he wakes up alarmed – and goes out to the kitchen for a midnight snack to soothe his nerves. Towards the end when the three men are under arrest, the investigator has a nightmarish dream about a sergeant whose brutal methods of torture are celebrated by a special holiday given to all policemen so they may avoid his ghost which comes back to haunt the prison. The investigator is awakened from his catnap by no other than the vile sergeant who in reality is his obedient underling. In such flights of fantasy (which even include one dream-within-a-dream) Buñuel explores the inherent violence of his characters, which is subordinated in everyday life to the ludicrous social niceties of a bourgeois existence. But juxtaposed with the violence is helplessness when confronted by an impossible situation requiring those same niceties, as when the young couple feel forced to accept the bishop who volunteers to be their gardener. Buñuel reveals their latent brutality through their violent dreams. His portrayal is a fantastic but nonetheless accurate and even sympathetic treatment of the bourgeoisie – men trapped by their attempts to conform to a reality which is ultimately external to them.

Buñuel's presentation of the bourgeoisie's dilemma is nothing less than kaleidoscopic. He mirrors the strange yet familiar behavior of the middle classes in a number of different and suggestive fragments. After all, the middle class lies close to his heart: as he said in connection with the movie, the bourgeoisie lies much more in his realm than does the proletariat. He is and has always been intrigued by the contradictions which this class, this mentality is unable to resolve. Thus, he recognizes a certain charm that they possess, but this charm they themselves would like to qualify as being of a discreet nature. Buñuel incorporates their very own standards into the title of his film, but in doing so he imparts to it an immediate ironic sense. They cannot both fulfill their social obligations and be faithful to their natural impulses. As the guests are due to arrive the young couple begin to make love. The guests turn up; the couple escape out the window to consummate their passion behind some bushes; the Ambassador fears a police trap, and the guests leave, again without their dinner.

Scenes of people eating abound in Buñuel's movies because he is always interested in depicting the most ordinary of daily actions, incorporating them in the most unusual tales. Bourgeois life is characterized by the exaggerated celebration of fundamental human activities – such as the ritualized group meal. The bourgeois dinner is exposed, as it were, in one of the dreams when the partners have just seated themselves, finally, around the table. To their great surprise and embarrassment the curtains are raised and they find themselves seated on a stage, watched by a full house. It is again their sense of privacy and decorum that makes them hurry off.

The Discreet Charm of the Bourgeoisie, more than any other recent Buñuel work, is surrealistic from its premise down to its smallest details. Dreams, for example, play an important part in the movie as a whole: they help above all to reveal suppressed violent forces which inhabit the unconscious. But since the Surrealists considered dreams to be a part of everyday life, they sought to abolish the dividing line between the conscious and unconscious realms. In a similar vein, Buñuel's dream sequences here grow out of real situations and it is only when they end up in peculiar conclusions followed by the dreamer waking with a start that we realize these events were the product of human fantasy.

It also happens that a totally incredible situation ends without such a clear explanation. The bishop who has become the young couple's gardener is called to administer a dying man's last rites. The man confesses that he had once poisoned a young boy's parents with arsenic. The clergyman realizes the victims in question were his own parents. With a certain professional integrity he administers the last rites, then slowly walks over to the side of the barn, picks up a gun and blows the dying man's brains out. Whether dream or reality, the event shakes us with its extreme violence, yet its incongruity evokes a certain laugh from deep within us.

The images that unfold often remain without explanation, and that is precisely how they were intended to strike us – immediately, deeply, without reference to a framework. A striking recurring image of the film, which becomes its final scene, is that of the six characters walking down a road. In talking about the meaning of this scene Buñuel explains the way he uses images:

> I immediately thought of a road – which reappears in the film as a leitmotif. And I thought that one could show these bourgeois first normal, a second time bored, a third time tired and wounded. Then I felt that it was necessary to conserve the image as is, in its innocence, in order not to elicit a symbolic interpretation, so that it could not be said: this is the end of the bourgeoisie, this is society which does not know where it's going. But symbols will certainly be found in this film, as always. I have never expressly used symbols. Here, there is neither good, nor evil, only people who walk on a road.

That almost obsessive image reinforces the theme in a visual way. It is surrealistic because of its specific meaninglessness, and its general impact.

The Discreet Charm of the Bourgeoisie is Buñuel's funniest film: its humor is totally surrealist in nature. The Ambassador of Miranda is being watched by a young revolutionary in front of his office. To get rid of her he shoots with a high-power rifle the walking toy dog she pretends to be selling. A puffy-cheeked peasant woman runs up to the bishop, as he is going to see a dying man, and confesses to him that she has always detested Jesus Christ. The military friends of the dope smugglers drop in on them at dinnertime when their maneuvers take them to the house. They light up joints but the smugglers embarrassedly admit they've never touched the stuff. When they admonish the colonel not to smoke he retorts, "The whole American army in Vietnam is doing it."

"That's why they end up bombing their own troops," cautions the smuggler.

"So much the better," gleams the colonel.

We are really taken aback to find a Buñuel movie which makes us laugh from beginning to end. But Buñuel has always created a jolting kind of humor. The bizarre sight of a man drawing a piano with donkey carcasses on top and two priests trailing behind in *Un Chien Andalou* may indeed symbolize the inhibitions society places on the love act, but it is also a terribly funny image. In *Los Olvidados* when Jaibo is about to kill a boy we see a tall skeleton of a building in the background. Only the producer's objections prevented Buñuel from placing a full orchestra on its steel beams. Black humor, the irrational, comedy in its most jarring form have always been a staple of the surrealist diet. In *The Discreet Charm of the Bourgeoisie* Buñuel has given us a work in which his surrealistic sense of humor emerges more fully than in any of his films since *L'Age d'Or*.

INTERRUPTION AS STYLE

JONATHAN ROSENBAUM

From *Sight and Sound*, vol. 42, no. 1, pp. 2–4. © 1973 by The British Film Institute. By permission

REPORTER: Who are your favorite characters in the movie?
BUÑUEL: The cockroaches. *(from an interview in Newsweek)*

'Once upon a time . . . ' begins *Un Chien Andalou*, in mockery of a narrative form that it seeks to obliterate, and from this title onward, Buñuel's cinema largely comprises a search for an alternative form to contain his passions. After dispensing with plot entirely in *Un Chien Andalou, L'Age d'Or* and *Las Hurdes*, his first three films, and remaining inactive as a director for the next fifteen years (1932–47), Buñuel has been wrestling ever since with the problem of reconciling his surrealistic and anarchistic reflexes to the logic of storylines. How does a sworn enemy of the bourgeoisie keep his identity while devoting himself to bourgeois forms in a bourgeois industry? Either by subverting these forms or by trying to adjust them to his own purposes; and much of the tension in Buñuel's work has come from the play between these two possibilities.

Buñuel can always tell a tale when he wants to, but the better part of his brilliance lies elsewhere. One never finds in his work that grace and economy of narration, that sheer pleasure in exposition, which informs the opening sequences of *Greed*, *La Règle du Jeu*, *The Magnificent Ambersons*, *Rear Window*, *Sansho Dayu* and *Au Hasard, Balthazar*. On the contrary, Buñuel's usual impulse is to interrupt a narrative line whenever he can find an adequate excuse for doing so – a joke, ironic detail or startling juxtaposition that deflects the plot's energies in another direction. A typical 'Buñuel touch' – the 'Last Supper' pose assumed by the beggars in *Viridiana* – has only a parenthetical relation to the action, however significant it may be thematically. And lengthier intrusions, like the dream sequences in *Los Olvidados*, tend to detach themselves from their surroundings as independent interludes, anecdotes or parables. For the greater part of his career, Buñuel's genius has mainly expressed itself in marginal notations and insertions. To my knowledge, his only previous attempt at an open narrative structure since 1932 has been *La Voie Lactée* – a picaresque religious (and anti-religious) pageant, much indebted to Godard's *Weekend*, which came uncomfortably close to being all notations and no text, like a string of Sunday school jokes.

If *Le Charme Discret de la Bourgeoisie* registers as the funniest Buñuel film since *L'Age d'Or*, probably the most relaxed *and* controlled film he has ever made, and arguably the first contemporary, global masterpiece to have come from France in the Seventies, this is chiefly because he has arrived at a form that covers his full range, permits him to say anything – a form that literally and figuratively lets him get away with murder. One cannot exactly call his new work a bolt from the blue. But its remarkable achievement is to weld together an assortment of his favourite themes, images and parlour tricks into a discourse that is essentially new. Luring us into the deceptive charms of narrative as well as those of his characters, he undermines the stability of both attractions by turning interruption into the basis of his art, keeping us aloft on the sheer exuberance of his amusement.

Seven years ago, Noël Burch observed that in *Le Journal d'une*

Femme de Chambre, Buñuel had at last discovered Form – a taste and talent for plastic composition and a 'musical' sense of the durations of shots and the 'articulations between sequences'; more generally, 'a rigorous compartmentalisation of the sequences, each of which follows its own carefully worked out, autonomous curve.' *Belle de Jour* reconfirmed this discovery, but *Le Charme Discret* announces still another step forward: at the age of 72, Buñuel has finally achieved Style.

Six friends – three men and three women – want to have a meal together, but something keeps going wrong. Four of them arrive at the Sénéchals' country house for dinner, and are told by Mme. Sénéchal that they've come a day early; repairing to a local restaurant, they discover that the manager has just died, his corpse laid our in an adjoining room – how can they eat *there* – so they plan a future lunch date. But each successive engagement is torpedoed: either M. and Mme. Sénéchal (Jean-Pierre Cassel and Stéphane Audran) are too busy making love to greet their guests, or the cavalry suddenly shows up at dinnertime between manoeuvres, or the police raid the premises and arrest everyone. Don Raphael Acosta (Fernando Rey), Ambassador of Miranda – a mythical, campy South American republic resembling several countries, particularly Spain – arranges a secret rendezvous in his flat with Mme. Thévenot (Delphine Seyrig), but M. Thévenot (Paul Frankeur) turns up at an inopportune moment. The three ladies – Mmes. Sénéchal and Thévenot and the latter's younger sister, Florence (Bulle Ogier) – meet for tea, and the waiter regretfully announces that the kitchen is out of tea, coffee, alcohol and everything else they try to order. Still other attempted get-togethers and disasters turn out to be dreams, or dreams of dreams. At one dinner party, the guests find themselves sitting on a stage before a festive audience, prompted with lines; another ends with Don Raphael, after a political quarrel, shooting his host; still another concludes with an unidentified group of men breaking in and machine-gunning the lot of them.

At three separate points in the film, including the final sequence, we see all six characters walking wordlessly down a road, somewhere between an unstated starting place and an equally mysterious destination – an image suggesting the continuation both of their class and of the picaresque narrative tradition that propels them forward.

Yet if the previous paragraph reads like a plot summary, it is deceptive. The nature and extent of Buñuel's interruptions guarantee the virtual absence of continuous plot. But we remain transfixed as though we were watching one: the sustained charm and glamour of the six characters fool us, much as they fool themselves. Their myths, behavior and appearance – seductive, illusory surface – carry us (and them) through the film with a sense of unbroken continuity and logic, a consistency that the rest of the universe and nature itself seem to rail against helplessly. Despite every attempt at annihilation, the myths of the bourgeoisie and of conventional narrative survive and prevail, a certainty that Buñuel reconciles himself to by regarding it as the funniest thing in the world.

Interruptions, of course, are a central fact about modern life; as I write this in a friend's apartment, the phone has been ringing about once every two paragraphs. Using this sort of comic annoyance as a structural tool, Buñuel can shoot as many arrows as he wants into our complacencies about narrative, the characters' complacencies about themselves. He exercises this principle of disruption in a multitude of ways, in matters large and small in the opening scene at the Sénéchals' house, Florence's dopey, indifferent, comic-strip face drifts irrelevantly into the foreground of a shot while other characters chatter about something else behind her, and similar displacements of emphasis abound everywhere.

Take the last attempted dinner. It begins with a red herring which leads us to suspect poisoning ('I prepared the soup with herbs from the garden'); the conversation is broken off for a cruel exchange with the maid about her age and broken engagement; and while M. Sénéchal demonstrates the correct method of carving lamb, Florence stubbornly insists on pursuing her deadpan astrological profile of Don Raphael. After the gang breaks in to shoot them all, our sense of their total demise – a Godardian image of overlapping corpses – is interrrupted when we realise that Don Raphael has hidden under the dinner table, and is reaching for a piece of lamb. Still crouching under the table, he bites savagely into the meat – a comic-terrifying reminder of the dream in *Los Olvidados* – and is finished off by a final blast of gunfire. Lest we suppose that this is the last possible interruption, we next see Don Raphael waking up from his nightmare. He gets out of bed, goes into the kitchen, and opens the refrigerator to take out a plate of lamb.

Every dream and interpolated story in the film carries some threat, knowledge or certainty of death – the central fact that all six characters ignore, and their charm and elegance seek to camouflage. Ghosts of murder victims and other phantoms of guilt parade through these inserted tales, but the discreet style of the bourgeoisie, boxing them in dreams and dinner anecdotes, holds them forever in check. To some extent, Buñuel shares this discretion in his failure to allude to his native Spain even once in the dialogue, although the pomp and brutality of the Franco regime are frequently evoked. (The recurrent gag of a siren, jet plane or another disturbance covering up a political declaration – a device familiar from Godard's *Made in USA* – acknowledges this sort of suppression.) But the secret of Buñuel's achieved style is balance, and for that he must lean more on irony – an expedient tactic of the bourgeoisie – than on the aggressions of the rebel classes; when he sought imbalance in *L'Age d'Or*, the revolutionary forces had the upper edge. An essential part of his method is to pitch the dialogue and acting somewhere between naturalism and parody, so that no gag is merely a gag, and each commonplace line or gesture becomes a potential gag. Absurdity and elegance, charm and hypocrisy become indistinguishably fused.

Another form of resolution is hinted at in the treatment of a secondary character, Monsignor Dufour (Julien Bertheau), a bishop who is hired by the Sénéchals as a gardener ('You've heard of worker-priests? There are worker-bishops too!'), and figures as clergy-in-residence at many of the abortive dinner parties. Late in the film, he is brought to the bed of an impoverished dying man – a gardener himself – by an old woman who asserts that she's hated Jesus Christ since she was a little girl, and promises to tell him why when she returns from delivering carrots. Dufour then proceeds to attend to the dying gardener, who confesses to having poisoned the bishop's wealthy parents when Dufour was a child. Dufour kindly and dutifully gives him absolution, then lifts up a nearby rifle and shoots the man through the skull. Thus, Buñuel appears to arrive at the conclusion that Catholicism, far from being the natural opponent of Surrealism, is the ultimate expression of it; and it seems strangely appropriate that after this scene both the bishop and the old woman with her promised explanation are abruptly dropped from the film, as though they've suddenly cancelled each other out.

Writing in 1962, Andrew Sarris remarked that Buñuel's camera has always viewed his characters from a middle distance, too close for cosmic groupings and too far away for self 'identification.' The singular achievement of Buñuel's crystallised style is to allow both these viewpoints to function – to let us keep our distance from the characters while repeatedly recognising our own behaviour in them. Cryptic throwaway lines, illogically repeated motifs and displacements in space and time give the film some of the abstractness of *Marienbad*, yet the richness of concretely observed social behaviour is often comparable to that in *La Règle du Jeu*. A similar mixture was potentially at work in *The Exterminating Angel* – the obvious companion-film to *Le Charme Discret*, with its guests unable to leave a room *after* finishing dinner. But despite a brilliant script, the uneven execution left too much of the conception unrealised.

Undoubtedly a great deal of credit for the dialogue of *Le Charme Discret* should go to Jean-Claude Carrière, who has worked on the scripts of all Buñuel's French films since *Le Journal d'une Femme de Chambre*: the precise banality of the small talk has a withering accuracy. Even more impressive is the way that Buñuel and Carrière have managed to weave in enough contemporary phenomena to make the film as up-to-date – and as surrealistic, in its crazy-quilt juxtapositions – as the latest global newspaper. Vietnam, Mao, Women's Lib, various forms of political corruption and international drug trafficking are all touched upon in witty and apt allusions. Fernando Rey unloading smuggled heroin from his diplomatic pouch is a hip reference to *The French Connection*, and much of the rest of the film works as a parody of icons and stances in modern cinema.

Florence's neuroticism – as evidenced by her loathing of cellos and her 'Euclid complex' – lampoons Ogier's role in *L'Amour Fou*; Audran's stiff elegance and country house harks back to *La Femme Infidèle*; while Seyrig's frozen, irrelevant smiles on every occasion are a comic variation of her ambiguous *Marienbad* expressions. And as I've already suggested, Godard has become a crucial reference-point in late Buñuel – not only in the parodies and allusions, but also in the use of an open form to accommodate these and other intrusions, the tendency to keep shifting the centre of attention.

A few years ago, Godard remarked of *Belle de Jour* that Buñuel seemed to be playing the cinema the way Bach played the organ.

The happy news of *Le Charme Discret* is that while most of the serious French cinema at present – Godard included – seems to be hard
at work performing painful duties, the Old Master is still playing –
effortlessly, freely, without fluffing a note.

WHY IS THE CO-EATUS
ALWAYS INTERRUPTUS?

JOHN SIMON

From *The New York Times*, February 25,
1973. © 1973 by The New York Times
Company. Reprinted by permission.

Luis Buñuel's *The Discreet Charm of the Bourgeoisie* presents me with a critical poser. Here is a film that has received rave
notices from all reviewers, top to bottom, and is doing well with
local audiences; yet I consider it absolutely worthless. Why?

The film operates on two levels: as an essentially realistic yet satirical portrait of the French bourgeoisie, and as a series of dreams
and visions constituting a surreal plane. Not only does the film
strike me as a failure on each of these levels, it does not even manage
to benefit from contrasting or dovetailing the two. I submit that
Buñuel, who has made some splendid and some dismal films, is now
an old, exhausted filmmaker, and that his besetting sins of lack of
discipline and indulgence in private obsessions have gotten quite
out of hand.

To begin with the satirical-realistic level: satire must, at the very
least, be funny. But *Bourgeoisie* is either groaning under old, obvious
jokes or coasting along barren stretches of mirthless nastiness. A
sextet of rich and decadent bourgeois, including one ambassador
from the imaginary Latin American country of Miranda, enjoy eating copiously and well. Yet, for one reason or another, their meals
get interrupted. Let's call this the co-eatus interruptus theme.

For example, they come to dinner at their friend's house on the
wrong day and must leave. They go, instead, to a country inn, but
find in an adjoining alcove the dead proprietor's body awaiting the
undertaker, and so decide to leave. Or they go, of an afternoon, to a
fashionable café-restaurant in Paris and, successively ordering tea,

coffee and hot chocolate, are told by the returning waiter that the place is out of each. So they leave.

Where is the joke or satire in that? No decent restaurant is ever out of all beverages, so the scene does not correspond to some ludicrous reality. But what about satiric-comical heightening? Does the scene, by indirection or hyperbole, succeed in ridiculing fancy restaurants? Or their waiters? Or their clientele? None of the above. Does it, then, make some sardonic point about French society? Not at all. Is it funny? No, only preposterous. In another scene the group sits down to dinner only to be interrupted by some officers, who are to be billeted with them and whose maneuvers have unexpectedly been moved ahead. Dinner is delayed while the hostess improvises additional food and tables, and the meal is about to start again. But now the other mock army attacks prematurely, the officers must leave, and we get an interruptus within an interruptus. Absurd, yes; funny, no.

And not meaningful either. What do these and other such scenes tell us? That the French bourgeoisie likes its food and takes it seriously, and hates to be thwarted in its enjoyment of it. So what? The Italian bourgeoisie is just as keen on eating, and so is the German and Austrian, and any other you care to name, with the possible exception of the English and American. But is this telling us anything new or enlightening or needful of iteration? What is so hilarious about people rattling off names of dishes or holding forth on the best way to make dry martinis? Nothing; yet from the way audiences are laughing you'd think the ushers were passing out laughing gas.

With interrupted eating comes also interrupted sex, the archetypal interruptus. A husband discovers his wife on the verge of adultery with his good friend the ambassador; or guests arrive for lunch just as the host and hostess feel so amorous that they must have instant intercourse – so they must climb out of the window and have it in the bushes. This is not only juvenile prurience, it does not even make satirical sense: if these solidly married bourgeois can still pant for each other so at high noon, all is not lost. Where the blood stirs, there is hope.

But where is the satire, where is the joke? Two people greedily pawing each other at an inopportune moment? Compared to that, a man slipping on a banana peel is Wildean wit and Swiftian satire.

On the surreal plane, the equivalent to the interruptus is the shaggy-dog story. In a sense, a dream is always over too soon, before the punchline of fulfillment can set in. But Buñuel shaggy-dogifies his dream or fantasy sequences in every possible way. A young lieutenant pops up from nowhere and relates a childhood vision in which his dead mother and her murdered lover appeared to the boy. They tell him that the dead and bloody man is his real father, and that the evil man he lives with is merely the killer of that true father. At the ghosts' urging, the boy poisons his pseudo-progenitor. He has had an unhappy childhood, says the lieutenant, and departs, never to be seen again.

Another man, a sergeant, is brought on to recount a dream of his. It is full of weird goings-on in a necropolis photographed and edited as in cheap horror movies; the events signify nothing meaningful or related to anything else in the film. The sergeant is asked to tell also his "train dream," but there is no more time for this. He has to leave, and we are left with a shaggy dog within a shaggy dog.

Again, a police commissioner we neither know nor care about has a dream about a bloody sergeant, allowing Buñuel to bring on yet another bloody corpse (the film is awash with blood, but you don't hear any of the antiviolence critics denouncing this one!) and to have a sado-comic scene in which the police torture a young rebel by means of an electrically charged piano, which, so to speak, plays him, and from which, suddenly, an army of cockroaches pours out – a shaggy-roach story.

Why should we care about the dreams of supernumeraries? A dream becomes interesting in relation to the waking personality of the dreamer, but if he remains a passing blank, of what concern are his grotesque dreams to us? Yet even the principal's dreams remain in this film unrevealing, unfunny, unconvincing. It would seem (as Buñuel has more or less admitted) that some of those dream episodes were originally intended as strange but real events – as, for example, in *The Milky Way* – but that the filmmaker lost his nerve and explained the thing away as dreams within dreams.

Typically, we'll see a character wake up after a grotesque dream, and another, equally grotesque, sequence begins. Then a second character is seen waking up, and he tells us that he dreamed both foregoing sequences, that even the first dream was dreamed by him, the second dreamer. Yet the protagonist of the second dream was really a third character, whose dream that should have been. If this doesn't make sense to you reading it, don't worry – it won't make sense viewing it, either.

The shaggy dogs spill over into the waking sequences. There is one in which an elderly peasant woman promises to tell a bishop why she hates the gentle Jesus, but is whisked off before she can do so. Again, the police commissioner receives a phone call from the minister of justice to release his prominent prisoners. Why? he asks. The minister explains, but the noise of a low-flying jet obliterates the explanation. Asked for a repeat, the minister wearily obliges, but another jet interferes. The frustrated commissioner passes the order on to his sergeant, who also requests an explanation. As the commissioner answers, the radiator pipes drown out his words – shaggy upon shaggy upon shaggy dog.

All the humor is pathetic. A bishop is summoned to give absolution to a dying old man. He turns out to be the gardener who, years ago, killed the bishop's parents who employed and tormented him. The bishop absolves the old man, then shoots him dead – another blood-spattered corpse. And people laugh at this! But they'll laugh at anything. We first glimpse the bishop innocently walking up to a front door to ring the bell; in the audience, hearty laughter. Why? Surely they have seen a soutane before, and the churchman is not walking on his hands or backward or hopping on one foot.

Then there is a visual refrain, a periodically repeated shot of the six main characters walking down a highway. This is no one's dream or vision and may be an auto-*hommage* to Buñuel's own *The Milky Way*, in which a highway was the connecting metaphor. Here, however, the three or four recurrences of the shot with incremental variations tell us no more than that our bourgeois sextet is trudging down the road of life with a different expression on each face. So what else is old? To resort to grandiose symbolism in order to say what plain narrative has already conveyed (and what, anyhow, is self-evident) is arrant pretentiousness.

Coitus or co-eatus interruptus and the shaggy-dog story are the two faces of the same debased coin. They are an impotent old man's cacklingly sadistic interference with his own fictional characters, and an exhausted mind's failed search for meaningful conclusions. Buñuel is merely rehashing his earlier and better films (themselves often enough marred by incoherence), without the fascinating love-hate or righteous indignation that informed them. We knew what was assailed in *Los Olvidados* or reduced to absurdity in *Simon of the Desert*. In *The Discreet Charm of the Bourgeoisie* we have not so much a shaggy as an old dog, unable to learn new tricks or even adequately recall old ones.

This latest Buñuel film is a haphazard concatenation of waking and dream sequences in which anything goes, and which would make just as much, or just as little, sense if they were put together in any other disorder. Since there is no plot and the characters are just pawns – oily businessman, dissembling diplomat, spaced-out debutante, haughty matron, frivolous wife – able performers are reduced to striking permanent attitudes and hoping they will add up to performances. The talented Delphine Seyrig, for instance, opts for one unrelieved smirk from beginning to end.

Why, then, such slavish adulation, placing the film on every Best List from high to low? Buñuel is a Grand Old Man – antifascist, anticlerical, antibourgeois – well into his seventies and still swinging. Secondly, he is European and has been through all those prestigiously arcane cults like surrealism, dadaism, fetishism, sadomasochism, and can provide nothing so shallow but that it is somehow chockful of profundities. Thirdly, his films are in a foreign language and must contain subtleties submerged in the subtitles. The reviewers, like good Pavlovian dogs, salivate away at the ring of Buñuel's name.

Audiences, in turn, have the unanimous rapture of the critics and all those awards to rely on. Dogs multiply: shaggy begets shaggy, Pavlovian conditions others into Pavlovians. *Dr. Strange-love*, a satire that did have meaning, predicted the world's end by hydrogen bomb. This Buñuel bomb merely ushers in the end of common sense in movie appreciation.

Credits

LE CHARME DISCRET DE LA BOURGEOISIE
(THE DISCREET CHARM OF THE BOURGEOISIE)

Color, France, 1972.
Original language: French.
Production house: Greenwich Film Production.
Producer: Serge Silberman.
Screenplay: Luis Buñuel with the collaboration of
    Jean-Claude Carrière.
Cinematography: Edmond Richard, in Eastmancolor.
Decoration: Pierre Guffroy.
Editing: Hélène Plemiannikov.
Assistant Directors: Pierre Lary, Arnie Gelbart.
Production manager: Ully Pickard.
Sound: Guy Villete.
Duration: 100 minutes.

CAST

Fernando Rey (Rafael de Acosta, the ambassador),
Jean-Pierre Cassel (Henri Sénèchal, businessman), Stéphane Au-

dran (Alice Sénéchal), Paul Frankeur (François Thévenot), Delphine Seyrig (Simone Thévenot), Bulle Ogier (Florence), Julien Bertheau (Monsignor Dufour, Bishop), Gerald Robard (Hubert de Rochecahin), Milena Vukotic (Inés, Sénéchal's maid), Claude Piéplu (the Colonel), Michel Piccoli (the Home Secretary), Muni (the peasant woman), Pierre Maguelon (the Chief of Police), François Maistre (Superintendent Deplus), Georges Douking (the dying gardener), María Gabriella Maione (the terrorist girl), Bernard Musson (manservant), Robert Le Béal (tailor).

COMPLIED BY YUNGSHUN TANG

Selective Bibliography

PUBLISHED SCRIPTS AND OTHER WORKS BY BUÑUEL

L'âge d'or and Un chien andalou. Trans. Marianne Alexandre. New York: Simon and Schuster, 1968.

Belle de jour, by Luis Buñuel and Jean-Claude Carrière. Trans. Robert Adkinson. New York: Simon and Schuster, 1971.

"*Le charme discret de la bourgeoisie* (découpage intégral par Luis Buñuel et Jean-Claude Carrière)." *L'Avant-Scène du cinéma,* no. 135 (April 1973): 11–48.

Un chien andalou. Foreword by Jean Vigo. London: Faber, 1994.

"*Un chien andalou,* a Scenario by Luis Buñuel and Salvador Dalí." In *Surrealism,* ed. Julien Levy, 64–74. New York: Black Sun Press, 1936.

"*La duchesse d'Aloe et Goya.*" Unproduced project. Trans. J. Sieger. *Postif,* no. 198 (October 1977): 9–17.

Goya: la duquesa de Alba y Goya: guion y sinopsis cinematografica de Luis Buñuel. Teruel: Instituto de Estudios Turolenses, 1992.

"*El* (script by Luis Buñuel and Luis Alcoriza)." *Image et son,* no. 187 (October 1965): 53–62.

El fantasma de la libertad, by Luis Buñuel and Jean-Claude Carrière. Barcelona: Aymá, S. A. Editora, 1974.

The Exterminating Angel, Nazarín and *Los olvidados.* Trans. Nicholas Fry. New York: Simon and Schuster, 1972.

"*Hamlet.*" *Cinématographe,* no. 92 (September–October 1983): 5–10.

198

"Hamlet (tragédie comique)." *Postif,* no. 272 (October 1983): 6–13.

Le journal d'une femme de chambre. Paris: Editions du Seuil, 1971.

Three Screenplays: Viridiana, The Exterminating Angel and Simon of the Desert. Trans. Piergiuseppe Bozzetti, Carol Martin-Sperry, and Anthony Pagden. New York: Orion Press, 1969.

Tristana. Trans. Nicholas Fry. New York: Simon and Schuster, 1971.

Buñuel, Luis. "Buster Keaton's *College."* In *The Shadow and Its Shadow,* ed. Paul Hammond, 34–35. London: BFI, 1978.

———. "Critique de *Napoléon* (Abel Gance)." *Cahiers d'art,* no. 3 (1927).

———. "Une girafe (texte surréaliste)." *Le surréalisme au service de la révolution* (May 1933).

———. *Goya de Luis Buñuel, 1928.* Paris: J. Damase, 1987.

———. *Là-bas.* Teruel: Instituto de Estudios Turolenses, 1990.

———. "Life among the Americans." *American Film* 8 (September 1983): 18+ [6p.].

———. "Luis Buñuel." *Cine cubano,* no. 102 (1982): 49–50.

———. "Luis Buñuel: la jalousie et la parano." *Visions,* no. 24 (December 1984): 29.

———. "A manera de despedida de un viejo amigo y maestro: Buñuel." *Cinemateca revista* 7, no. 39 (November 1983): 44–47.

———. *Mi último suspiro* (Mon dernier soupir). Trans. Ana María de la Fuente. Barcelona: Plaza & Janes, 1982.

———. *Mon dernier soupir.* Paris: Éditions Robert Laffont, 1982.

———. *My Last Sigh.* Trans. Abigail Israel. New York: Vintage, 1983.

———. "Out of a Cinema Credo." *New York Times,* 18 March 1962, sec. 2, 29–30.

———. *Poemas (inéditos).* Santa Cruz de Tenerife: Carlos E. Pinto, 1981.

———. "Poesía y cine." *Nuestro cine,* no. 66 (October 1967): 20–22.

———. "Poésie et cinéma." *Cinema 59,* no. 37 (June 1959): 70–74.

———. "Preface to *Un chien andalou."* *La révolution surréaliste,* no. 12 (December 1929).

———. "Réponse à un questionnaire surréaliste sur l'amour." *La révolution surréaliste,* no. 12 (December 1929).

———. "Une soirée au Studio des Ursulines." *Postif,* no. 118 (Summer 1970): 52–54.

———. "A Statement." *Film Culture,* no. 21 (Summer 1960): 41. Rpt. in *Film Makers on Film Making: Statements on Their Art by Their Directors,* ed. Harry M. Geduld, 175–176. Bloomington: Indiana University Press, 1970.

———. "Sur Nazarín." *Cinema 61,* no. 52 (1961).

Buñuel, Luis, and Jean-Claude Carrière. *Le Moine.* Unproduced project (1965). Paris: Eric Losfeld, 1971.

Buñuel, Luis, and Deborah Treisman. "Gags." *Grand Street* 14, no. 4 (Spring 1996): 16.

Buñuel, Luis, and Garrett White. "Why I Don't Wear a Watch." *Grand Street* 15, no. 3 (Winter 1997): 19.

Larrea, Jean, and Luis Buñuel *"Illisible, fils de flûte:* synopsis d'un scénario non réalisé." *Postif,* nos. 50–52 (March 1963): 12–14.

Logette, Lucien, *"Espagne 1937."* Unproduced project. *Jeune cinéma,* no. 225 (January 1994): 11–17.

BOOKS AND PARTS OF BOOKS ON BUÑUEL AND PARTICULAR FILMS

Abel, Richard. *"La coquille et le clergyman* (1928) and *Un chien andalou* (1929)." In *French Cinema: The First Wave, 1915–1929,* 475–485. Princeton: Princeton University Press, 1984.

Aranda, José Francisco. *Luis Buñuel: A Critical Biography.* Trans. and ed. David Robinson. New York: Da Capo Press, [1976] 1985.

Baxter, John. *Buñuel.* London: Fourth Estate, 1994.

Bazin, André. *The Cinema of Cruelty: From Buñuel to Hitchcock.* Ed. François Truffaut and trans. Sabine d'Estree. New York: Seaver Books, 1982.

Besas, Peter. "Bardem, Berlanga, and Buñuel into the Breach." In *Behind the Spanish Lens: Spanish Cinema under Fascism and Democracy,* 31–52. Denver, Colo.: Arden Press, 1985.

Breton, André. *Manifestoes of Surrealism.* Trans. Richard Seaver and Helen R. Lane. Ann Arbor: University of Michigan Press, 1969.
  What Is Surrealism?: Selected Writings. New York: Monad, 1978.

Buache, Freddy. *The Cinema of Luis Buñuel.* Trans. Peter Graham. New York: A. S. Barnes; London: Tantivy, 1973.

Cohen, Margaret. *Profane Illumination: Walter Benjamin and the Paris of Surrealist Revolution.* Berkeley: University of California Press, 1993.

Conley, Tom. "Documentary Surrealism: *On Land without Bread."* In *Dada and Surrealist Film,* ed. Rudolf E. Kuenzli, 176–198. New York: Willis Locker & Owens, [1987] 1996.

Conrad, Randall. *Luis Buñuel: Surrealist and Filmmaker.* Boston: Museum of Modern Art, 1974. Mimeograph.

de la Colina, José, and Tomás Pérez Turrent. *Objects of Desire: Conversations with Luis Buñuel.* Ed. and trans. Paul Lenti. New York: Marsilio Publishers, 1992.

Durgnat, Raymond. *Luis Buñuel.* Berkeley: University of California Press, 1977.

Edwards, Gwynne. *The Discreet Art of Luis Buñuel: A Reading of His Films.* London: Maion Boyars, 1982.

Indecent Exposures: Buñuel, Saura, Erice & Almodóvar. London: Maion Boyars, 1982.

Eidsvik, Charles. "Dark Laughter: Buñuel's *Tristana* (1970) from the Novel by Benito Pérez Galdós." In *Modern European Filmmakers and the Art of Adaptation,* ed. Andrew Horton and Joan Magretta, 173–187. New York: Frederick Ungar, 1981.

Evans, Peter William. *The Films of Luis Buñuel: Subjectivity and Desire.* Oxford: Clarendon Press, 1995.

Farber, Manny. "Luis Buñuel." In *Negative Space: Manny Farber on the Movies,* 275–281. London: Studio Vista, 1971.

Fernandez, Henry C. "The Influence of Galdós on the Films of Luis Buñuel." Ph.D. diss., Indiana University, 1976.

Fiddian, Robin W., and Peter W. Evans. "*Viridiana* and the Death Instinct." In *Challenges to Authority: Fiction and Film in Contemporary Spain,* 61–70. London: Tamesis Books, 1988.

Higginbotham, Virginia. *Luis Buñuel.* Boston: Twayne, 1979.

Kinder, Marsha. "Exile and Ideological Reinscription: The Unique Case of Luis Buñuel." In *Blood Cinema: The Reconstruction of National Identity in Spain,* 278–338. Berkeley: University of California Press, 1993.

Kinder, Marsha, and Beverle Houston. "*Un chien andalou*" and "*Land without Bread.*" In *Close-Up: A Critical Perspective on Film,* 41–43, 106–109. New York: Harcourt Brace Jovanovich, 1972.

"Subject and Object in *Last Year at Marienbad* and *The Exterminating Angel:* A Mutual Creation." In *Self and Cinema,* 241–284. Pleasantville, N.Y.: Redgrave, 1980.

Kovács, Steven. "The Fulfillment of Surrealist Hopes: Dalí and Buñuel Appear." In *From Enchantment to Rage: The Story of Surrealist Cinema,* 183–249. London: Fairleigh Dickinson University Press, 1980.

Kyrou, Ado. *Luis Buñuel: An Introduction.* Trans. Adrienne Foulke. New York: Simon and Schuster, 1963.

Mellen, Joan. "Buñuel's *Tristana.*" In *Women and Their Sexuality in the New Film,* 191–202. New York: Horizon Press, 1973.

ed. *The World of Luis Buñuel: Essays in Criticism.* New York: Oxford University Press, 1978.

Oudart, Jean-Pierre. "Word Play, Master Play." Review of *Tristana.* In *Cahiers du Cinéma, 1969–1972: The Politics of Representation,* ed. Nick Browne, 137–145. Cambridge, Mass.: Harvard University Press, 1990.

Partridge, Colin J. *Tristana: Buñuel's Film and Galdós' Novel: A Case Study in the Relation between Literature and Film*. Lewiston, N.Y.: Edwin Mellen Press, 1995.

Paz, Octavio. "Luis Buñuel." In *Alternating Current*, trans. Helen R. Lane, 104–110. New York: Viking Press, 1973.

Rees, Margaret A., ed. *Luis Buñuel: A Symposium*. Leeds: Trinity and All Saints' College, 1983.

Reyes Nevares, Beatriz. "Luis Buñuel." In *The Mexican Cinema: Interviews with Thirteen Directors*, trans. Elizabeth Gard and Carl J. Mora, 55–62. Albuquerque: University of New Mexico Press, 1976.

Sánchez Vidal, Agustín. "Góngora, Buñuel, the Spanish Avant-Garde and the Centenary of Goya's Death." In *The Spanish Avant-Garde*, ed. Derek Harris, 110–122. Manchester: Manchester University Press, 1995.

Sandro, Paul. *Diversions of Pleasure: Luis Buñuel and the Crises of Desire*. Columbus: Ohio State University Press, 1987.

Sarris, Andrew. "Luis Buñuel." In *Interviews with Film Directors*, ed. Andrew Sarris, 65–74. New York: Bobbs-Merrill, 1967.

Stam, Robert. "Hitchcock and Buñuel: Authority, Desire, and the Absurd." In *Hitchcock's Rereleased Films from Rope to Vertigo*, ed. Walter Raubicheck and Walter Srebnick, 116–146. Detroit: Wayne State University Press, 1991.

Stauffacher, Frank. *Notes on the Making of* Un chien andalou: *Cinema*. San Francisco: Museum of Modern Art, 1947.

Talens, Jenaro. *The Branded Eye: Buñuel's Un chien andalou*. Minneapolis: University of Minnesota Press, 1993.

Wall, James M., ed. *Three European Directors: François Truffaut, Fellini's Film Journey, Luis Buñuel and the Death of God*. Grand Rapids, Mich.: William B. Eerdmans, 1973.

Williams, Linda. *Figures of Desire: A Theory and Analysis of Surrealist Film*. Urbana: University of Illinois Press, 1981.

Wood, Michael. "The Corruption of Accidents: Buñuel's *That Obscure Object of Desire* (1977) from the novel *The Woman and the Puppet* by Pierre Louÿs." In *Modern European Filmmakers and the Art of Adaptation*, ed. Andrew Horton and Joan Magretta, 329–340. New York: Frederick Ungar, 1981.

SPECIAL ISSUES OF JOURNALS

l'Avant-Scène du cinéma, nos. 27–28 (June–July 1963), special issue on "*Un chien andalou, L'âge d'or, L'ange exterminateur*"; 36 (April 1964), special issue on "Luis Buñuel"; 89 (February 1969), special issue on "*Nazarín*: Film chrétien ou terrible blasphème"; 94–95 (July – September 1969), special issue on "Spécial Buñuel: *La voie lactée/Simon du désert*"; 110 (January 1971), special issue on "*Tristana*"; 135 (April 1973), special issue on "*Le charme discret de la bourgeoisie*"; 137 (June 1973), special issue on "*Los olvidados*"; 151 (October 1974), special issue on "*Le fantôme de la liberté*"; 206 (April 1978), special issue on "*Belle de jour*"; 315–316 (November 1983), special issue on "Buñuel: l'âge d'or filmographie écrits"; 344 (November 1985), special issue on "*Cet obscur objet du désir*"; 428 (January 1994), special issue on "*Viridiana.*"

Cahiers du cinéma, no. 191 (June 1967), special issue on "Cannes, Pierre Perrault, Luis Buñuel"; 212 (May 1969), featuring *Simon du désert* and *La voie lactée*; 223 (August–September 1970), featuring *Tristana*.

Cercle du cinéma de l'A.G.E.T. (Toulouse) (1963); (1964), special issue on "Pour Buñuel."

Cine cubano (Havana), nos. 78–80 (1973), special issue on "Santiago Alvarez, Luis Buñuel, Migail Romm."

Ciné nuevo (Mexico), nos. 4–5 (November 1961), features *Illisible fils de flûte*.

Cinemages, no. 1 (1995), special issue on "Luis Buñuel."

Cinématographe (Paris), no. 92 (1983), special issue on "Dossier: Luis Buñuel."

Études cinématographiques, nos. 20–21 (1963), special issue on "Luis Buñuel"; 22–23 (1963), special issue on "Luis Buñuel"; 38–39 (1965), special issue on "Surréalisme et cinéma"; 40–42 (1965), special issue on "Surréalisme et cinéma."

Jeune cinéma (Paris), no. 134 (1981), special issue on "Surréalisme et cinéma."

La méthode, no. 7 (January 1962), special issue on "Luis Buñuel."

Movietone News, no. 39 (February 1975), special issue on "Luis Buñuel."

Postif, no. 10 (1954), special issue on "Le cinéma mexicain/Buñuel"; 42 (November 1961), special issue on "Luis Buñuel"; 108 (September 1969), special issue on "Luis Buñuel, Gordon Douglas, Hyère"; 146 (January 1973), special issue on "Luis Buñuel/Robert Mulligan," featuring *Le charme discret de la bourgeoisie*; 162 (October 1974), special issue on "Buñuel, Rivette, Saura, Science Fiction," featuring *Le fantôme de la liberté*; 272 (October 1983), special issue on "Buñuel, Fellini, Animation, Grande-Bretagne"; 391 (September 1993), the dossier on "Buñuel au Mexique"; 392 (October 1993), the dossier on "Buñuel de l'Espagne à la France."

Premier plan, no. 13 (1960), special issue on "Luis Buñuel," ed. Freddy Buache; 33 (1964), special issue on "Luis Buñuel," ed. Freddy Buache.

Revue du cinéma image et son (Paris, a.k.a. *Image et son*), no. 101 (April 1957), documents on *Cela s'appelle l'aurore*; 108 (January 1958), documents on *La mort en ce jardín*; 157 (December 1962), special issue on "Luis Buñuel"; 250 (May 1971), special issue on "Luis Buñuel."

PERIODICAL ARTICLES

Anderson, L. G. Review of *Los olvidados*. *Monthly Film Bulletin* 19 (June 1952): 76.

Aranda, José Francisco. "Back from the Wilderness." *Films and Filming* 8, no. 2 (November 1961): 29–30, 45.

"Surrealist and Spanish Giant." *Films and Filming* 8, no. 1 (October 1961): 17–18, 39.

Arena, BBC. "The Life and Times of Don Luis Buñuel." Produced by Alan Yentob and directed by Anthony Wall, 11 February 1984.

Armes, Roy. "Cinema: Film Theory and Practice: Buñuel, Bresson, Tati." *London Magazine* 15 (April–May 1975): 96–101.

Aub, Max, and Margaret Sayers Pelen. "Religious, Eroticism, Death." Interview with Buñuel. *Grand Street* 14, no. 4 (Spring 1996): 8.

Aubrey, Daniel, and J. M. Lacor. "Luis Buñuel." Interview. *Film Quarterly* 12, no. 2 (Winter 1958): 7–9.

Badder, D. J. "Luis Buñuel." *Film Dope*, no. 5 (July 1974): 44–46.

Banner, Michael. "Leaders of the Banned: *Un chien andalou*." *Melody Maker*, 72, no. 24 (June 1995): 42.

Barcia, J. Rubia. "Luis Buñuel's *Los olvidados*." *Quarterly of Film, Radio, TV 7*, no. 4 (Summer 1953): 392–401.

Beck, Henry Cabot. "Reel to Reel: *The Young One*." *Village Voice*, 6 October 1992, 69.

Bellow, Saul. "Buñuel's Unsparing Vision." *Horizon* 5, no. 2 (November 1962): 110–112.

Belton, John. "Medieval Modernism: Buñuel's Autobiography." *Millennium*, nos. 14–15 (Fall–Winter 1984–1985): 28–34.

Bergroth, Trevor, and Michael Koller. Review of *The Milky Way*. *Filmviews* 31, no. 127 (Autumn 1986): 38.

Besas, Peter. "Spanish Fest Honors Buñuel, a First since the Civil War." *Variety*, 27 December 21, 1976, 4.

Biskind, Peter. "New and Recommended: *Los olvidados*," *Premiere* 3, no. 1 (September 1989): 106.

Borau, José Luis. "Without Weapons." *Quarterly Review of Film Studies* 8, no. 2 (Spring 1983): 85–90.

"A Woman without a Piano, a Book without a Mark." *Quarterly Review of Film and Video* 13, no. 4 (December 1991): 9–16.

Brennan, Simon. "Classics/Foreign: *Belle de jour.*" *Premiere* 9, no. 5 (January 1996): 113.

Brown, Georgia. "Tricks of the Trade: *Belle de jour.*" *Village Voice*, 4 July 1995, 49.

"Buñuel Marks 50th Year as Filmmaker." *Variety*, 4 May 1977, 5+.

"Buñuel, 74, Still Highly Active; Films Display Creative Tone." *Variety*, 2 October 1974, 30.

"Buñuel, 77, Attains Comm'l Status; His *Desire* a Paris Hit." Review of *That Obscure Object of Desire*. *Variety*, 14 September 1977, 2.

"Buñuel, 77, to Roll Remake of 'Woman.' " *Variety*, 24 November 1976, 6.

"Buñuel's Mexican for Audio Brandon." *Variety*, 11 February 1976, 28.

Burgess, Jackson. Review of *Simon of the Desert*. *Film Quarterly* 19, no. 2 (Winter 1965–1966): 47–48.

Canby, Vincent. "Film: Buñuel's Bronte." Review of *Abismos de pasión*. *New York Times*, 27 December 1983, C11.

"Film: From Buñuel, *Los ambiciosos*, at the Public." *New York Times*, 12 February 1988, C13(L), 18(N).

"Film: *Garden* Offers Glimpses of Genius." Review of *La mort en ce jardín* (Death in the Garden). *New York Times*, 26 August 1977, C6.

"Luis Buñuel – Much of the Fun is in Surprise." Review of *Le fantôme de la liberté*. *New York Times*, 20 October 1974, sec. 2, 17.

Review of *Susana*. *New York Times*, 8 November 1983, 22(N), C9(L).

Review of *Wuthering Heights*. *New York Times*, 27 December 1983, 24 (N), C11 (L).

"Screen: Buñuel at Peak in *Archibaldo.*" *New York Times*, 16 September 1977, C9.

"Screen: Buñuel's Mexican Western." Review of *El rio y la muerte* (The River and Death). *New York Times*, 9 September 1977, C9.

"Screen: *El bruto*, a 1952 Melodrama by Buñuel." *New York Times*, 21 September 1983, C22.

"A Short Confession by Luis Buñuel." *New York Times*, 23 January 1985, 16 (N), C14 (L).

"Uncovering Luis Buñuel's Mexican Treasures." *New York Times*, 18 January 1976, sec. 2, 13.

Cargin, P. "Faces in the Glass." Review of *Cet obscur objet du désir*. *Film*, no. 62 (June 1978): 10.

Review of *The Phantom of Liberty*. *Film*, no. 23 (February 1975): 20.

Casciero, Alberto. "Provocateur of Surreal Screens." *Americas* 45, no. 3 (May–June 1993): 40–47.

Clarens, Carlos. "Chance Meetings: *Le fantôme de la liberté.*" *Sight and Sound* 44, no. 1 (1975): 12–13.

Coleman, John. "Films: Masked Balls." Review of *L'âge d'or. New Statesman*, 4 January 1980, 31.

"Rare & Ranging." Review of *The Phantom of Liberty. New Statesman*, 7 March 1975, 318.

"The World Well Lost." Review of *Cet obscur objet du désir. New Statesman* 95 (March 1978): 441.

Conley, Tom. "Documentary Surrealism: On *Land without Bread.*" *Dada/ Surrealism*, no. 15 (1986).

Conrad, Randall. " 'I Am Not a Producer!' – Working with Buñuel: A Conversation with Serge Silberman." *Film Quarterly* 33, no. 1 (1979): 2–11.

" 'The Minister of the Interior Is on the Telephone' – The Early Films of Luis Buñuel." *Cineaste* 7, no. 3 (1976): 3–14.

"No Blacks or Whites: The Making of Luis Buñuel's *The Young One.*" *Cineaste* 20, no. 3 (1994): 28–34.

Corn, Alfred. "Quentin Crisp Meets Buñuel." *ARTnews* 93, no. 4 (April 1994): 159.

Cox, Alex. "Bug-Eyed Buñuel." *Sight and Sound*, no. 5 (March 1995): 61.

Cox, Harvey. "The Death of God and the Future of Theology." *New Theology*, no. 4 (1967): 243–253.

Crowther, Bosley. Review of *Los olvidados. New York Times Film Review*, 25 March 1952, 2.

Cuperman, P., and O. Shipiro. "Re-constructing Buñuel." *Lamp* (1986): 23–31.

D'Arcy, S. Review of *The Phantom of Liberty. Films Illustrated* 4 (February 1975): 206.

Dare, Michael. "2nd Features: *Illusion Travels by Streetcar.*" *Billboard* 103, no. 12 (March 1991): 42.

Dean, Peter. "Video: *The Diary of a Chambermaid.*" *Sight and Sound* 5, no. 4 (April 1993): 68.

"Video: *The Exterminating Angel.*" *Sight and Sound* 5, no. 3 (March 1995): 63.

"Video: *The Milky Way.*" *Sight and Sound* 3, no. 8 (August 1993):61.

"Video: *Phantom of Liberty.*" *Sight and Sound* 5, no. 4 (April 1993): 69.

"Video: *Simon of the Desert.*" *Sight and Sound* 5, no. 3 (March 1995): 62.

"Video: *Tristana.*" *Sight and Sound* 3, no. 8 (August 1993): 62.

Denby, David. "Discreet, Charming, Funny: *Belle de jour.*" *New York*, 17 July 1995, 48–49.

"Movies: Golden Anniversary." Features *L'âge d'or. New York*, 5 May 1980, 71–72.

D'Lugo, Marvin. "Glances of Desire in *Belle de jour.*" *Film Criticism* 2, nos. 2–3 (Winter – Spring 1978): 84–89.

Doniol-Valcroze, Jacques, and André Bazin. "Conversation with Buñuel." *Sight and Sound* 24, no. 4 (Spring 1955): 181–185. Abridged from *Cahiers du cinéma*, no. 36 (June 1954): 2–14.

Drummond, Phillip. "Textual Space in *Un chien andalou.*" *Screen* 18, no. 3 (1977): 55–119.

Dudley, F. X., and H. Klein. "The Feminine Screen of Luis Buñuel." *Lamp* (1985): 75–80.

Durgnat, Raymond. Review of *The Milky Way. Film Comment* 10 (July–August 1974): 37–42.

Review of *Tristana. Film Comment* 10 (September–October 1974): 54–62.

"Theory of Theory – and Buñuel the Joker." *Film Quarterly*, no. 44 (Fall 1990): 32–44.

Eder, R. "Critic's Notebook: Surrealism Made Real." *New York Times*, 18 January 1976, sec. 2, 13.

Everson, W. K. Review of *That Obscure Object of Desire. Films in Review* 29 (January 1978): 50–51.

Faust, M. "Classic on Laser: *Belle de jour.*" *Video* 19, no. 10 (February 1996): 76.

Fernández, Enrique. "Film: et tu, Bruto?" Review of *El bruto. Village Voice*, 27 September 1983, 60.

"Film Spanish Steps." Review of *Las hurdes. Village Voice*, 20 December 1988, 93–94.

"A Recipe for Andalusian Chicken." *Film Criticism* 2, nos. 2–3 (Winter–Spring 1978): 78–83.

Fieschi, Jean-André. "The Angel and the Beast: Luis Buñuel's Mexican Sketches." *Cahiers du cinéma in English*, no. 4 (1966): 19–25.

Flatley, Guy. "New in Video: *Belle de jour.*" *Cosmopolitan* 220, no. 3 (March 1996): 38.

Fragola, Anthony N. "Buñuel's Re-vision of *Wuthering Heights*: The Triumph of *L'amour fou* over Hollywood Romanticism." Review of *Abismos de pasión. Literature-Film Quarterly* 22, no. 1 (January 1994): 50–56.

Fuentes, Carlos. "Luis Buñuel: The Macabre Master of Movie-Making." *Show*, no. 3 (November 1963).

García Abrines, Luis. "Rebirth of Buñuel." *Yale French Studies*, no. 17 (Summer 1956): 54–66.

García Riera, Emilio. "The Eternal Rebellion of Luis Buñuel." *Film Culture*, no. 21 (Summer 1960): 42–57.

"The Films of Luis Buñuel." *Film Culture*, no. 21 (Summer 1960): 58–59.

Gilliatt, Penelope. "The Current Cinema: Buñuel, Brilliant on a Shoestring." Review of *La ilusión viaja en tranvía* (A Tram-Ride of Dreams). *New Yorker*, 29 August 1977, 65–67.

"Long Live the Living: A Profile of Luis Buñuel." *New Yorker*, 5 December 1977, 53–72.

Gliatto, Tom. "Picks and Pans: *Belle de jour*." *People Weekly*, 24 July 1995, 13–14.

Goldstein, Ruth M. Review of *The Adventures of Robinson Crusoe*. *Film News* 34 (March–April 1977): 27.

Gow, Gordon. Review of *Nazarín*. *Films and Filming* 10, no. 1 (October 1963): 23.

Review of *That Obscure Object of Desire*. *Films and Filming* 24 (May 1978): 32–33.

"The Great Ones: *Robinson Crusoe*." *Classic Film Collector*, no. 54 (Spring 1977): 28–29.

Grossvogel, Donald I. "Buñuel's Obsessed Camera: *Tristana* Dismembered." *Diacritics*, no. 2 (Spring 1972): 51–56.

Hammond, Robert M. "Luis Alcoriza and the Films of Luis Buñuel." *Film Heritage* 1, no. 1 (Autumn 1965): 25–34.

Hamrah, A. S. Review of *Belle de jour* and *That Obscure Object of Desire*. *Une Reader*, no. 74 (March 1996): 139–140.

Harcourt, Peter. "Luis Buñuel: Spaniard & Surrealist." *Film Quarterly* 20, no. 3 (Spring 1967): 2–19. Rpt. in Peter Harcourt, *Six European Directors*, 102–134. Baltimore: Penguin, 1976.

Hatch, Robert. Review of *That Obscure Object of Desire*. *Nation*, 26 November 1977, 572–573.

Hedges, Inez. "Substitutionary Narration in the Cinema?" Features *Tristana*. *Sub-stance*, no. 9 (January 1974): 45–57.

Hoberman, Jim. "Film: Hoodoo You Love?" Review of *La fiévre monte à El Pao*. *Village Voice*, 16 February 1988, 78.

"Film: Passion Pit." Review of *Abismos de pasión*. *Village Voice*, 3 January 1984, 52.

"Golden Oldie." Review of *L'âge d'or*. *Village Voice*, 16 August 1994, 43.

"Take Two: *Los olvidados*." *American Film* 8 (June 1983): 14–15.

Hogue, Peter. "The 'Commercial' Life of Luis Buñuel." Review of *Ensayo de un crimen*. *Movietone News*, no. 51 (August 1976): 1–3+.

Hull, David Stewart. Review of *Viridiana*. *Film Quarterly* 15, no.2 (Winter 1961–1962): 55–56.

Humphries, Reynold. "Lacan and the Ostrich: Desire and Narration in Buñuel's *Le fantôme de la liberté*." *American Imago* 52, no. 2 (Summer 1995): 191–203.

Indiana, Gary. "Going Back to Buñuel." *Village Voice*, 8 April 1997, 8.

Insdorf, Annette. "After 50 Years, a Buñuel Classic Returns." *New York Times*, 27 April 1980, sec. 2, 15–16.

Irwin, Gayle. "Luis Buñuel's Postmodern Explicador: Film, Story and Narrative Space." *Canadian Journal of Film Studies* 4, no. 1 (1995): 27–47.

James, C. "Critic's Choice: A Beauty, a Beast and a Dog That Isn't." Review of *Un chien andalou*. *New York Times*, 17 April 1992, C8.

"Film View: No Depth on *Wuthering Heights*." Review of *Abismos de pasión*. *New York Times*, 9 April 1989, sec. 2, 11–12.

Jobb, Julian. Review of *Tristana*. *Sight and Sound* 40, no. 2 (Spring 1971): 103.

Jones, E. T. "Desire under the helms of Rohmer and Buñuel: *Claire's Knee and That Obscure Object of Desire*." *Literature/Film Quarterly* 9, no. 1 (1981): 3–8.

Kael, Pauline. "The Current Cinema: Cutting Light." Review of *That Obscure Object of Desire*. *New Yorker*, 19 December 1977, 128–130.

Kanesaka, Kenji. "Interview with Luis Buñuel." *Film Culture*, no. 24 (Spring 1962): 75.

"A Visit to Buñuel." *Film Culture*, no. 41 (Summer 1966): 60–65.

Kauffmann, Stanley. "Shocks, Past and Present." Features *L'âge d'or*. *New Republic*, 17 May 1980, 26–27.

Kellerman, Stewart. Review of *Le fantôme de la liberté*. *New York Times*, 27 November 1988, H34.

Kenny, Glenn. "Laser Discs: *Cet obscur objet du désir*." *Video Review* 11, no. 11 (February 1991): 78.

"The Power to Reorient." *Film Comment* 29 (July–August 1993): 86–88.

Kermode, Mark. Video Review of *Viridiana*. *Sight and Sound* 5, no. 3 (March 1995): 59.

Kernam, Margot S. Review of *Belle de jour*. *Film Quarterly* 23, no. 1 (Fall 1969): 38–41.

Kinder, Marsha. "The Tyranny of Convention in *The Phantom of Liberty*." *Film Quarterly* 28 (Summer 1975): 20–25.

Kirkup, J. "Cinema: Luis Buñuel: Mysteries of the Blood." *London Magazine* 22 (November 1982): 64–69.

Knight, Arthur. "The Films of Luis Buñuel." *Saturday Review* (July 1954): 27.

Kovács, Katherine S. "Pierre Louÿs and Luis Buñuel: Two Visions of Obscure Objects." *Cinema Journal* 19, no. 1 (Fall 1979): 86–89. Rpt. in *Cinema Examined*, ed. Richard Dyer MacCann and Jack C. Ellis, 282–233. New York: E. P. Dutton, 1982.

"The Plain in Spain: Geography and National Identity in Spanish Cinema." Features *Las hurdes. Quarterly Review of Film and Video* 13, no. 4 (1991): 17–46.

Krebs, Josef. "Now in Stores: *Belle de jour.*" *Video* 19, no. 9 (January 1996): 99.

Krohn, B. "Reissues: The Buñuel Classics." *Boxoffice* 120 (February 1984): R25–26.

Lambert, Gavin. Review of *Nazarín. Film Quarterly* 13, no. 3 (Spring 1960): 30–31.

Lennon, Peter. "Fetishiana: Luis Buñuel Talks to Peter Lennon." *Guardian,* 7 January 1964.

Lord, John. Review of *Los olvidados. Lumière* (Melbourne), no. 33 (April–May 1974): 31.

Lyon, E. H. "Luis Buñuel: The Process of Dissociation in Three Films." *Cinema Journal* 13, no. 1 (1973): 45–48.

McGillivray, D. Review of *The Phantom of Liberty. Films and Filming* 21 (April 1975): 36.

McVay, Douglas. Review of *The Phantom of Liberty. Focus on Film,* no. 20 (Spring 1975): 6–9.

Maddison, John. Review of *Los olvidados. Sight and Sound* 21, no. 4 (April–June 1952): 167–168.

Madsen, A. "Buñuel's *Phantom of Liberty.*" *Sight and Sound* 43, no. 3 (Summer 1974): 170–171.

Maltin, Leonard. Review of *Belle de jour. Modern Maturity* 39, no. 3 (May 1996): 32.

Maslin, Janet. "Film: Buñuel's Line." Review of *La ilusión viaja en tranvía. New York Times,* 19 August 1977, C9.

"Film: The *Madcap* Family Plotters." Review of *The Great Madcap* (El gran calavera). *New York Times,* 5 August 1977, C7.

Review of *Belle de jour. New York Times,* 25 June 1995, sec. 2, H15.

Review of *Daughter of Deceit* (La hija del engaño). *New York Times,* 12 August 1977, C11.

"A Vision of Eroticism among the Straitlaced." Review of rereleased *Belle de jour. New York Times,* 25 June 1995, H15.

Mathur, Paul. Video Review of *Viridiana*. *Melody Maker* 72, no. 6 (February 1995): 15.

Mayersberg, P. "The Happy Ending of Luis Buñuel." *Sight and Sound* 52, no. 4 (1983): 258–259.

Millar, Daniel. "Luis Buñuel: Naturalist and Supernaturalist." *Screen Education*, no. 43 (March–April 1968): 64–71.

Milne, Tom. "The Mexican Buñuel." *Sight and Sound* 35, no. 1 (Winter 1965–1966): 36–39.

Review of *El. Monthly Film Bulletin* 35 (February 1968): 19–20.

Review of *Le fantôme de la liberté*. *Monthly Film Bulletin* 42 (February 1975): 30–31.

Review of *Nazarín*. *Monthly Film Bulletin* 30 (October 1963): 141.

Review of *That Obscure Object of Desire*. *Monthly Film Bulletin* 45 (March 1978): 41–42.

Morris, M. Review of *The Phantom of Liberty*. *Cinema Papers*, no. 2 (July–August 1975): 157.

Morse, David. Review of *Tristana*. *Monogram*, no. 5 (1974): 19–20.

Mortimore, Roger. "Buñuel, Sáenz de Heredia, and Filmófono." *Sight and Sound*, no. 44 (Summer 1975): 180–182.

Morton, J. "A Great Spanish Film Director." *Contemporary Review* 244 (February 1984):111.

Moskowitz, G. Review of *Le fantôme de la liberté*. *Variety*, 28 August 1974, 20.

Mussman, Toby. "Early Surrealist Expression in the Film." *Film Culture*, no. 41 (Summer 1966): 8–16.

Naremore, J. "Expressive Coherence and the *Acted Image*." Features *Cet obscure objet du désir*. *Studies in the Literary Imagination* 19, no. 1 (1986): 39–54.

"National Film Theatre: Buñuel and Capra – Two Men and Their Art." *Film* (London) 2, no. 6 (September 1973): 21.

"New Buñuel Film to Roll in Spain." Review of *Cet obscur objet du désir*. *Variety*, 29 December 1976, 29.

Nowell-Smith, Geoffrey. Review of *Nazarín*. *Sight and Sound* 32, no. 4 (Autumn 1963): 194–195.

Oswald, L. "Figure/Discourse: Configurations of Desire in *Un chien andalou*." *Semiotica* 33, nos. 1–2 (1981): 105–122.

Overbey, David L. Review of *Cet obscur objet du désir*. *Sight and Sound* 47, no. 1 (Winter 1977–1978): 7–8.

Paz, Octavio. Review of *Nazarín*. *Film Culture*, no. 21 (Summer 1960): 60–61.

Pearson, Harry. Review of *Belle de jour*. *Films in Review*, no. 46 (November–December 1995): 98–99.

Pena, Richard. "¡Que viva Mexico!: *El* (This Strange Passion)." *Film Comment* 31, no. 6 (November 1995): 29.

"¡Que viva Mexico!: *Los olvidados* (The Young and the Damned)." *Film Comment* 31, no. 6 (November 1995): 29.

Pérez, G. "The Thread of the Disconcerting: A Note on Buñuel's Narrative." *Sight and Sound* 52, no. 1 (1982–1983): 58–61.

Perry, J. W. "*L'âge d'or* and *Un chien andalou.*" *Filmfax*, no. 40 (August–September 1993): 62–67.

Pittman, Randy. Review of *Illusion Travels by Streetcar*. *Library Journal* 116, no. 9 (May 1991): 124.

Popkin, M. "*Wuthering Heights* and Its Spirit." Review of *Abismos de pasión*. *Literature/Film Quarterly* 15, no. 2 (1987): 116–122.

Prouse, Derek. "Interviewing Buñuel." *Sight and Sound* 29, no. 3 (Summer 1960): 118–119.

"Puzzling Theft and Fire: Buñuel's *Desire* Film Victim – But Just Why?" Review of *Cet obscur objet du désir*. *Variety*, 15 March 1978, 38.

Rainer, Peter. Review of *Los olvidados/Nazarín*. *American Film* 14, no. 9 (July 1989): 64–65.

Reilly, C. P. Review of *The Phantom of Liberté*. *Films in Review* 25 (December 1974): 625–626.

Review of *Belle de jour*. *New York Times*, 15 December 1995, B7 (N), D18 (L).

Review of *Diary of a Chambermaid*. *New York Times*, 26 March 1989, H26.

Review of *The Phantom of Liberté*. *Independent Film Journal* 74, no. 11 (October 30, 1974): 2.

Review of *The Phantom of Liberty*. *Film*, no. 105 (April–May 1982): 33.

Review of *That Obscure Object of Desire*. *New York Times*, 5 May 1995, B8 (N), D17 (L).

Rich, B. Ruby. "Meet Jeanne Buñuel." *Sight and Sound*, no. 5 (August 1995): 20–23.

Robinson, David. "Buñuel and Louÿs." Review of *Cet obscur objet du désir*. *Sight and Sound* 47, no. 3 (1978): 160.

"The Old Surrealist." *London Magazine* (November 1962): 66–72.

Romney, Jonathan. "Delirium Diluted." *New Statesman and Society* 5, no. 214 (August 1992): 31–32.

Roof, G. "Un-passionne-appel-au-meurtre: Murder and Artistic Experience in *Un chien andalou.*" *Romance Quarterly* 41, no. 4 (Fall 1994): 209–218.

Ross, M. B. "A House of Cards: A Case for Analogy in Luis Buñuel." *Lamp* (1985): 61–70.

Rotha, Paul. Review of *Viridiana*. *Films and Filming* 8, no. 9 (June 1962): 32.

Roud, Richard. "New York Film Festival Preview: Richard Roud on *The*

Spectre of Liberty." Review of *Le fantôme de la liberté. Film Comment* 10 (September – October 1974): 34–35.

Rubia Varcia, J. "Luis Buñuel's *Los olvidados." Quarterly of Film, Radio and Television* 7, no. 4 (1953): 392–401.

Rubinstein, E. "Visit to a Familiar Planet Buñuel among the Hurdanos." *Cinema Journal* 22, no. 4 (Summer 1983): 3–17.

Sandro Paul. "Textuality of the Subject in *Belle de jour." Substance,* no. 26 (1980): 43–56.

Sarris, Andrew. "Films in Focus: Buñuel at the Beginning." *Village Voice,* 5 May 1980, 39.

"Luis Buñuel: The Devil and the Nun – *Viridiana." Movie,* no. 1 (1962): 14–16. Rpt. in Andrew Sarris, *Confessions of a Cultist: On the Cinema, 1955–1969,* New York: Simon & Schuster, 1971; *Renaissance of the Film,* ed. Julius Bellone, 330–339, London: Collier-Macmillan, 1970.

"Luis Buñuel: Forms + Phantoms." Review of *Le fantôme de la liberté. Village Voice,* 31 October 1974, 99.

"Rental Tapes: *Illusion Travels by Streetcar." Video Review* 12, no. 7 (October 1991): 120.

Scharfman, Ronnie. "Deconstruction Goes to the Movies: Buñuel's *Cet obscur objet du désir." French Review* 53, no. 3 (February 1980): 351–358.

Seger, Rufus. "Luis Buñuel: Reality and Illusion." *Anarchy,* no. 6 (August 1961): 183–189.

"Set Paris Tribute for Luis Buñuel." *Variety,* 3 November 1982, 37.

Shandy, Tristram. "Another Look at Buñuel: The Tragic Eye." *Anarchy,* no. 6 (August 1961): 183–189.

Smith, Paul Julian. "Shocks and Prejudices." *Sight and Sound,* no. 5 (August 1995): 24–26.

Sobchack, Vivian. "Synthetic Vision: The Dialectical Imperative of Buñuel's *Las hurdes." Millennium,* nos. 7–9 (Fall–Winter 1980–1981): 140–150.

Sonnenberg, Ben. "Black Comedies: *The Criminal Life of Archibaldo de la Cruz." Nation,* 31 January 1994, 140.

Spence, Martin. "Green Slime and *Devotion." Sight and Sound* 56, no. 3 (Summer 1987): 215–217.

Stam, Robert. "Hitchcock and Buñuel: Desire and the Law." *Studies in the Literary Imagination* 16, no. 1 (1983): 7–27.

Sterritt, David. "An Original Vision: Luis Buñuel." *Christian Science Monitor,* 4 August 1983, 16.

Review of *Objects of Desire: Conversations with Luis Buñuel,* by José de la Colina and Tomás Pérez Turrent. *Christian Science Monitor,* 15 July 1993, 13.

Review of *Tristana*. *Christian Science Monitor*, 17 January 1997, 15.

Review of *The Young One*. *Christian Science Monitor*, 23 June 1994, 10.

Stolz, George. "Surrealism in Spain." Features *Un chien andalou*. *ARTnews* 94, no. 5 (May 1995): 166.

Suleiman, Susan. "Between the Street and the Salon: The Dilemma of Surrealist Politics in the 1930's." *Visual Anthropology Review* 7, no. 1 (1991): 39–50.

"Freedom and Necessity: Narrative Structure in *The Phantom of Liberty*." *Quarterly Review of Film Studies* 3, no. 3 (Summer 1978): 277–296.

Sultanik, A. "Is the Revolution Over?" Review of *Cet obscur objet du désir*. *Midstream* 24 (February 1978): 88–89.

Taves, Brian. "Whose Hand?: Correcting a Buñuel Myth." *Sight and Sound* 56, no. 3 (Summer 1987): 210–211.

Taylor, J. R. "Luis Buñuel."*Films and Filming*, no. 349 (October 1983): 7–9.

Thiher, A. "Surrealism's Enduring Bite: *Un chien andalou*." *Literature/Flim Quarterly* 5, no. 1 (1977): 38–49.

Thomas, Kevin. "Four Buñuel Rarities at Fox Venice."*Los Angeles Times*, 27 October 1983, 3.

Review of *Una mujer sin amor*. *Los Angeles Times*, 11 November 1983, 9.

Review of *Susana*. *Los Angeles Times*, 2 November 1983, 2.

"Time Stands Still for La *Belle*." *Los Angeles Times*, 24 June 1995, Fl.

Thomas, Nicholas. "Colonial Surrealism: Luis Buñuel's: *Land without Bread*." *Third Text*, no. 26 (Spring 1994): 125–132.

Tynan, Kenneth. "Movie Crazy." Review of *Los olvidados*. *Sight and Sound* 20, no. 1 (May 1951): 4.

Van der Vliet, Gina. "Luscious Jackson Video Inspired by Buñuel Film." *Billboard* 108, no. 54 (December 1996): 76.

Van Gelder, Lawrence. Review of *L'âge d'or*. *New York Times*, 18 August 1985, H2O.

Vas, Robert, Review of *Ensayo de un crimen*. *Monthly Film Bulletin* 27 (December 1960): 164.

Review of *Viridiana*. *Monthly Film Bulletin* 29 (May 1962): 65.

Walker, Ian. "Buñuel's Half Century: Once upon a Time." *Sight and Sound* 47, no. 1 (1977–1978): 2–5.

Weiler, A. H. Review of *Simon of the Desert*. *New York Times*, 12 February 1969, C33.

Weiss, Jason. "The Power to Imagine." *Cineaste* 13, no. 1 (1983): 6–11.

Westerbeck, C. L., Jr. "Obscenery." Review of *Le fantôme de la liberté*. *Commonweal* 101 (November 1974): 190–191.

"Year of the Women." Review of *Cet obscur objet du désir*. *Commonweal* 105 (February 1978): 117–118.

Williams, Linda R. "Dream Rhetoric and Film Rhetoric: Metaphor and Metonomy in *Un chien andalou.*" *Semiotica* 33, nos. 1–2 (1981): 86–103.

"An Eye for an Eye: Why Is the Violation of the Eye So Terrifying in Films from Buñuel to *The Terminator,*" *Sight and Sound* 4, no. 4 (April 1994): 14–16.

"The Prologue to *Un chien andalou*: A Surrealist Film Metaphor." *Screen* 17, no. 4 (Winter 1976–1977): 24–33.

Willis, Donald C. "Buñuel's Half Century: *Nazarín*: Buñuel's Comic Hero Revisited." *Sight and Sound* 47, no. 1 (1977–1978): 5–7.

Wilson, Peter. "Immersed in Films." *Sight and Sound* 3, no. 1 (January 1993): 35.

Wood, Michael. "Buñuel's Private Lessons." Review of *Cet obscur objet du désir. New York Review of Books* 24 (February 1978): 39–42.

"Double Lives." Review of *Belle de jour. Sight and Sound* 1, no. 9 (January 1992): 20–23.

Wright, Basil. Review of *The Criminal Life of Archibaldo de la Cruz. Sight and Sound* 25, no. 2 (Autumn 1955): 87–88.

Yeats, E. D. "Image and Body: The Optical Alignment of Walter Benjamin and Luis Buñuel." *Journal of European Studies* 23, no. 91 (September 1993): 251–282.

Young, Vernon. "Buñuel and Antonioni." *Hudson Review* 15, no. 2 (Summer 1962): 274–281.

Zimmerman, P. D. "Down and Freedom." Review of *Le fantôme de la liberté. Newsweek*, 4 November 1974, 92.

THE DISCREET CHARM OF THE BOURGEOISIE (NOT INCLUDING THE ESSAYS IN SPECIAL ISSUES)

Ahrens, Julie. "Getting What You Need: Changing Surrealist Vision in Buñuel's *Un chien andalou, The Discreet Charm of the Bourgeoisie,* and *That Obscure Object of Desire.*" *Movietone News*, nos. 58–59 (August 1978): 17–21.

Babington, Bruce, and Peter W. Evans. "The Life of the Interior: Dreams in the Films of Luis Buñuel." *Critical Quarterly* 27, no. 4 (1985): 5–20.

Bonneville, L. Review. *Sequences*, no. 72 (April 1973): 36–37.

Carrière, Jean-Claude. "Deux extraits du scénario *Le charme discret de la bourgeoisie.*" *Revue belge du cinéma* 18 (Winter 1986): 54–58.

Eberwein, Robert. "The Collective Dream in *The Discreet Charm of the Bourgeoisie.*" In *Film and the Dream Screen*, 183–191. Princeton: Princeton University Press, 1984.

"Entretiens avec Luis Buñuel: *Le charme discret de la bourgeoisie.*" *Cahiers du cinéma*, no. 464 (February 1993): 36.

George, G. L. "The Discreet Charm of Luis Buñuel." *Action* 9 (November–December 1974): 26–29.

Gitlin, T. "Buñuel, Peckinpah, Rohmer, and Tanner." *Performance* 1 (May–June 1973): 65–73.

Gow, Gordon. Review. *Films and Filming* 19 (March 1973): 45.

Jousse, Thierry. "Buñuel face à ce qui se dérobe." Review. *Cahiers du cinéma*, no. 464 (February 1993): 28–32.

Kaminsky, Stuart M. Review. *Cinefantastique* 3, no. 1 (1973): 33.

Kermode, Mark. Video Review of *Belle de jour, Le charme discret de la bourgeoisie, Cet obscur objet du désir. Sight and Sound* 2, no. 8 (December 1992): 61.

Kovács, Steven. Review. *Film Quarterly* 26, no. 2 (1972–1973): 14–17.

Leduc, J. Review. *Cinéma Quebec* 2 (March–April 1973): 53.

Lefèvre, Raymond. Review. *Revue du cinéma*, nos. 276–277 (October 1973): 72–73.

Minish, G. Review. *Take One* 3 (November–December 1971): 26–27.

Paris, James Reid. Review. In *The Great French Films*, 270. Secaucus, N.J.: Citadel Press, 1983.

Pauly, Rebecca. "A Revolution Is Not a Dinner Party: The Discreet Charm of Buñuel's Bourgeoisie." *Literature-Film Quarterly* 22, no. 4 (October 1994): 232–237.

Ramsey, Cynthia. *The Problem of Dual Consciousness: The Structures of Dream and Reality in the Films of Luis Buñuel*. Ann Arbor: University Microfilm International, 1983.

Reilley, C. P. Review. *Films in Review* 24 (January 1973): 54–55.

Review. *Films and Filming* 19 (March 1973): 52–53.

Rosenbaum, Jonathan. "Interruption as Style: *Le charme discret de la bourgeoisie.*" *Sight and Sound* 42, no. 1 (Winter 1972–1973): 2–8.

Letters to Robin Wood. "Letters: Response to 'The Skull Beneath the Skin: Some Indiscreet Charms of Narrativity' (*Cineaction*, no. 11)." *Cineaction*, no. 12 (Spring 1988): 64.

Sandro, Paul. "The Management of Destiny in Narrative Form." Review of *The Exterminating Angel* and *The Discreet Charm of the Bourgeoisie. Cine-Tracts* 4, no. 1 (Spring 1981): 50–56.

Schmidt, N. "Montage et scénario." Review. *CinemAction*, no. 72 (1994): 98–104.

Wood, Michael. "The Discreet Charm of Luis Buñuel."*American Film* 7 (September 1982): 34–39.

Notes on Contributors

José Luis Borau is a distinguished Spanish filmmaker (writer, director, producer) whose films include *Brandy, Crimen de doble filo, Hay que matar a B, Furtivos, La sabina, Río abajo, Tata mía, Celia*, and *Niño nadie* and whose own *Mi querida señorita* (which he produced and cowrote with director Jaime de Armiñán) was nominated for best foreign film the same year that *The Discreet Charm of the Bourgeoisie* won the Oscar in that category. He is also well known as a teacher of screenwriting who helped train a whole generation of Spanish filmmakers and who produced many important films directed by others. He is currently the president of the Spanish Academy of the Motion Picture Arts (the group responsible for giving out the Goya Awards, which are comparable to the Oscars).

Juan Roberto Mora Catlett is a professor of direction and editing at the Film School of Mexico's National Autonomous University (Mexico City), where he held the post of academic secretary from 1978 to 1985. He is also an award-winning filmmaker who has won the Great Special Award of the Jury at the Latin-American Film Festival in Trieste in 1992 for his feature, *Return to Aztlan*; two Mexican Film Academy Awards, one in 1987 for best screenplay and the other in 1982 for best editing; the Third Experimental Feature Film Festival Award for best screenplay in 1987; and the Ninth Ibero-American Film Festival Gold Columbus Award for best documentary in Huelva, Spain, in 1983. He also received a Guggenheim Fellowship in 1986–1987 and was a member of Mexico's National System of Creators of Art from 1994 to 1996.

MARVIN D'LUGO is professor of film studies at Clark University in Worcester, Massachusetts. He is one of the most distinguished North American scholars writing on Spanish cinema. He is the author of *Carlos Saura: The Practice of Seeing* (Princeton University Press, 1991), *Guide to the Cinema of Spain* (Westport, Conn.: Greenwood Press, 1997), and has published many seminal essays on Spanish and Latin American cinema, literature, and culture.

VICTOR FUENTES was born in Madrid. He is professor of nineteenth- and twentieth-century Spanish literature at the University of California, Santa Barbara. He has published numerous studies on literary history and criticism, cinema and the relationship between film and literature. His publications include *La marcha del pueblo en las letras españolas: 1917–1936*, *El cántico material y espiritual de César Vallejo*, *Benjamín Jarnés: Bio-Grafía y metaficción*, and *Buñuel en Mexico*.

MARSHA KINDER is professor of critical studies in the school of cinema-television at the University of Southern California, where she teaches courses on Buñuel, Spanish media culture, international cinema, and narrative theory. She has been a contributing editor to *Film Quarterly* since 1977. Her two most recent books are *Refiguring Spain: Cinema, Media, Representation* (Duke University Press, 1997) and *Blood Cinema: The Reconstruction of National Identity in Spain* (University of California, 1993), with a companion bilingual CD-ROM, which is the first in an electronic series on national media cultures that she is editing for the University of Southern California Electronic Press. Currently she is director of the Labyrinth Project, a research initiative at the Annenberg Center for Communication that is producing multimedia works that expand the language of interactive narrative and that use Buñuel's films as one of their models.

JOHN RECHY is a well-known Mexican-American novelist whose works include *City of Night, Numbers, The Sexual Outlaw, Bodies and Souls, Marilyn's Daughter, The Miraculous Day of Amalia Gómez, Our Lady of Babylon,* and *The Coming of the Night.* He is an instructor in the masters program in professional writing at the University of Southern California where he teaches a film course for writers that prominently features the works of Buñuel. He was the 1998 recipient of PEN West's Lifetime Achievement Award.

AGUSTÍN SÁNCHEZ VIDAL is currently professor of the history of cinema and other audiovisual media at the University of Zaragoza, where he has taught Spanish literature for over twenty years. Not only is he one of Spain's most preeminent film scholars, but he is recognized worldwide as the most distinguished and prolific scholar on the works of Luis Buñuel. Between 1976 and 1980 he worked in collaboration with Buñuel on his *Obra Literaria* (1982). He has published many other books, including *El cine de Carlos Saura* (1988), *Borau* (1990), *El cine de Florián Rey* (1991), *El cine de Segundo de Chomón* (1992), and *El mundo de Buñuel* (1993). In 1988 his book *Buñuel, Lorca, Dalí: el enigma sin fin* won the prestigious Mirror of Spain award given by the Editorial Planeta. He has also contributed to many collective works on the avant-garde, such as the catalog for the Buñuel Retrospective for the 1984 Venice Film Festival, *Trent'anni di avanguardía spagnola* (Jaca Book, Milan, 1987), *Spanish Masterpieces of the 20th Century* (Seibu Museum of Art, Tokyo, 1989), *The Surrealist Adventure in Spain* (Ottawa Hispanic Studies, Canada, 1991), the monograph that the Pompidou Center dedicated to Buñuel's *La edad de oro* in 1993, the catalog for the Buñuel exposition at the Bonn Center of the Arts in 1994, and the catalog for the *Salvador Dalí:*

The Early Years retrospective organized jointly in 1994 by the Centro Reina Sofía Museum in Madrid, the Hayward Gallery of London, and the New York Metropolitan Museum of Art.

YUNGSHUN TANG is a Taiwanese-Chinese scholar who is completing a doctoral degree in critical studies in the school of cinema-television at the University of Southern California in Los Angeles. His dissertation is on the representation of masculinity in American cinema.

JAMES TOBIAS is an interaction designer who has been a member of the research staff at the Interval Research Corporation in Palo Alto, California. Prior to receiving a master's degree in interactive telecommunications from New York University's Tisch School of the Arts, he lived for six years in Japan, where he was employed as linguistics programmer for Fujitsu Ltd.'s Artificial Intelligence Division and, in addition, composed music for piano and performed with choreographer Anzu Furukawa, among others. He currently lives in Los Angeles where he is pursuing a doctorate in critical studies at the University of Southern California.

HARMONY H. WU is a doctoral candidate in the division of critical studies in the school of cinema-television at the University of Southern California in Los Angeles. She received her B.A. from Amherst College, where she wrote an honors thesis on the films of Pedro Almodóvar, and subsequently studied in Spain. Her dissertation will focus on horror and genre hybridity, with feminist and cross-cultural perspectives. Her recent work is included in *Visible Nations: Latin American Cinema and Video*, edited by Chon Noriega (forthcoming from University of Minnesota Press).

Index

Printed in the United Kingdom
by Lightning Source UK Ltd.
123379UK00002B/205-207/A

9 780521 568319